A DROP OF MIDNIGHT

A DROP OF MIDNIGHT

A MEMOIR

JASON DIAKITÉ

TRANSLATED BY RACHEL WILLSON-BROYLES

AMAZON **CROSSING**

Previously published as *En Droppe Midnatt* by Albert Bonniers Förlag in Sweden in
2016. Translated from Swedish by Rachel Willson-Broyles. First published in English
by Amazon Crossing in 2020.

Published by Amazon Crossing, Seattle

www.apub.com

Amazon, the Amazon logo, and Amazon Crossing are trademarks of Amazon.com, Inc., or its affiliates.

ISBN-13: 9781542017077 (hardcover)
ISBN-10: 1542017076 (hardcover)

ISBN-13: 9781542016704 (paperback)
ISBN-10: 1542016703 (paperback)

Cover design by Philip Pascuzzo

Cover illustrated by Ronald Wimberly

Printed in the United States of America

First edition

Libation
To my forefathers and foremothers
I stand on the shoulders of your sacrifices and your
resolute courage.

Ubuntu

You may shoot me with your words,
You may cut me with your eyes,
You may kill me with your hatefulness,
But still, like air, I'll rise.

Maya Angelou

IT AIN'T WHERE YOU FROM IT'S WHERE YOU AT

His shoes were always shined. Even in the autumn of his old age, when he'd lost all his hair. As the cancer in his prostate consumed his organs ever faster. As he spent his days waiting for the end in his favorite sunken red chair with the plastic cover, his shoes were always shined.

My grandfather, Solomon Warren Robinson, known as Silas, sure could dance and sure knew how to dress. During the week, he was a waiter on the Pullman train between New York and Philadelphia. He never missed a day of work. No cold, no aching joints, swollen feet, or existential crises could keep him from fulfilling his duty.

Silas was born in the small town of Allendale in the subtropical state of South Carolina. His mother and his twin brother died during the birth. Silas and his older brother, Wade, grew up in the home of their maternal aunt. He never knew his father. When he was nine, his aunt's gruff husband declared that there was no point in sending a little nigger to school.

"Books are worthless. If you're going to live here, you'll work and contribute to the household."

Grandpa quit school in the third grade. He had been born in 1907, and slavery had in theory been abolished more than forty years earlier, but in 1896, the court decision in Plessy v. Ferguson established "separate but equal" as the law of the land, and American apartheid was a fact.

The plantations and estates around Allendale remained standing proudly—monumental reminders that nothing had truly changed. The endless fields of cotton still needed to be harvested each season, and the hands that picked the cotton were still black. But when Grandpa was little, it wasn't the whip that snapped over his back in the fields. In post-emancipation South Carolina, grinding poverty was far more effective than any whip.

The only belonging I have of my grandfather's is a sandy-colored trench coat. It's so worn with time I have to be extremely careful when I put it on. The lining is falling to pieces, and the pockets are full of holes. But when Silas bought it, it was an investment. He worked hard for every cent. The only money he had was what he saved from his jobs as a cotton picker, a shoe shiner, a waiter. It was just enough for food and lodging.

The coat must have been important to him. In it, he was no longer one of the barefoot, rag-clad black bodies working themselves to death in the fields of the South. I can picture Grandpa sizing up the coat in the mirror and feeling pride swell in his chest. I can picture it matching his shiny shoes and wide-brimmed hat. He always dressed elegantly as a signal to all he passed on the Harlem boulevards: here comes a sophisticated big-city man who has managed to move up in the world. Up, north, away from the muddy cotton fields—up to the stable pavements of Harlem at the age of thirteen.

The coat. Woven of the same cotton he and all his family before him were forced to pick from dawn to dusk.

In my spacious apartment in central Stockholm, far from the segregated world where Grandpa grew up, the coat prompts me to wonder: *Who am I? Who are my people? Where is my home?*

I spent my entire upbringing in the southern Swedish city of Lund searching for an answer. An unambiguous, coherent image of who I was. I wished for white skin, a people, an origin, a collective narrative, and a history. A homeland.

Where was I supposed to start? As I created my identity, it became a patchwork quilt, a mosaic of irregular shards and pieces I meticulously tried to meld together into Jason Michael Bosak Diakité. I was never American, never Swedish, never white but never black either. I was a no-man's-land in the world.

I have a complex system of roots that branches across continents, ethnicities, classes, colors, and eras. I am Jason, son of the black Madubuko Diakité and the white Elaine Bosak. I am all the countries my forefathers came from and were shipped to in chains. I am all the colors and shades of their skin. I am their rage and their longing, their hardships, successes, and dreams. I am the intersection of Slovakia, Germany, France, Africa, South Carolina. Of white, black, and Cherokee. I am the meeting of Bosak, Schneidmüller, Hauser, Privat, Robinson, Davis, and Miller. The sum of Mom's Slavic German roots and Dad's African ones molded in the social democracy of Sweden.

Must I have just *one* home? Must I have just *one* origin? Is that to make it easier for those around me, or to flat out appease them? To make it simpler for them to put a label on me, measure me, place me, fence me in, and judge me?

Is that why I have spent so much time tormenting myself with these questions of identity? So I can give a simple answer when someone asks where I come from?

Maybe. It's human nature to want clear answers. Obvious boundaries between good and evil, light and dark, right and wrong, friend and enemy, "us" and "them." As if humans cannot exist otherwise.

Can't I have many origins, identities, homes?

I believed for a long time that I didn't have a choice because that was just how the world, and people, worked. I imagined that if you were Swedish, you were white, the same as if you came from Scranton, Pennsylvania, like my mother. But if you were from Harlem, you were black, like Dad and his family.

The phrase "nigger shit" was hurled after me time and again on the playground in elementary school. My uncle shouts, "Hey, Puerto Rico!" every time we meet. I'm often asked if I'm from Morocco, Thailand, India, Ecuador, Cuba, or Ethiopia.

"Jason—isn't that Arabic for 'Jesus'?" asked one middle-aged man in the small Swedish town of Harlösa.

My name signals, to Swedes, that I am something different. That I'm not one of us.

"'Diakité,' what kind of name is that?" asked the cashier at a department store in New York.

Only, she pronounced it like "the architect."

"'Diakité' comes from the Fula people, or Fulani, as they're also called," I responded, glad that she was curious. "The name is as common in Guinea, Burkina Faso, Mali, Senegal, The Gambia, and Nigeria as 'Williams' or 'Jones' are in the US."

The cashier just shrugged.

All those hours I spent, as a nine-year-old, staring at the white flecks on the back of my right hand, thinking maybe there was something white under my brown skin. Maybe the white spots would grow and make me into who I wanted to be. White?

I also remember the contagious beats of hip-hop and the cocky pride in having black skin. Public Enemy's and Boogie Down Productions' powerful messages of standing up against the system and being proud of who you are and where you're from.

I remember the most glaring moment when I felt like an outsider, when I truly felt I would never be accepted as "one of us" by my fellow Swedes—despite all the awards, praise, applause, gold records, and the love of fans: I was on the second floor of the Parliament House in Stockholm, just about to give my acceptance speech for the 5i12 Movement's anti-racism prize. My legs, hands, and vocal cords trembling, I stood before the cameras and the microphones, before the gathered politicians, journalists, and friends, and my speech became a desperate plea for acceptance. For Sweden to be my home.

One week earlier, I had released a song called "Svarta duvor och vita liljor" ("Black Doves and White Lilies") together with rap group Kartellen. In one line I rap, "beat Jimmie blue and yellow and hoist him up the flagpole"—a metaphor for what I think of Jimmie Åkesson and his Sweden Democrat party, who demanded the right to determine who and what is Swedish. The song unleashed a flood of threats and hate on social media. The newspapers called it a threat to democracy. As a result, the speaker of parliament boycotted the awards ceremony and exiled us to a tiny room on the second floor.

I'm not sure I'd ever felt so unwelcome in this place I thought was my homeland. I was born here, I speak the language fluently, I carry Swedish culture within me.

I have been steeped in the quintessentially Swedish experience. I've laughed at the comedy of Hasse and Tage; sung Bellman's epistles at the top of my lungs; read about Nils Holgersson and his wonderful adventures in Sweden; hopped like a frog around midsummer poles; eaten falafel in Malmö; learned to recite the list of kings; plodded through Strindberg's *The People of Hemsö*; cursed the weather with Persian cab drivers; jumped the turnstiles in the subway; and danced to *schlager* stars Herreys and Carola. I have run up the Brösarp hills and puked in the park on Walpurgis Night. I've been enchanted by the northern lights and drained of blood by mosquitoes during the long, bright nights of the midnight sun.

Yet I have always carried around the nagging feeling that I am only a guest in someone else's home. May I really open the fridge and help myself to whatever I find? I have to be careful not to knock over someone's vase or accidentally break something fragile. May I have permission to stay here as long as I like? Will the color of my skin always follow me like a shadow that can be turned against me at any moment, can become the only thing that defines me? Can I manage not to be reduced to Other?

Who am I?

Grandpa always dressed impeccably and held his head high. He used lye in his hair to burn out his curls and make it straight, make himself whiter. But did he ever dream of something bigger than his life as a waiter? If he did, what dream twinkled there on the horizon? What sorts of questions nagged at Grandpa? Did he wonder who he was during his long Sunday walks along the broad avenues of Harlem? Was Grandpa ever ashamed of his golden-brown skin and his simple upbringing? What fears did he carry with him?

Standing before the mirror in my home in Stockholm, wearing Grandpa's worn coat, I realize that I need to travel to the places where he grew up. I have to find this last bit of mortar to secure the mosaic of my identity. I have to go to the place where he was born. I have to go to South Carolina.

COUSIN WILLIE

I rub at my eye for a long time to get the last of the grit that lingers just where my eyelid ends and the bridge of my nose begins, grit left behind by an insufficient amount of sleep. I lay in bed with my laptop on my belly until four in the morning, trying and failing to settle down enough to fall asleep. It's getting harder and harder to tear myself away from the internet. Hours trickle by as I surf everything from music blogs to auction sites to news outlets.

Now it's just past eleven a.m., and I'm sitting at the kitchen table in my robe, my computer once again on and casting its white glow over me. Winter refuses to release Stockholm from its grip. It's February 2015. Gray. The world seems to be living under a thick wool blanket of low-hanging clouds. Last February, I counted only two afternoons when those of us in the North could see blue sky. It's the same story this year. The feeling of endless winter is amplified when I open a window to air the place out. The cold quickly finds its way into my kitchen. I hug myself, rubbing my shoulders, and search for an old clip on my computer. The grainy black-and-white video shows blues legend Sonny Boy Williamson II soulfully singing "Nine Below Zero" to an all-white audience.

> She wait till it got nine below zero, and put me down
> for another man

Sonny Boy rocks back and forth in time with the music, takes out his harmonica, and makes it sound more sincere than the most achingly sad lament. I get up and close the window; a more thorough airing out will have to wait until the sun finds its way back to these northerly latitudes and thaws some of the frost on the ground and the people.

I'm going to need a cup of coffee to deal with this morning. Although it's almost midday, there are hardly any people on the sidewalk below my window. Sweden still hasn't chanced waking from its hibernation.

As Sonny Boy's song fades out, I realize I need something a little peppier, so I put on D'Angelo's new album *Black Messiah*.

When I hear the first lines of "Ain't That Easy," I feel warmth spread through the room.

My one-year-old nephew has fallen ill with a type of arthritis. He's been in the hospital for several weeks, and my family is just about falling apart. My seasonal depression is exacerbated by the fact that I haven't written a song in almost six months. I'm lost. Last month I turned forty.

What have I accomplished in life, really? Sure, I've had a few magical concerts and memories. But the phrase "life is short" is starting to feel inadequate. Life is also long. What should I do with the rest of my years? I've dedicated my life to my career. For the past twenty years, that's been my excuse for everything and my absolute number-one priority. I prioritized music over my family, friends, and relationships. Now it feels like that career, and my accompanying self-image, are dissolving like a veil of smoke in a sudden breeze. My writer's block and my failed marriage are crystal clear signs my life is heading down the wrong track. I firmly believed my only chance of security was a home, a relationship, a family I created. But it seems that on the road of love, I'm a helplessly bad driver.

The baobab tree I bought in Senegal last year, which has lived in a pot in my bedroom since, has come down with some strange disease. Its delicate green leaves are covered in white crystals. *Shit, I hope it doesn't die,* I have time to think before returning to my brooding.

Should I keep battling to force out some relevant rap lyrics and spend all four seasons touring, or is it time to take a chance on something else? Should I open a bookstore, or finally get a law degree like Dad thinks I should, or study history?

As a kid, I wanted to be a pastor; when I got a little older, I dreamed of becoming a stockbroker on Wall Street. In my teen years, I switched to thinking I would one day be a lawyer. But all those other dreams withered away when I discovered hip-hop. Since that day, there was only one dream: I wanted to be a rapper.

Out of nowhere, I recall that I parked on the street outside the night before but never paid for the spot. I have to move the car. I don't want to find yet another yellow ticket on the windshield. The ultimate waste. I smile inwardly at how trivial life can be.

I retie the belt of my robe so it covers my chilly skin more thoroughly. I should get a pair of slippers too. I laugh at my impending old-man ways, but the distraction doesn't last and soon my train of thought returns to the right track. *What if I never manage to write a good song again? Shit.* I don't have the strength to think about that anymore today; it's February and the most important thing is just making it through this day with some basic level of energy intact.

Life is too short for me to waste it on sleepless nights and slow winter mornings, and too long not to dream of greater things than writing new lyrics, going to the next gig, and thinking about what sneakers to buy next. I slowly push down the plunger of my French press and pour a cup of steaming coffee. *I have to get out of here,* I think as D'Angelo sings.

D'Angelo's electric guitar brings me a certain measure of comfort in my listlessness, and the coffee spreads its earthy, nutty scent through the kitchen, perking up my brain cells a little bit. Maybe today I'll find a drop of inspiration.

I push the thought away even as it appears; inspiration never shows up when I'm looking for it. Looking for it is more like an exercise in not searching. I sit down at the computer. I have to check my email.

My phone dings from the counter next to the fruit bowl full of shriveled apples and one very brown banana. I rise from the kitchen chair and walk over to retrieve the phone.

Hope we can tlk soon. Luv Dad. This text means Dad's feeling lonely. But it's also his reminder: I've forgotten to call him for a few days.

My dad, Madubuko, would have preferred that I didn't move to Stockholm. He would much rather have had me stay in Malmö. Close to him.

Loneliness is a common thread running through Dad's life. His loneliness often cries out from between the lines of his texts; sometimes he even states it flat out: *I'm so lonely, Jason, where are you and when are you coming here?* With each text like that, I feel the same guilt. That I'm not enough, that I'm an inadequate son.

Dad has lots of friends, but really what he likes most of all is to have someone just listen to him. In that respect, I'm his favorite. He never runs out of lessons in life wisdom, and he always has something important to tell me, something he feels I need to know about life. Most of the time I respond by saying I've heard it a thousand times. I don't quite know where Dad's chronic loneliness comes from. He's said so many times that he doesn't belong in Sweden, that it's about time for him to move home to New York once and for all. God knows he's tried. He must have moved back three times during my life, only to return to Sweden after six months or a year.

Dad often sat around the kitchen table in Lund with his friends George, Stanley, Don Clayborn, and Don Franklin, spending hours grumbling about Lund and Sweden: the weather, the people, the politics . . . everything was so much worse than back home. When the conversation really reached peak levels, one of the older men might turn to me and ask, "You're Swedish, Jason, what do you think?" My face was always one big question mark. You mean I'm not the same as all of you?

Time and again, Dad said he was going to send me to live in Harlem, so I could learn about the street and how things really are. "Boy, you need to learn some street smarts."

Despite their laments, the gentlemen always found their way back to Lund. Whenever one of them had just returned from a trip, they all dropped by Dad's kitchen for an effusive report about how wonderful it was to visit the homeland. About new music or the most recent political incident. Sometimes my dad and his friends met in the newspaper reading room of the city library in Lund. They read papers from all over the world and had lively debates about events and developments in far-off places like Washington, DC; Algiers; Paris; or San Francisco.

Dad's love for Sweden has always been strongest during the periods he's lived in New York. There, he longs for the secure embrace of the welfare state, but back in Sweden, he won't stop talking about returning to the US. Has his exile lasted so long that he, too, feels homeless, restless? Perhaps that question unites us: Where is my home?

I breathe out a few times, take a sip of coffee, and try to gather my thoughts and my patience before I dial the number. The fact is, for the past few weeks, I've been nagging Dad to tell me about my great-grandfather: what his name was, when he was born, the sort of work he did, how he lived . . . I've pressed him for details about our family's origins in the impoverished American South.

Each time, all he'll say is that he doesn't know and that my questions are impossible to answer because he has no relatives left who could share those details with us. It's as if he won't even try to recall stories he's heard about Grandpa's family or think about where we might start looking for answers. He probably doesn't want to look.

The other day he dropped me a line to tell me about a man he called Cousin Willie. My dad and his siblings call him "cousin," but he's actually my grandfather's cousin. In the South, though, cousins are cousins. As far back as I can remember, Dad has told tall tales about his many cousins. He claims to have well over a hundred of them. Some are second or third cousins, some are once or twice removed, but they're all cousins just the same.

Cousin Willie is the child of one of my grandfather's mother's thirteen sisters. Willie's grandchildren had sent a letter to Dad inviting him to a party in celebration of the old man's one-hundredth birthday, to be held on March 10. The party is supposed to take place in Aiken, South Carolina. It's a small town near the even smaller community of Allendale, where my grandfather Silas Robinson grew up, and which is likely the place where my ancestors were slaves only two generations before Grandpa.

Cousin Willie was born in 1915, right into the poverty that reigned over black people in the South. This was the year after World War I broke out and fifty years after slavery was officially abolished. Two years later, President Woodrow Wilson decided that the United States would enter the war. In the South, black men were drafted at far higher rates than white men, which highlights the degree to which black lives were considered more expendable. Not only that, but having land-owning black men off at war meant their land was available for seizure by white interests.

"Jim Crow," the nickname for state laws that circumvented federal laws in order to deny the black population the same rights their white fellow citizens enjoyed, was in full force in 1915. The following year was also the start of the Great Migration—the mass exodus of black folks from the agricultural fields, injustices, and lynchings of the South to the northern industrial centers and the promise of a better life. According to African American writer Isabel Wilkerson, this migration went on until 1970.

In 1915, my grandfather was eight years old. He had already been working as a cotton picker for several years and would only spend one more year attending school. He would teach himself to read and write later, in his teens. That same year, *The Birth of a Nation*, a racist film praised by the Ku Klux Klan, was shown on screens all over the country and was, in fact, the first movie ever to be shown in the White House. Lynchings were becoming ever more common, and acts of terror against black people increased dramatically. It was nothing out of the ordinary when approximately fifteen thousand people gathered in Waco, Texas, in May of 1916 to watch as an eighteen-year-old black man, Jesse Washington, was burned alive.

Perhaps the century-old man named Willie knows the name of my great-grandfather? He's the last living witness, the last link to the slave generation, and he would surely have stories about our family and this dark era for African Americans.

I am surprised at the strength of my newfound desire to explore my roots. Imagine getting to see South Carolina with my own eyes. Imagine getting to see the impoverished neighborhoods, the waving Confederate flags, the Spanish moss hanging from the stately trees, and the old plantations. All I've really experienced of my family's homeland is New York; Los Angeles; Scranton; Washington, DC; San Francisco; Boston; and Portland. Mostly prosperous cities along the coasts. I've never explored that other United States. I've only seen it on TV. The crazy Christian right, people who don't know where Europe is, places in the interior US where hope died with the downfall of industry or, in some cases, was never even allowed to sprout. What if I can find the graves of my grandfather's family, or the fields where they worked?

"Dad, we really have to go."

Dad sighed. "But, Jason, I don't know if I have the strength. I'm old now."

"Not compared to Cousin Willie. How many people make it to one hundred? To him, you're probably just a kid."

"I don't know if I can deal with meeting all those people. We're talking folks who don't know any other life besides being poor and black in one of the most reactionary parts of the American South. Nothing has changed in the South. You have no idea what I've been through down there."

Dad sighed again, heavier this time.

"Or more accurately, things change so slowly that you can hardly tell. The question is, what happens faster—the wind eroding a cliff, or cultures and attitudes shifting in the rural South?"

"Sure, Dad, but that doesn't mean we wouldn't get anything out of going, does it? The experience of seeing what reality looks like for the parts of our family who stayed in the South would be valuable in itself."

But none of my arguments seem to reach Dad. In fact, each time Cousin Willie's party in South Carolina comes up, he appears even more determined not to go. It feels pointless trying to pep up someone who seems to no longer find joy in new discoveries.

Now he's texting me and he wants to talk. I learned long ago that if I don't call, Dad will only end up feeling more forgotten, more alone. So I tell myself I won't nag him about the trip. But . . . shit! I just don't want to accept that I might miss the chance to create new bonds with my family in the US simply because of his reluctance.

I have to try to convince him, I think as I press my finger to the word "Dad" on my screen. As the phone rings, I hurry to find the headset so I can connect it before Dad answers. I have to turn down the music too.

I press one white earbud into my right ear and walk to the kitchen window.

"Hey, Jason," Dad says, sounding lethargic. "How are you?"

"I'm fine, Dad. How are you?"

"I'm tired. I'm having so many problems with the authorities I work with. I mean, I'm working my ass off to give as complete a picture as I can of who these asylum seekers are. I sit there for hours, interviewing them about what they experienced in their homelands. It really takes a lot of time. Then, when I send the invoice to the authorities, they always dispute the number of hours. I don't think I've ever gotten paid for more than half the hours I've put in. And now they've gone and blacklisted me."

"What do you mean, 'blacklisted'?" I interject, upset. "Why?"

Dad raises his voice because now we're getting into one of his favorite topics to complain about. I picture him shaking a finger to emphasize each word in his version of events.

"Well, I was dealing with the case of a Roma man, and when I asked him what date his application was due, he said January fourteenth. I made sure the application was in on that day. But according to the authorities, it was due on the tenth. Now they're saying I'm unreliable. Like it's my fault the man gave me the wrong date."

"Shit, that sucks, Dad. Isn't there anything you can do?"

"I wrote a letter to one of the managers, but she says the rules are that if a representative doesn't follow the guidelines, they're blacklisted for six months. That means I can still take clients, but the authorities won't send any to me. I have to find them myself. But how many asylum seekers can I find on my own? How many . . . ?"

I'm sure he's sitting in his easy chair, rolling his eyes until his face collapses into a tired grimace. This has always been an uphill battle for him in Sweden. The struggle to be treated fairly. Dad blames his troubles with the universities in Lund and Stockholm, which delayed and impeded his doctoral studies, as well as his failure to secure a permanent position back when he was working as an English teacher for the school district in Lund in the 1980s, on his black skin. He often points out that black people don't get as much respect as whites do in this country. Even so, he loves Sweden.

"I need the money," Dad continues. "It's just a headache. I can't understand the authorities in this country."

If it's not the Migration Agency or the Faculty of Law, it's the Social Democrats or the Centre Against Racism. There's always some agency to complain about. Over the years, in my conversations with Dad, I've learned to keep quiet and listen, but I don't always manage to bite my tongue. I often go on the offensive and try to find a way to overturn my father's arguments and urge him not to be so pessimistic. I tell him that not *everything* has to do with skin color; it's not the cause of every problem. This, in turn, leads to long, draining disputes that seldom come to any conclusion. Next conversation we have, we start the whole process over again.

But today I know better. I let Dad complain.

He tells me that the camshaft on his pride and joy, his green Lexus, is broken, and the repairs will cost many thousands of kronor. But the Lexus is still the best car in the world, he assures me. It took him years to save up for it, after a lifetime of owning old, beat-up cars. Now he can gaze proudly through the pristine windshield of his Lexus as he drives down the streets of Malmö and Lund. But how can he afford to keep it up now that the authorities are contesting his invoices, his back is bad, he has trouble walking, and he can't work as much?

"You have to help me buy a cane. I need one now that I'm so old."

"Sure, Dad, we can go buy a cane next time I visit."

"OK, as long as you don't put off visiting me for too long, Jason. Who knows how much longer I'll live."

"Dispense with the drama, Dad," I respond, annoyed. "If you walk around telling yourself you're old, you'll age twice as fast. Can't you see that?"

Dad responds with silence.

"I got in an argument with Hilmi," he says after a moment. Hilmi, a South African surgeon, is my godfather.

Another of Dad's habits, which drives me insane, is that as soon as we touch on a sensitive subject in our conversations, he changes the topic to something more trivial.

"That happens with some regularity," I point out. "I'm sure you'll patch things up."

My patience is coming to an end. I have to wrap up this conversation before I say something mean and we have a falling-out. Again.

"Dad," I interject in a pause while he takes a breath, "why can't we just go to Cousin Willie's birthday party? What if I never get to meet him?"

"I have a bad heart, you know that. I don't want to go to South Carolina and end up having another heart attack."

I know deep down that nothing wears at my father's heart more than his feelings of guilt toward his family. Every time he talks to a cousin, a niece, a sister at home in the US, his brow knits and the wrinkles gather across his forehead. His exile. The great distance from his homeland. The thousands of miles between him and the city of his birth, his streets and corners and the folks he always calls "my people."

"Don't you miss your native country, Dad?"

"Yes, I do, Jason. Every day."

Dad sighs.

"But in some ways, I abandoned my family," he says in an attempt to rouse my sympathy. "I had to. Otherwise, I never would have made it out of the ghetto. Out of Harlem, away from the decay and destructiveness. But I've never been able to shed the guilt."

Dad's words echo what Kendrick Lamar says in "Mortal Man," his beautiful expression of survivor's guilt.

My dad was a pioneer in his family, just like his father before him. Not only did he marry a middle-class white woman, he moved to Europe. To many of my relatives, Europe is some vague, unknown concept they might have seen flicker by on the TV now and then. It's not just that they lack an understanding of the world; they aren't particularly interested in gaining one. They can't afford to think of the world beyond the ghettos of the United States.

But for me, it's important to find my roots. Since I was eight or nine, I've wondered who I really am, or rather, what I am. I'm not white or black; I'm not American or Swedish. I'm rootless. It hurts me that

Dad doesn't want to, or can't, see how complex the question of identity has been in my life. It's like he doesn't understand how impossible it's been for me to maneuver through a world where I have so often been considered neither black enough to be black nor white enough to be white. Maybe he thinks that the safe streets of Lund have spared me from learning what racism feels like.

A number of episodes flash by. Like that warm summer night years ago when I was having a beer with a few friends at a sidewalk café on Stortorget, joking around, and a guy at the table next to ours hissed, "Can't you shut your mouth, you little nigger?" I ended up beaten bloody, crying in the restaurant bathroom.

Or that night in Malmö when a friend and I walked past a night-club called Kramers Hörna, and the largest of the four bouncers shouted at us, "Look, here come the monkeys!" He laughed scornfully and made loud monkey noises. My friend made a move toward him, as if to show he was ready for a fight. And the bouncer just said, "Want some of this, you fucking little nigger? Come over here and I'll give you a taste."

Or the half-empty bar in Trondheim, Norway, when a large man knocked me roughly on the shoulder. The guy was at least three heads taller than me, and his chest was the size of a wheelbarrow. "We don't want any of your kind in here," he said in a superior tone, fixing his watery gaze on me. "I have just as much right as anyone else to be here, you fucking gorilla," I responded. That punch—it was like he'd thrown a sewing machine at my chest, and I flew backward, straight into the bar.

Just as that racist gorilla was about to bring his fist down on me again, the bouncer stepped in, got an iron grip on my arm, and hustled me out.

I blink, and another memory pops up. One evening when I was little, the neighbors were watching me while Mom worked late. One neighbor lady was chatting about the local gossip, travel plans, and garden work with her husband. The conversation turned to their jobs.

The neighbor lady was complaining about the schedule at the hospital, where she worked nights as a nurse, and said, "It's real nigger work." No one around the table reacted. My eight-year-old self had no words. I couldn't even put my finger on how that word landed inside me. But at last the neighbor lady seemed to realize what she'd said, so she turned to me: "Oh, that's just a phrase. You know, a way to say it's a really crappy job."

All those sorts of incidents and episodes left definite traces in me; they clued me in. Let me know I'm not like them, I'm not like the white people.

Dad notices how quiet I've gotten on the other end of the line and starts over in a more conciliatory tone.

"Jason, son, you do have roots. You know perfectly well who your parents are, and we've always—"

"But, Dad," I interrupt.

His pet peeve, in conversations with his son, is being interrupted.

"I'm not trying to blame anyone," I say. "You know that. I just want to see where I come from, or at least see that part of my origins."

"But I don't want to see where I come from," Dad counters. "Why can't you understand that I just want to forget all that poverty and misery? I don't want to relive the racism there. I really don't want to go back to South Carolina."

Dad raises his voice: "Why do you keep insisting you want to go track down old nigger graves that were paved over into parking lots ages ago? Why?"

I don't know what to say; I realize this conversation isn't going anywhere. Instead, we both fall silent, which is a rare occurrence in my family. We've forgotten how important silence can be. It's room to let our thoughts settle. Usually, we talk our way through everything and think about it later. Maybe that's why we so often say things we come to regret.

"OK, Dad," I say after a moment. "I hear you, and I respect your feelings. We won't go to South Carolina."

There's no way he could miss the disappointment in my voice.

But the question looping through my mind is: *Why don't you go by yourself, Jason?* It's awfully easy for me to accuse my dad of refusing to face his fears. Why don't I face my own? But can I really just show up to see these relatives I don't know and say, "Hi, I'm your Swedish cousin Jason"? Surely they would faint. Or say that they don't have any Latinos or Indians in their family.

I hang up and sit back down at the kitchen table. I spent our entire conversation pacing back and forth, all over the apartment. The more involved I become in a phone call, or the more upsetting it is, the more I wander around. Soon I will have worn a path into the hardwood floor. I turn up D'Angelo again and start glancing through my emails.

Just over a month later, I'm sitting in Dad's living room in Malmö. The faint spring sunshine can barely find its way through the thick white curtains. As always, the TV is on. It's either Al Jazeera or the BBC. But it's almost always the news. The laptop is open on the small brown table beside Dad's favorite black easy chair in front of the TV. There are books everywhere, most of them with Post-its stuck inside. Dad only reads nonfiction.

He's wearing blue jeans and a blue shirt. He is color blind and is never quite sure what colors he has on; as a result, I've seen him in some fantastic outfits over the years. A half-eaten apple sits next to the computer, and there's a big bowl of tangerines on the coffee table. Dad loves tangerines. He goes to the Arabic grocery on Sevedsplan and buys several pounds' worth every week. Those he doesn't eat are given away. "Here. They're good. Eat." It's his constant mantra. During the course of one visit, I'm asked if I want a tangerine probably seven times. If I say no to an offer of food or fruit, he just waits and asks me again twenty minutes later. "There's chicken in the fridge, Jason. Eat." There's always chicken in the fridge at Dad's. Unless it's already on the table. Chicken and jurisprudence might be the two things Dad loves most in the world, aside from his wife.

The floor is covered in a large Oriental carpet, all blue, green, and red. Dad and my godfather Hilmi love carpets. Carpets and cars. If I were to buy a carpet without asking their advice first, they would just shake their heads and say, "You paid too much. If you'd talked to us first, you would have known where to buy. When will you understand, you have to start listening to your elders?" When I was about to buy my first car, Dad went on and on about how I had to learn all about cars before I even set foot in a dealership. "Don't stay ignorant, read up."

Dad owns maybe six pairs of reading glasses, and he keeps their cases strategically placed throughout his home and car, and in various jackets. He never goes without slippers; it's a rule of his. He always wears slippers at home and has any number of pairs. When he visits a friend's house, he always brings a bag containing a pair of slippers.

The large wall to the left of Dad's throne is covered in white shelves from floor to ceiling, corner to corner. On them, books and framed pictures compete for space. Five pictures of me at my graduation. Pictures of Grandpa Silas; my grandmother, who everyone called Madame; Uncle Obi; Aunt Chinyelu; Aunt Juanetta; Great-Grandmother BM—Madame's mother; Dad's wife, Monique; and even more pictures of me: as a child, on a horse, on a skateboard. I'm probably in about half of the photos in his apartment. His only son. The one who is supposed to carry on the family name. Even though I didn't become the lawyer Dad wanted me to, I still hold the place of honor on the shelf. Besides Dad's easy chair, the room holds two big black leather sofas, a display cabinet full of glasses and china, and a big black dining table surrounded by eight chairs. The table is covered with documents and another laptop. Dad owns more computers than anyone I know. He has three right now, but I remember times when he had five. The fax machine, his two printers, the paper shredder, the filing cabinet, and the shelf full of binders are in the office right next to the room we're sitting in now.

Dad loves administration. Being in control. Knowing what's up. Organization. He finds me lacking in that department. He's always asking if I've done this or that, handled one thing or the other. As if I might not be competent enough to keep track of my own life. But those questions have ebbed over the years—a little, at least.

I sit in the leather sofa beside Dad's chair, in the dim light, and tell him that I want to write a book about him and our family. He wrinkles his nose, shakes his head, and opens his eyes wide.

He dismisses the idea. "Nobody's gonna buy a book like that," he repeats several times. And then, teasing, with an ironic smile: "You should write a crime novel instead, something people wanna read."

Now I'm convinced: I have to write about us.

"Our family's history is something we should be proud of, not put on display for people to gawk at," Dad adds, shaking his head firmly. "These are private matters. I know you love talking to journalists, Jason. But you'll never find me sitting around talking about my private life with some reporter. I promise you that."

He flashes a satisfied smile.

Dad has always been very proud. He's concerned with how black people in general, and how he as a black man in particular, are seen and portrayed. It is a matter of the utmost importance to him. Vital.

"I don't want you to write a book about how poor my parents were and how they were such victims of their era. We must not appear poor. We aren't victims."

Dad raises a finger in the air. Then he grips the thick armrest of the black chair and leans forward.

"Do you see these books?" he asks.

He points at the row of books to his left: thick volumes like T. J. English's *Savage City* and thinner ones like Michelle Alexander's *The*

New Jim Crow. It's a long succession of books about, and usually by, black people.

"All these books took time to write. Each book took years. Years of research and hard work. Do you understand that?"

Dad's gaze finds its way over the top edge of his reading glasses and he gives me a look, the one that says, *You still have so much to learn, son.* But with love.

"Do you know what? It took time to read them too. And I've done that. Writing a book isn't child's play."

Dad jabs his index finger into his thigh again and again as if to emphasize that this is the crux of his argument. I don't contradict him this time either.

Last year I nagged and nagged him to watch *12 Years a Slave*. He refused; he kept saying, "Everyone knows slavery was horrible. We've all seen it in movies and read about it in books. People are sick of that topic."

There was something fragile about Dad's half-closed eyes and wrinkled forehead. As if he didn't have the strength to look at images of slavery, I thought, and wondered why.

"Why not focus on the positive things African Americans do today?" he argued. "The problem with hip-hop is that it holds up a magnifying glass to the most dysfunctional parts of the ghetto, and African Americans' complete lack of a chance in life. They inherit hopelessness. The hopelessness that's forged into the bricks and concrete of the ghetto, that drips down the facades of the buildings, impregnating everything and everyone that lives there. Even the grass is browner in the ghetto. People ought to tell the stories of what African Americans have managed to accomplish *despite* slavery."

Dad smacked his palm against his knee.

I snapped back that I thought he definitely should see *12 Years a Slave*.

After all, the unpolished rawness and uncompromising energy of hip-hop have their roots in slavery. Just like some of the sweetest forms of expression the human race has ever invented, like jazz and blues. They were born out of misery but were so infectiously captivating and full of such bold emotions that they permeated everything else—contemporary music, fashion, art, the way people talk, the way people walk, the way people *are*. The fact that "diss" and "cool" have become words in the Swedish language, and are now even in the Swedish Academy's official dictionary, is proof of how powerful African American music and culture is.

But Dad refused to see the movie.

And now he's just as stubborn when it comes to my plan to write about our family.

"No one wants to read a book about poor black people in the South. Write about your music, write about something that will contribute to the world, something with a message."

As if to move away from the sensitive topic, he says, "Jason, I got a letter from Cousin Willie's daughter today. He died. He passed away a few weeks after his birthday party."

"What, Dad . . . he's dead?"

"Cousin Willie passed away. No one knows why. He was old. Old people die."

With that, all the answers I've been hoping for are gone forever. I sigh and gaze out at the bare trees in Rörsjö Park under the gray quilt of clouds outside Dad's living room window.

HARLEM, GEORGIA

"Have I ever told you about the time I got arrested in South Carolina?" Dad asks out of the blue.

We're sitting at a café in the middle of the Caroli City shopping center in Malmö in January 2015, and grit on the tiled floor rasps and crunches under the shoppers' winter boots. Dad's eyes sweep over the stream of people. So far, we have neither received the coffee we ordered nor managed to hit that nerve that stimulates a deep conversation between father and son.

I haven't said anything more about my desire to travel to South Carolina and dig into our family history. And he hasn't brought it up either; instead, we're chewing on pleasantries and exchanging tidbits of information about our everyday lives.

He asks me how my car is running. Annoyed, I reply that it's running fine. I ask how his back is doing; he says it's fine. So, how's work? Oh, things are fine for both of us, thanks. My head is full of thoughts about the funk I've fallen into. Why doesn't he ask how my marriage is? He knows I'm in the midst of a crisis. Shit, shouldn't Dad be more interested in the important parts of his son's life, not just how his car is running?

This stiff, hesitant conversation is the last thing I want. Why can't I have a deeper talk with him? Dammit, why am I always so harsh and impatient with him? Why can't I stop being dismissive of him as soon as the conversation isn't on my own terms? My conscience is chafing at me. Do I look down on him? Or does he just *think* I do? Why can't I reply cheerfully to his ordinary questions, share details, without immediately going to DEFCON 3?

He's all bundled up. He always is. His blue winter coat looks two sizes too big; if it weren't, he wouldn't be able to button it over his stomach. Surrounded by his bulky blue woolen beanie and the large coat, his face looks so small that you might think he's twenty years younger than he is. With his scarf still wound tightly around his neck, he continues to tell me about his memory from the South.

The waitress is balancing two very full mugs of coffee, which she cautiously sets before us.

"You know I was with a woman named Betty, right?" Dad asks as I try to take a sip of the hot coffee. "That was before your mom, Jason."

"Yes, I know," I respond without bothering to hide my irritation.

As soon as our conversations touch on his earlier marriage or relationships, I turn into a mama's boy and judge him extra hard.

"Anyway, Betty had three kids. I was only twenty-four, and my mother and grandmother didn't think she was anything worth betting on. But she was a good person. Very poor. Very black and very friendly. I lived in the heart of Harlem in New York. Betty was from the Harlem no one had ever heard of, in Georgia, a place lots of black people fled from in search of a better life. The name was the same, but there were worlds of difference between them. Her Harlem was a place to escape from; my Harlem was a place people escaped to. I knew I would never be able to live in Harlem, Georgia. No chance I would settle in the South. Voluntarily submit to the deadly racism that lived on there? No way. I'd had enough of the South after my military service in Georgia, Texas, and Kentucky."

Dad looks me straight in the eye and won't drop his gaze until I show him, with slow nods, that I am giving him my full attention.

"But I kept seeing her anyway."

Dad folds his hands over his stomach, leans back, and goes on with a dreamy gaze and a small smile that suggests he must have really liked Betty, no matter where she lived.

"Betty was good, she had to live a pretty boring life because she had three kids, and a routine was just what I needed. She made sure that food was on the table at the same time every day. The food part was important, you know. Anyone who gives you food is also giving you love. By the way . . . does your wife cook for you?"

"For the thousandth time, Dad, that attitude is so antiquated I can't even handle it."

Dad nods in concern.

"Just keep telling your story," I say in an impatient tone that's almost exclusively reserved for my father.

A tone I suspect says a lot about my opinions on his choice of topic and likely leaves tiny scars inside both him and me. Papercuts on our souls. But I can't stop myself.

"After a while, Betty had to move home to the South. She'd already left, and I had promised to drive a few boxes down to her. You have to understand, son, that this was 1965, the height of the civil rights movement. Black Panthers, Martin Luther King. The year Malcolm X was shot. Did I ever tell you your aunt and your cousins were at the Audubon Ballroom when Malcolm was shot by Elijah Muhammad's henchmen? Sai and Bibi were probably too little to remember, but your aunt Chinyelu remembers. Her husband at the time, John Farris, was one of Malcolm's bodyguards. It was a terrible time. Black heroes were being murdered. Kennedy had been assassinated too, and the police and the Ku Klux Klan were terrorizing black people all over the country. I felt so fucking resigned after Malcolm was killed. I tried to drive uptown to Washington Heights to rescue your aunt from the chaos. But it was impossible to get through the traffic. It was late, late at night before I got hold of Chinyelu. She couldn't believe it—that Malcolm X had been murdered. She was heartbroken and shaken. She'd been sitting there with Sai and Bibi, and she still hadn't recovered from the shock of what might have happened to her children if the killers had aimed their weapons at the audience."

"What? Why didn't you ever tell me this?" I ask.

"You were always in such a hurry," he responds with a crooked smile. "If you'd taken the time to listen to me, I would have told you."

I just shake my head at this exchange, so typical of the two of us.

The café, the tile floor, the cooling coffee, the streams of people, the sale signs, the noise, and my life crises suddenly seem very distant.

"We'd been so hopeful for so long," he slowly continues. "We knew that we were right, of course, all us African Americans. The injustices had been going on for a ridiculously long time. For God's sake, a hundred years had passed since Lincoln declared the slaves free. But the terror and endless oppression went on and on."

His voice rises again, and an ancient desire to fight blazes up in my so warmly dressed father. He returns to his story about Betty.

"I had a car, one my mother had leased through her business. And, Jason, her business, you know I worked there too, it was a legitimate operation. Your mother always says your grandmother was a hustler, but renting out rooms to poor people was perfectly legal."

Dad's sudden defensiveness leads my thoughts to my grandmother. Who was she, really? How much of a hustler was she? How many dubious shortcuts did she take in life?

Dad's tales of her battle for civil rights and her unshakable belief in black nationalism and freedom for the African American people often portray her as a bit too saintly. But I've also heard my mother's slightly harsher pronouncements about Madame. That she was a bad, irresponsible mother. That she was into shady business up in Harlem. That she was flat-out racist toward my mother and never forgave her son for being a traitor to his race and marrying a white woman. Stories my dad seldom wants to acknowledge, but which I know have branded his soul.

"So I packed my records in the car. Back then, I lived with your aunt and Bibi and Sai in a large apartment on 110th Street and Eighth Avenue. I only took the records I thought I'd need most while I was in the 'other' Harlem. Some Coltrane, Miles Davis, a few Monk LPs."

He laughs.

"Y'know, if I had to sit around in the godforsaken South, I needed to bring a little chicken soup for the soul. I packed my bags too. I didn't know how long I would be staying in Georgia, but I thought it might be a few months. I took my best shirts and two or three suits. I wasn't wearing just any old shoes on my feet, son. It was a pair of Church's. Black wing-tip brogues. They cost fifty dollars. That was a lot of money back then. My father, may he rest in peace, thought it was crazy to spend fifty dollars on a pair of shoes. He had certainly never spent that much on footwear, and still your grandpa was always elegantly dressed, with special emphasis on his shoes. 'You can just buy a pair from Florsheim for four dollars,' he angrily pointed out. 'Sure, Dad,' I said dismissively, 'but these are *handmade* shoes, which means they cost a little more.' He just laughed at me and mumbled that I was too young and dumb to know what was good for me. But, Jason, you always had to look sharp in Harlem. Always, every day. Shirt, tie, jacket—and most important of all, a pair of stylish shoes. It was a matter of pride."

Dad catches my eye just as he says the word "pride." As if to reassure himself that he has transmitted yet another important life lesson to his son. He unbuttons his coat. A sign that we'll be sticking around this harshly lit mall café for a good long time.

"It's all about how we present ourselves, it's all about appearances," Dad admonishes. "That determines what sort of respect the rest of the world will show you. I thought I was careful to raise you to always dress properly, but your hip-hop generation doesn't really understand the importance of that. Y'all walk around in untucked, oversize T-shirts and pants that sag down and don't even cover your asses. You look like jailbirds, or at least people who are begging to become jailbirds."

I just smile and think about how Dad is showing the same lack of understanding as his own dad showed him when he bought a fifty-dollar pair of kicks.

"In our day, dignity was important. You didn't want to look poor. We may have been poor in a financial sense, but spiritually we weren't. It was a time of striving for something greater."

"OK, Dad, but things are different now," I point out. "Plus, I don't wear baggy jeans anymore. Haven't you noticed? And it's just not necessary to tuck in your shirt nowadays."

"Sure, sure." He laughs, waving one hand dismissively before he goes on. "Anyway, I drove downtown to Betty's old apartment. It was on Third and Avenue B, or maybe it was Avenue C. You know how bad things were in Alphabet City in the seventies and eighties; I've told you before. But in 1965 . . . well, it wasn't the ghetto, anyway. I parked the car down on the street and ran up the four flights of stairs to Betty's little hole-in-the-wall to grab the last of her boxes. And wouldn't you know it, when I get back down to the street with the very last box, some goddamn junkie has broken one of the back-seat windows and lifted everything that wasn't attached to the car. My records and clothes; Betty's boxes. Typical New York. My city."

Dad shakes his head. His eyes reveal the love-hate relationship he has to the place he comes from. The city is harsh and brutal, but also action-packed and fantastic. His good-natured smile hints that even the memory of the belongings he lost is a thread that links him to the place he so often talks about and misses. His home.

"Don't bury me here, Jason," Dad says pensively. "I can't spend eternity in an old gray cemetery in Lund or Malmö. I've been away from my people for too long. At least lay me to rest among my own."

I've heard Dad say this any number of times, but never with such honesty and sorrow. We lock gazes for a long time as we sit there in silence. Dad lowers his eyes to stare at the table and observe his own hand for a moment, then looks up again, takes a breath, and pleads, "Take me home when I die."

"I will, Dad, I promise. You'll be buried in America."

He nods, quiet but pleased that his wish has been sown in his son. Then he shifts gears and continues, excited: "So the big city had plans of its own for my records and Betty's boxes. You were always getting stuff stolen out of your car in New York; I've lost so many records over the years. I know Sweden isn't as bad. But I'm still paranoid."

All my life I've heard him say that you should never sit with your back to the door in a restaurant. Never trust anyone on the street and always be aware of your surroundings.

"'Screw it,' I thought. I still had one of Betty's boxes and I wanted to see her. So, I was annoyed, but I drove to the nearest police station and reported the theft before I headed south. So naïve! What was I thinking? A young black man, in 1965, in a rented car with a broken window."

He chuckles at the memory of his own foolhardiness.

"But I was young and awfully dumb. I suppose I was full of the same arrogance I so often see in you. That attitude you young folks have: 'nothing bad could happen to me!'"

All I can do is roll my eyes at his teasing and urge him to go on with his story.

"Somewhere outside Lexington, South Carolina, I was stopped by a state trooper. You know, one of those white, small-time tyrants with a crew cut and a pistol who knows he's got all the power on his side. Especially in an encounter with a black man. They *still* shoot young black men, and women, and even children—and get away with it!"

The tone and volume of Dad's voice peaks, and he doesn't seem to care that the customers at the next table in this little café are sending glances his way, eyeing the old black man whose clothes are too big.

"'Well, well,' that fucking cracker cop snorted," Dad goes on. "'This doesn't look so good, does it? You say the car is a rental. How'd this window get broken?' It was lucky I'd filed a police report back in New York, and I also had proof that the car was rented under my name. I triumphantly handed the paper to the officer, and he stared at it for a long time."

He snorts loudly and snaps his fingers.

"That easy!" he shouts so unexpectedly that the woman behind us jumps. "Those papers might as well have been written in Chinese. It was 1965! In South Carolina. The only thing that cracker saw was a young nigger in a car. Finally, the officer said he wasn't letting me go. Another officer hopped out of the patrol car, which was behind mine, and said I had to get out of the vehicle. One of them drove my car, and I had to ride in the back seat of the troopers' cruiser. We were driving down back roads and I had no idea where we were going, but suddenly we arrived at a small airport. 'There's an Avis desk here,' said the officer. 'Let's go have a talk with them and see what's what.' 'OK, Officer,' I said obediently. I knew enough to tone down my earlier cockiness. Back then, they would hang young black men for nothing!"

Dad's voice rises another notch. I love seeing him so indignant and passionate. He so seldom talks about his most emotional memories.

"You could disappear, and no one would ever find you again. After a while, the trooper came out with the same stern look he'd been wearing when he stopped me on the highway. 'Nope, we're driving into town and dropping you with the sheriff. He can decide what to do with you,' said the crew-cut officer. 'Shit,' I thought. With the state police, at least you had a chance, but with the sheriff in a small town in South Carolina back then . . . anyway, we arrived at the sheriff's office and I had to take a seat in a shabby, bare waiting room. My car was right outside. I could see it through the window."

Dad gives a heavy sigh at the memory. His coat has come off and his knitted hat is on the round metal table. But his scarf is still tied around his neck. He takes a sip of the cooling coffee and goes on.

"The trooper went in and had a good long talk with the sheriff. I spotted an older man in striped clothing who was sweeping the worn wooden floors of the office. This was actually the second time that an old black janitor saved my ass. The man stopped sweeping and came up to me to ask what I'd done. I swore my innocence and told him the whole story in detail. 'That doesn't matter, son,' the old janitor said, giving me knowing look. 'All you need to know is that you're in a real mess right now. They're going to put you away for something, they don't need any real reason to punish a nigger from the North. Suddenly you're chained to fifty other men, digging ditches along the highway all day long. You can count on at least thirty days, or maybe they'll come up with something even worse.' The man leaned on the handle of his broom and thought for a moment. 'The best thing you can do right now is run,' he said, and went back to sweeping the floor. I stood up and walked around the waiting room a little. There was no one there but the cleaning man and me, so I approached the door very slowly. When I got close enough, I opened it and ran as fast as I could. Shit, I was running for my life. Down the block and through a yard. Soon I got to a gas station where I saw a brother about to get in his car. I took a chance and jumped in the back seat. The man was scared at first, but when he saw the fear on my face, he at least let me explain what I was up to. 'Please, mister, can you help me?' I begged. I told him the short version of what was going on and asked if he could drive me someplace where I could find a phone. Given the circumstances, the man was very kind. He drove me to his home, where he let me use the phone and even gave me some food."

Dad pauses and looks around at the shoppers of Caroli City as they buzz past. I suspect a variety show of memories is playing in his head. He continues, his voice just as intense.

"I'll say it again, folks who give you food are good people. That's one thing that can be said for the South: neither slavery nor the Klan could destroy the hospitality. After I ate, I called my mother in New York. But, of course, the line was busy, so I called Betty and explained what had happened. I asked her to keep trying to contact Madame. The kind man offered to drop me off along the highway where the bus usually stopped. I could get on there and transfer to a bus to Harlem in the next town. So suddenly there I was, standing on a highway in South Carolina, only a couple miles from Allendale, where your grandfather was born, running from the law."

He laughs as if the incident is still completely unbelievable.

"But at least I still had my Church's shoes," Dad says, pleased. "I'll tell you again, Jason, it's important to look sharp on every occasion in life. The world will treat you with the same amount of respect as you treat yourself. Sharp!"

My father has a tendency to bang his fist on the table to emphasize what he considers important information. In this case, he nearly over-turns his half-empty coffee mug.

"So there I stood in my fancy shoes, and you know what? I saw the bus coming, getting closer, and then . . . it just leaves me in a cloud of dust."

Dad shakes his head.

"Wild horses couldn't drag me back to that fucked-up state. 'Why did I leave New York?' I thought in a panic. What happened next was even worse. Suddenly I see the sheriff and some of his men driving down the road, three cars in all. The sheriff hopped out and said, 'Boy, guess we've got a problem with you. Now get in the car.' The way the sheriff called me 'boy,' I knew I was dealing with the worst kind of cop. Six policemen against little old me. As politely and subserviently as an African American could possibly address a white officer back then, I said, 'Yes, sir.' Just like a slave. It was just, 'yes suh, no suh, yes suh, no suh.' Dogs were treated better than blacks in the South in those days."

Dad stops to watch me for a moment. As if he's waiting for a reac-tion. Maybe he wants me to understand how horrible the South is. I start to speak, but I don't quite know what to say.

"Go on, Dad," is all I manage.

"So there I was, back in the sheriff's office," he says. "After a while, the sheriff walks into the interrogation room. 'Boy, I don't know who you are or what kind of shit you're stirring up in my town, but I got a call from Washington about you.' *Huh? What's all this?* I thought. The sheriff said, 'So here's the deal: an agent from the FBI is coming to have a talk with you, you troublemaker.' Jason, you know your grandmother worked at the Embassy of Guinea for a while and in Guinea too. You know she spoke fluent French, right?"

"I had no idea, Dad," I respond.

"Well, she did," Dad says proudly. "Your grandmother was very smart. After all, she was a hustler."

Dad smiles in that mysterious way he often does when he's talking about his mother and grandmother. Whether she was a hustler or not depends on his mood.

"After Betty explained what had happened to me, Madame called the FBI in Washington and said she was calling from the Embassy of Guinea and her son had run into trouble outside Lexington, South Carolina, for some tiny thing."

Even her own children called her Madame. They were never, *never* allowed to call her Mom or Mother.

"Lucky for me, Madame could hustle. When the man from the FBI finally showed up, he said I was free to go, and he would help me get a motel room for the night. I called Betty again. She would ask her uncle to drive the eighty miles from Harlem, Georgia, first thing the next morning. The FBI agent thought I could just get back in my rental car, but I absolutely refused. I suspected the sheriff and his men had planted something in the car so they could stop me again as soon as the FBI man left. I was sure they wanted revenge. It was late at night by the time I arrived at the motel in the black part of town. Southern cities are still divided up into black and white parts, often demarcated by the train tracks. Once the FBI agent left, I was once again a lone black man in a dusty backwater in the American South. I paced back and forth in the room. Every possible scenario flashed through my mind. Maybe the sheriff would alert the Klan. What if they came to get me in the middle of the night? No one would ever hear from me again. Just another vanished nigger in the South."

Dad holds up his hands and shakes his head.

"No, sir. No way in hell. I walked down behind the motel and saw a big tree. *Fuck it,* I thought, and climbed as high up in the tree as I could. I sat down on a thick branch where I would be well hidden. There, at least, I was relatively safe. That's where I spent the night, Jason. In a tree, with my handmade black leather shoes on my feet. So much for looking sharp. I still ended up a tree like a fucking monkey."

Once again, Dad lets his eyes wander over the brightly lit mall passageway outside the little café.

How can the country where he was treated like a dog with no rights also be the country he calls home? How has this sort of experience shaped Dad? How has it affected his understanding of his skin color and his identity? I realize, too, that this must be the sort of experience that has caused him and his friends to see the world in black and white. That never let them forget the difference in living conditions that come with having black skin. My experiences with racism in Sweden pale in comparison to the lack of rights black people in the United States endure.

I become even more convinced that I want to know more. Much more. I want to gather stories, memories. I have to hold on to this inheritance so I can pass it on to future generations. One day I, too, will be part of history. The history that belongs not only to those of us who have lived already, but also to those yet to be born.

I say none of this to Dad, who's still looking around as people swarm past us. Dad notices me trying to catch his eye and shifts in his chair.

"So, anyway, there I was, up a fucking tree. Terrified of being lynched and cursing my own foolishness. What was I *thinking*? 1965 . . ."

Dad stops talking. His gaze seems to go blank again, and he says in a lower voice, "I just wanted to get out of there as fast as I could. At last I made it to Harlem, Georgia. Knowing full well that I couldn't stay there with Betty. But also with the feeling that I didn't even want to stay in a country where I had to live in fear of the authorities. Your mom was the first person I met who showed me there was a different life. Beyond Harlem. You know, Jason, I didn't set foot in South Carolina again until 2002, and to be perfectly honest, I still felt uncomfortable entering the state. Some things have changed, but that goddamn racism in the South—it lives on."

THE CHOIR SINGS

My earliest memory is of my mother's crying face. I'm standing in my crib, holding on to the slats, looking up at her. Tears are running down her cheeks, and she's shouting something at my dad, who's standing in the doorway. I am one year old.

Shortly after that, they divorce. My dad, the hot-tempered visionary who dreamed of getting an education and devoted his energy to uplifting black people, and my artistic, energetic mom, who left her exciting life in New York in 1969 to support him as he chased his dreams in little Lund in the peculiar country of Sweden.

Elaine came from a well-respected, loving family in the sleepy coal-mining city of Scranton, Pennsylvania. She was well educated, and by the age of twenty-four, she had already traveled all over the world. The predictable existence for smart white girls in Scranton in that era was not for her—she wanted to live her life on different terms.

Perhaps Elaine and Madubuko were each other's ticket to that other life they so fervently dreamed of. Perhaps their respective differences were the soil that fertilized their unlikely love. In 1966, it wasn't a common sight to see black boys and white girls walking hand in hand on city streets, standing together in line for a movie, sitting at restaurants or on park benches, or whispering intimate words to each other. Could skin color have mattered to my parents? Could Mom's white skin have signaled to Dad that, with her by his side, he would find a way out of

Harlem and gain access to the big world outside? Did Dad's black skin spark Mom's desire for something other than a safe middle-class existence? Or did they not see skin color at all—were they just two young people who found each other in that big city?

It's March, and I'm in a snowless Skåne, visiting my family for the fourth time since New Year's. My one-year-old nephew, Rion, is still in the hospital, and the doctors aren't yet sure how grave his arthritic disease is, just that it is very serious. Mom has been taking care of Rion's sister, Stella, since my sister and brother-in-law are spending day and night at his bedside, and I come down to see them and lend a hand as often as I can. Before I drove to Skåne, I warned Mom that I wanted to interview her.

"Oh, OK, so what do you want to know? And why?"

"Nothing major, Mom," I assured her. "Just a few simple questions. Nothing to be nervous about."

My parents are extremely private people. I recall how uneasy they were the first time I participated in Swedish Radio's *Sommar i P1*, a program that is wildly popular in summertime when a different person each day gets ninety minutes to speak about whatever they want. They didn't like the idea that I would talk about my personal life live on the air. It was bad enough that their son had chosen a very public career—they are not interested in having their lives put under the microscope. The second time I was on the show, I sent the relevant parts of the manuscript to them for their approval. Their responses were curt and unenthusiastic. "Fine, fine, if you want to talk about this, well . . ."

Now I'm sitting in Mom's living room. She's on the sofa with her foot up on a stool—she recently had surgery—and I've pulled up a chair. Mom's shoulders tense when I pull my phone out.

"Oh, are you going to record me?" she asks.

"I want to write a book about our family's history and what brought us to Sweden," I reply.

She looks at me in surprise.

"It's important to me to write down your story while you're all still young enough to tell it," I say with a wink.

She doesn't seem enthused in the least about discussing her background and her life. But at the same time, she loves to talk, so once we get going, her words flow like water down a mountain.

"Well, I underwent a transformation of my own. A lot happened in my life in the 1950s and '60s. I went from a simple small-town life in Scranton to four eventful years at college in Syracuse, and then I spent two years in a small village in the Philippines, in the Peace Corps. I was an aid worker and mainly taught English to the villagers. Before I moved to New York, I spent 1964 traveling all over Asia. My friend Bill was the one who suggested I look for a job as a social worker with the New York State Training School for Girls. My job was to place young girls in foster homes, then follow up and make sure they were doing well. Back then, I wasn't very familiar with New York, and I thought the city was enormously exciting. I bought a subway map and set out. My zones were Bedford-Stuyvesant and East New York, which were financially and socially hard-hit parts of Brooklyn. At the time, it was unusual for white people to go there. But I was naïve, which probably saved me. It was like it never occurred to me that there was anything strange about going to the ghetto. I did try to look like I knew where I was going, and I never looked people in the eye. I'd learned that much. Actually, there was only ever one time I felt threatened. One of my clients and three other girls had been placed in a foster home, and we had found out that the foster mother was prostituting the girls. She was basically running a brothel."

Mom reaches for a blanket to put over her legs. As she carefully spreads it out, she continues.

"The foster mother threatened me with two big German shepherds when I showed up at her door in my social-worker shoes."

"What kind of shoes were those?"

"Gum soles, they were called. Real nerd shoes, hardly anyone walked around in them. I'm sure you could tell I was a social worker from a mile away. Here comes the little white twenty-five-year-old in her gum soles in the middle of East New York."

Mom laughs.

"Anyway, the lady said that the dogs didn't like white people and hinted that she would sic them on me if I didn't get out of there. I hurried back to the office and told my boss what had happened. Later, we went over with the police, retrieved the girls, and placed them in better homes. I lived in Manhattan, on Avenue C. It was a crazy place, full of junkies and prostitutes. It wasn't exactly safe either. But you got used to New York quickly. It was an intense but wonderful city to be young in."

Mom's current home is far from the hectic pulse of Manhattan. She lives on the outskirts of Lund, in a leafy development of row houses called Djingis Khan: a collection of boxy, wooden two-story homes that stand among oaks, hackberry trees, and lilac hedges. The development was built as student housing in 1972 and was an enclave for immigrants and leftists from the start. It's the same neighborhood my dad lived in for most of my upbringing. Djingis Khan—named after a famous play put on by the students at Lund University, which in turn took its name from the most ruthless ruler and successful conqueror in human history—is the geographical location that most strongly signifies home for me.

Mom has both a garden and an allotment there. On the windowsill in her cozy living room are rows of potted hoya plants. A red sofa marks the center of the room and is flanked by two lovely wooden lamps. On the walls are marionettes from Indonesia, masks from the Philippines, and sculptures she's made herself out of crooked driftwood fashioned to look like birds in flight. Mom's apartment is neater than Dad's; there aren't as many books and papers scattered about. Unlike Dad, Mom prefers antique furniture and decorates her home with artifacts from her many travels. She has good taste, my mom. I'd like to believe I inherited that from her.

It feels as though the foliage outside extends into the house. She notices me looking at her plants.

"Look how healthy my baobab trees are," she says proudly. "Both the one you bought me in Senegal and the one I got from Lisa."

"No doubt about it, Mom, you have a green thumb. But keep telling the story!"

"Anyway, I met your dad while I was looking for one of my clients who had run away from her foster home. I found out that the girl was in Harlem, on 110th Street. OK, no problem, I headed uptown and rang the bell. It was your aunt Chinyelu's apartment. A real slum, Jason. The buildings are nice now, but back then, the paint was peeling in the hallways and every other light bulb was missing. The stairwell stank of piss and shit. There was trash everywhere. Junkies on the stairs and rats in the corners. But in any case, there I was on the third floor and the door was opened by a very stylishly dressed young man. He had a three-piece gray wool sharkskin suit on. He was good-looking too. It was a large apartment with big windows overlooking Central Park. There was almost nothing inside. No furniture. No rugs, no pictures on the walls. It was impoverished. As Harlem had been for a long time. It's only recently that gentrification brought in the people with money to spend on fixing up those grand old buildings . . ."

She snorts and rolls her eyes.

"Your dad looked at me in surprise. 'I'm looking for Patricia,' I said. He invited me in, and I got a good feeling about him. I simply trusted him right off the bat. He had kind eyes and gorgeous hands. I don't know why, but I've always been attracted to beautiful hands."

Mom smiles dreamily. I know she's had three great loves in her life, three pairs of hands to which she has entrusted her heart.

"Their shape, the texture of the skin, the web of veins across their backs, the slenderness of the fingers . . . I can't put my finger on what makes a nice hand so nice, but when I see a pair of nice hands, I know it right away. Madubuko was living there at the time, and he told me his sister had found Patricia in the stairwell. She had nowhere else to go and had made her way there to sleep. But it was extremely dangerous for a fourteen-year-old girl, so your aunt had invited her to stay in her apartment. My job was to investigate the situation in the apartment to see if your aunt could be approved to be Patricia's guardian. And she was, but after six months or so, Patricia ran away from her too. We never found her again. But there and then, in your aunt's apartment, that very first time we met, your dad and I started talking about music and the clubs in Greenwich Village. I mostly just wanted to talk about the Beatles, but I understood by your father's bewildered look that he preferred a different kind of music. I honestly think Madubuko was a little shocked to meet a white girl who was so enthusiastic about talking to him. I told him about everything I liked about New York and that I love the theater. 'Oh, so do I,' said your dad. But it just felt like a come-on."

Mom stops in the middle of her story and observes my self-conscious expression. Does she see my dad in me? Does she think I toss out lines all the time too?

"Yeah, Dad probably wasn't as smooth as he thought." I grin.

"But he was charming, so why not? I said I really wanted to see *Man of La Mancha*. The musical version of *Don Quixote*. It was having a really long run back then. So we exchanged numbers and decided to see it together."

Dad was definitely hitting on Mom. No way he was a regular theatergoer in the New York of the sixties. Maybe I'm mistaken, but it doesn't jibe with the man I know, who doesn't even like to read fiction. Did she really believe him?

"I knew he was just trying to serve up smooth lines, he was snowing me," she says with a smile, then continues in a more serious tone.

"Several years later when I brought your dad on his first trip to Europe, we went to the area where Cervantes's book takes place. One day, we stopped at a small hotel in the Spanish countryside. I hopped out of the car, ran in, and asked if they had any rooms available. The little old man behind the counter was very accommodating and said there were plenty of rooms. When I came back with your dad and our luggage, it was like the old man was a completely different person. He snapped that there weren't any free rooms at all. That I'd gotten it all wrong. Goddamn . . ."

Mom's face twists in disgust.

"I never could get used to the racism. Your dad couldn't either, but that time he was so dejected that he didn't say anything. At the market in the little village, we bought a rabbit, some vegetables, and a bottle of wine and drove out into the country and parked our little Citroën Deux Chevaux in a meadow at the edge of the forest. I made rabbit stew, and then we took the seats out of the car and slept in sleeping bags on the metal floor. It was a wonderful night. We didn't stay at any hotels for the rest of that trip. Instead, we repeated our little ritual with the seats every night. Oh, Jason, I'm just babbling . . ."

"No, Mom, keep going. I want to know everything!"

Mom seems delighted at how raptly I'm listening to her memories, and after smoothing the blanket over her legs, she's ready to go on.

"That day in your aunt's apartment in Harlem, I also told your dad that a man had dropped all his papers on the bus a week or so earlier and I'd helped him pick them up. As thanks, he had invited me to lunch afterward. 'You're not from here?' your dad asked. 'Nope.' I laughed. 'You shouldn't be so naïve,' he said. Your dad taught me that. That it's healthier not to be so trusting. But it also made me feel afraid, like I constantly had to be on guard. I think that sort of fear can attract misfortune somehow. 'This isn't a rose garden, Elaine.' That was something your father was always saying."

"So, it was sort of like double-edged wisdom?"

She nods.

"His reality and the one I came from were worlds apart. I hadn't been brought up with fear, the idea that I should always be watching my back. I grew up in a nice single-family home in a small town where everyone knew me and my family. I'd also traveled all over Asia on my own, so I thought I knew how to survive. But Madubuko and I had completely different ideas about reality. Not just how we understood the world around us, but how differently the world viewed us individually and as a couple. After work, I kicked off my social worker shoes and put on nice clothes. I had accounts at Bergdorf Goodman and Saks. I lived a life of luxury compared to your dad. Yet we found each other in that huge city, like two planktons who happen to meet in the stomach of a blue whale. I had dated black men before I met Madubuko. So had some of my friends. We wanted to break out of the strict, narrow norms of the 1950s. My God, the civil rights movement was in full swing. I was sympathetic to it, but I wasn't an active participant. But I was involved in the anti-war movement, protesting the Vietnam War. I helped distribute literature, handed out flyers, and demonstrated. Only after I met your dad did I realize how much my white perspective shaped my view of American society. My father paid for college for my siblings and me. I got a great education and lived in a sorority house with servants who waited on us. Still, I wasn't completely oblivious. My classmates and I had demonstrated outside the dean's office when he decided anyone who dated a black person would be required to inform their parents. My best friend, Linda, was with a black man who also went to Syracuse, and it was hard to wrap our minds around his stories of how much trouble he'd had trying to find a place to live, just because of the color of his skin. And here we lived in a big old mansion in the heart of the city. Talk about guilt. It made me feel ashamed of my skin color. Since your dad had lived in Nigeria, we hung out with a lot of exiled Nigerians in New York, ate Nigerian food, and danced to highlife music."

My grandmother, Madame, was responsible for Dad's knowledge of Nigerian culture. Madame was a Pan-Africanist, an activist, and a black nationalist. She was convinced that it would be best for the black citizens of America to move back to Africa. So when she got married for the third time, in the 1950s, to a Nigerian journalist, she sent her four children there so they would be spared the oppression of the United States and develop an African identity, and the pride she believed would result.

"It was during those days I started to identify with black people," Mom says. "For a while, I even believed I *was* black. I was fascinated by black skin, and I often looked in the mirror, surprised to find that I wasn't black. That's how much I wanted to take part in Madubuko's thoughts, feelings, and experiences."

Mom's words make me think of all the times I stood in front of the wardrobe mirror as a kid, trying to see the opposite. I tried to see a white Jason. It strikes me that I never told either of my parents about my confused identity. I don't get much farther in that thought before Mom starts in on another memory.

"The first time I met your grandmother, I was struck by her vanity. Your dad introduced her as his older sister. But I knew she wasn't. She also talked in this corny, fake British accent, which I found strange. And she often wore a mink coat. It was so contradictory that this extremely vocal and intelligent woman put on such artificial airs, so easy to see right through. She wasn't a very good mother. Maybe if she'd gotten more love from her mother, she would have been better at loving her own children. Madame was very dark, while her sister Bessie was light-skinned. Your great-grandmother BM was a tiny woman, but she was tough. She was Native American, and I remember her whole apartment smelled like mothballs. She had strategically arranged them under the big faux Persian rug in the living room to keep it from being eaten up by bugs. And then, in the middle of all this, I show up: a white woman

45

with designer jewelry, expensive silk stockings, and a miniskirt. I was basically unacceptable in every way."

Mom laughs. I imagine she hasn't thought back on this for a very long time.

As Mom takes a sip of her tea, I think about a framed black-and-white photo I have of three short-haired women in knee-length skirts. My great-grandmother in the middle, her daughter Madame on her right, and to the left, Bessie, four shades lighter—the belated child BM had during another relationship. They're sitting on a rococo sofa, and there's a glimpse of a rug at their feet. I imagine the scent of mothballs. No one in the picture is smiling. Bessie's head is turned toward BM, who is looking straight into the camera with a grim expression. Madame is holding BM's right hand in both her own with what appears to be a tight grip.

After a while, Mom shakes herself as if to resurface from the distant memories, and she cheerfully tells me about the time she had to hide under a coat in the back seat of my grandmother's car in Harlem so Madame wouldn't be seen with a white person in the car.

"Was my grandfather the same when you met him for the first time?" I wonder.

"Your grandfather was a quiet man, but he was lovely—and he made food for me too. The first time he made me breakfast, he cooked brains and eggs. Yeesh . . . fried calf brains and scrambled eggs. I'd never seen a breakfast like that. By the way, did you know . . ." She trails off.

"Know what?"

"Your grandmother refused to come to our wedding. She hated the thought of your dad marrying a white woman. But BM actually did show up. Your dad didn't get much love or intimacy in his life. His parents did their best, but they were more severe than I was used to. There was no coddling, no talking about feelings. It was no sure thing, surviving in Harlem. Aside from in music, there was no room for feelings and gentle words."

I find it moving that Mom can still be so understanding about the fact that Dad's family had such a hard time showing each other love. It must have been hard for her to accept.

"When I told my family I'd met your dad, the news exploded like a bomb. My uncle Bob thought I should break up with him. 'It's impossible for whites and blacks to live together,' he claimed. Bob didn't consider himself a racist, just a person with normal ideas about what was socially and culturally acceptable. He even had the gall to tell me, 'I don't approve of your relationship, Elaine.'"

Mom chuckles, and I ask eagerly, "But what did Grandpa think of it?"

She takes a deep breath and responds.

"At first, he felt the same way. Madubuko wrote a formal letter to him to ask for my hand, but your grandpa didn't answer and wouldn't even speak to me for a long time. But suddenly, one day, he called me up and said he wanted your dad and me to come to Scranton. When we got off the bus at the station, he was already there. I wanted to jump in the front seat next to Dad, I'd missed him so much, but he asked us to sit in back, and he drove us in his silver Oldsmobile like a chauffeur. His voice was quiet but serious: 'I want to apologize,' he said. 'I've been acting like a racist, but I want you two to know that if you want to get married, you have my full support. I accept you, Madubuko, and I'm ashamed of my behavior. I want both of you to hear me say this right now, so we don't have to talk about it anymore later.'"

Mom's voice breaks. Her gaze disappears into the distance, and I can see how much she misses her dad, how the sadness seizes her. She runs her hands through her hair as if she doesn't quite know what to do with them. At last, she laces her fingers behind her head and leans back on the sofa. It's as if she's holding pain, happiness, warmth, and longing inside her all at once.

When she looks up at me again, her eyes are full of a tenderness I seldom see in her.

"I saw Dad's face in the rearview mirror and the tears trickling down his cheeks. That was why he didn't want me next to him in the passenger seat. He knew he was going to get more emotional than he was comfortable with, and he didn't want me to see him cry."

It's the first time I've heard this story, and I have to fight to keep the floodgates closed. I'm touched by how emotional Mom is getting about such a crucial moment in her life. It also makes me think of my maternal grandfather, a man who also always dressed elegantly, with his black beret, a man who spoke fluent French and liked to sing Slovak folk songs. I remember Grandpa's two-tone shoes with their white and brown leather. The man who taught me to play cribbage and always believed in me. The man who always said that one fine day I would attend Princeton, just as he had.

There's a photograph of my two grandfathers standing in front of my maternal grandpa's house outside Scranton. The picture must be from 1969. It's in color, and the two men seem to be trying to outdo each other's smiles. They're wearing similarly elegant, shiny shoes. I've heard they liked each other—they respected one another's work ethic, and, I'm guessing, style.

My mom's maternal grandfather, Michael Bosak, fled rural Slovakia at the age of sixteen and came to the United States in 1886, through Ellis Island, to build a better life in the New World. Both he and my dad's father had fled poverty as teenagers on their own.

It's a beautiful moment I share with Mom, here in her living room, and it further strengthens my desire to dig deeper into my family history. Mom smiles lovingly and breaks the silence as if she has just come across a forgotten shard of memory.

"Now that I think about it, I hardly ever saw my father cry," she recalls. "But he cried that time. Hardly a day goes by that I don't think about him or Mom. I was so proud of him in that moment. When your dad and I got divorced many years later, your grandpa said it was much worse than when I asked him to accept that we were going to get married: 'I stood up for the two of you to all my friends and relatives who were protesting the marriage so loudly and saying that a relationship between a white person and a black person could never last. Now you're proving them right. And they're going to make sure I know it.' My only response was, 'Dad, maybe I just married the wrong black person.'"

I laugh until my chest hurts, and Mom joins in just as loudly.

"But I'm proud that I opened my brother's and sisters' eyes to the fact that it's not skin color that defines a person," she says at last. "Later, when I met Roland—a white Swedish man—they were forced to accept it when we lived together and had a child without being married. I've always been a rebel."

As we sit in Mom's apartment in Djingis Khan in Lund, I'm reminded that Lund is where Mom was called "nigger whore" on the street. Lund was where she most clearly felt the difference between walking hand in hand with a black man and with a white man. But New York had toughened her up. Once, when a white man in Little Italy shouted "you nigger whore" after her on the street, Dad calmly walked around to the trunk of his car, took out a crowbar, walked up to the car the man was in, and slammed the crowbar as hard as he could into the windshield, shattering it. Then he walked calmly back to his car, where Mom was standing, and said, "Come on, Elaine, let's go."

"We weren't surprised by the reactions in New York, because the lines were so sharply drawn between black and white. But to experience the same ignorance, the same fear, the same hate, in Sweden weighed heavy on us. We realized we would never be able to escape the color of our skin . . ." Elaine says.

This conversation rips a hole inside me. I see the sad nine-year-old lying there at night, inconsolable, wondering why he exists and asking his mom, "Why do I look like this? What am I?" And her well-meaning face when she replies, "You are a beautiful boy and don't let anybody tell you any different. And I love you very much."

In these late-winter weeks of March, the memories land at the bottom of my soul. The emotions from my childhood pop up inside me before I fall asleep, as I stare out the bus window, as I walk home from the grocery store, as I take care of the recycling, pay bills, fold the laundry, brush my teeth; they show up right before I go onstage. The memories haunt me full force. As if I was saving them until I got strong enough to handle it, to feel them again. The memories are strongest when I return to Lund and wander around the streets, wander among the buildings and byways that shaped me.

My sister Anja is born in 1981. To a white mother and a white father. I am six. When we go to restaurants, walk around town, go on vacation, I feel like I don't fit into the image of our family. I don't look like I belong with them.

I'm sure Mom loves my sister more; they look just like each other. It doesn't matter how much tenderness and attention Mom shows me; from the age of eight, my self-image tells me my skin color is something ugly. I have a hard time loving myself. This is the start of a drawn-out identity crisis. A process that will follow me through life like a shadow.

When I'm six, at daycare at my cousin Bibi's house, a cute girl named Maria calls me a brown midget. I'm speechless; I just keep playing. But later I gather the courage to ask Bibi how come I'm brown.

"Your mom spilled coffee on you when you were a baby," she answers. "That's why you're brown."

I contemplate my mom's clumsiness for a while and then go back to playing.

I become more and more self-conscious and inquisitive about my skin color, and when I'm seven, Dad says, "Jason, don't ever let anyone call you a mulatto. That's a very bad word."

He walks over to the bookshelf, as he so often does. When I ask him tough questions, he always refers me to a book where I can find the answer, instead of just telling me. Education and culture are fundamental parts of my father's role as a parent. Dad places the encyclopedia on the table, pages quickly through it, stops his index finger on one page, reads silently, and then says, "Here you can see that 'mulatto' comes from the word 'mule.' Never let anyone call you 'mule' or 'half breed,' or belittle your heritage in any other way. You're black, be proud of that."

It takes many years for me to understand what he means.

When I'm a teenager, I ask him how he ended up in Sweden, and Dad tells me it was a coincidence. He'd been accepted into film school in Copenhagen. In the years leading up to that, he had become interested in making movies and had done a few in the US. He dreamed of becoming a documentary filmmaker.

"One day, walking down Strøget in Copenhagen, I ran into another black man. Well, of course, I stopped to talk to him. He was from Zambia and eagerly welcomed me to Scandinavia and told me I would be better off going to the neighboring country, Sweden, which was only a short ferry trip away. There, he said, they practically gave away university educations, and best of all you could study in English, unlike in Copenhagen, where I had to learn Danish in order to study. I could hardly believe my ears: anyone at all could study anything at all, for free. And in English."

The same day he arrived in Lund, in 1968, he enrolled at the university.

"Back then," Dad remembers one day, "we could take as many credits as we wanted to and could handle each semester. Jason, your godfather Hilmi got a bachelor's degree with a major in the history of economics in a year and a half. At the age of twenty! Education, Jason, education . . . An education and the dignity it gives you is something no one can take away."

So Dad left Harlem for Copenhagen and then left Copenhagen for Sweden. As far as I know, he's been registered at Lund University ever since. Fifty-five years later, he still pays the term fee and keeps his student union membership card in his wallet.

In sixth grade, I become friends with Alex, a kid in my class. He doesn't play soccer or handball, and he's not in the popular crowd at school. Yet he gets respect from just about everybody.

Alex lives in Gräddhyllan, a small neighborhood whose name means "top shelf"—home of the most lavish mansions on the east side of Lund. He has a Ping-Pong table and a pool table; he goes skiing during winter and Easter breaks, and he goes on vacation to the US and London. To me, Alex is super cool, and I secretly wish I could live his life, be white and rich.

One day I barely have time to step through Alex's door before he says, "My parents are going to Denmark."

His parents aren't like mine. They have expensive clothes, expensive habits, serious faces, and they travel a lot. All alone in that big house, we play Ping-Pong and pool and run around.

"Wanna see my dad's liquor cabinet?" Alex asks slyly after we finish a game of Ping-Pong.

He goes over to a large cupboard in the kitchen, opens the door, and takes out a green bottle.

"This is banana liqueur," he says. "Pisang Ambon."

We drink it straight from the bottle. After each gulp, we alternate exchanging pleased glances and laughs. Soon Alex takes out another bottle.

"This is sake. My dad bought it in Japan."

Alex pours a little sake into a cup and says we have to kneel to drink it. That's how they do it in Japan.

We get on our knees on the brown tile floor, facing each other, with the cup of sake between us. Alex bends forward like a Muslim placing his forehead to the floor in prayer and picks up the cup of sake, raises his head and the glass, and takes a sip.

"You have to say *kampai*," Alex informs me.

I do as he says. We sample and taste our way through Alex's dad's liquor cabinet. Our fits of laughter get longer and longer until we're rolling around on the floor. Our wrestling match is interrupted by even more peals of laughter until Alex says we should go buy some *snus*. When I do my first packet of the snuff, I feel numb all over, and also like I'm embracing a forbidden adventure. A few minutes later, I'm puking all over a building outside the shop that sold us the *snus*. With traces of vomit on my chin, I tell Alex I have to go home.

Around eight in the evening, I walk into my mother's kitchen and loudly declare what's going on.

"Mom, I'm drunk."

I stagger to the living room and lie down on the sofa. Mom follows me, looking at me with an expression of amused shock. I lean over the armrest of the big blue corner sofa, grab a pillow, and blow my nose violently on it.

"What on earth are you doing?" Mom shouts. "How could you get drunk?"

Mom is relatively lenient, but when Dad is called over an hour or so later, it's a different story. He chews me out and says he's very disappointed in me, angry at how far over the line my behavior is. He thought he raised me better than that. How could I even think of doing something so stupid? Dammit, he's going to call Alex's parents and tell them a thing or two.

I'm sick for two days after our night of drinking. We never become very close friends, but Alex is always nice to me, which means that the cooler guys in our class tease me less.

"I don't understand why Magnus and those guys tease you so much," Alex says one day. "You're not even black."

In that moment, I love Alex. Finally, a white boy who sees that I'm not black. If he can see my whiteness, then other people must be able to as well.

When my mother's partner, Roland, mentions that he used to tape down his wavy hair to make it as straight as Paul McCartney's, I try to do the same. I fight with the transparent pieces of tape for a long time to get them to stick to my scalp. Every morning, I wake up full of expectation. Instead, I find little hairy bits of tape in my bed. My curls persist in curling. I try hair gel, combs, and water, but I can never get a side part to stay.

At the hairdresser, I always point at the pictures of the all-white men with hairstyles that are fashionable in the eighties, like Tom Cruise in *Top Gun* or synth-pop singer Howard Jones on the cover of the album *Dream into Action*, and say, "I want to look like that."

I get the same response every time: "That won't work with your hair."

Until my classmates discover Eddie Murphy, Michael Jackson is the only black celebrity people know of. In 1986, when I look at the cover of *Off the Wall* and compare it to the picture that adorns *Bad*, I can clearly see that I'm not the only one trying to erase and escape my skin color.

Michael Jackson's face and fate, later in life, are perhaps the most candid display of self-hatred ever. Even though he was the biggest star of all time and a billionaire several times over, he never managed to escape from the self-contempt his brown skin evoked from the white eyes with which he observed himself.

Michael Jackson is the biggest idol I've ever had. But during my teen years, he gives me nothing in terms of being a black role model. Instead, he only amplifies the unhealthy self-image I already possess—no matter how many white gloves I put on, how much I moonwalk in front of the mirror and daydream myself away.

For a long time, I've tried to make myself invisible in school. I dress like everyone else, talk about the same movies, join in on games of soccer and *brännboll* and *innebandy*. I've even chimed in on teasing Stefan for being the first one to grow pubic hair, Emma for the weird way she dresses, and Ingrid because she cries so easily. The tiniest difference is a target for oppression, and I'm as ruthless toward them as my tormentors are toward me. All to keep from being noticed. All to keep from finding myself in the bullies' crosshairs.

So now I've heard from Alex that he can see something the bullies can't. That I'm white. After all, I have those flecks of pigment on my left hand. A cluster of white spots that looks like a map of an archipelago. I sometimes stare at those spots for a long time, imagining that if they were more numerous, I would have been white.

I close my eyes and try to imagine what I'd look like if I were white. Sometimes I even feel like the marks have grown. That the whiteness inside me is spreading. But it never does. Those white flecks are locked in an eternal stalemate with a sea of brown.

Alex remains, however, the only white person who ever suggests I am white.

"Nigger shit."

For several years, this is my middle name. What could be blacker than the feces of a black person? It would have been bad enough just to be called "shit." But apparently, middle-schoolers understand that shit from a nigger must be more disgusting than white people's.

One duo, Magnus and Agge, calls me this during many recesses, and my only defenses are my fists. But I can't punch their words away. They bore their way in under my reddish-brown skin.

No matter how invisible I am, they can still reveal my true self. How did Magnus and Agge learn these words? Nigger shit. Nigger. Nigger bastard. You fucking nigger. Each time I hear those words, it's as if they lay open my insides, which indeed contain the grossest thing ever: nigger shit.

I learn early on that the kindness of little white boys has its limits. Any day without such nicknames cast after me is a good day. But I always know that tomorrow I might be reminded of my skin color again, and of what it looks like. No one else in the class ever reacts to the fact that Magnus and Agge call me nigger so often. Do they think I'm a nigger shit too?

And so they pass—the days, weeks, months, and years in the asphalt schoolyard of my school, Tunaskolan, and in its whitish-beige corridors and classrooms. One day, I'm playing with my tormentors; the next day, we fight after one of them throws those words in my face.

One afternoon, as the recess bell rings, we all run into the small hallway outside our classroom. In it stands a big gray barrel full of plastic field-hockey sticks. The early bird gets the worm. Everyone is assigned their own stick, but you lose yours if someone else takes it. I grab one a split second before Magnus does.

"That's my stick," he says sharply.

"But I got it first," I respond.

"It's mine," he says, raising his voice. "Let go, fucking nigger shit!"

I don't let go of the handle of the plastic stick, and Magnus doesn't either. Our tussle is in full swing. Magnus is at least four inches taller than me and manages to work it out of my hands. I am left by the barrel to find another decent stick. I notice Miriam standing right behind me. She's merely waited for the scuffle to end so she can grab her stick. Miriam doesn't look at me; she just finds hers and heads for the playground.

Ever since we played Truth or Dare in second grade and I got to kiss Miriam, I've had a crush on her. All the guys in my class have a crush on Miriam. She has long blonde hair and intensely blue eyes. *She heard what Magnus called me,* I think. *No way such a beautiful girl would lower herself to like a nigger shit like me. So humiliating. I'm so small.*

I daydream all the time. I dream of the day I'll show up at school and everyone will want to play with me. And Miriam will want to kiss me again.

The playground of Tunaskolan is for more than playing. The choir of bullies might start droning on at any moment. The tiniest mistake I make, the tiniest misstep, and I'll hear those words again. There is nothing I can do to bring down or disturb the pigmentocracy that rules the classroom, the halls, the gym, the cafeteria, the schoolyard, or the hockey field.

There are only three brown-skinned students in the whole middle school: Monica, the cute girl from Brazil; Ben, adopted from India; and me. Ben and I are friends by geography. We're neighbors. His adoptive mom won't let him be at home during the daytime on weekends or school breaks. He has a small space in the chilly, unfinished, concrete basement in his adoptive parents' big red house. When he can't find any playmates, he hangs out there, in the dark.

Ben and I swipe apples and plums from neighborhood yards; we climb trees, ride bikes, and fight. He's the year below me in school, but since we're friends, we hang out on the playground. So often that my choir of bullies sings to him too.

"Why the hell are they calling me 'nigger bastard'? I'm from India," he says, honestly surprised. "I suppose it's just because I hang out with you."

I have no response, no comfort, no explanation to give him. Ben lies a lot; I do too. I lie about my dad. That he's actually a rich filmmaker, or that my real dad lives in New York and has met Eddie Murphy, that he has four cars.

Besides having nonwhite skin at Tunaskolan, it's not exactly a plus if your parents are or seem poor. Then you get called "socialist bastard" or even straight-up "commie." The few times I allow my parents to pick me up from school, they always arrive in their beat-up cars. Dad in his worn-out white Volvo Amazon or his rusty black Simca, and Mom in her red wreck of a Renault 16. The other kids are picked up in Mercedes, Volvo 740s, or BMWs. I hunker down as low as I can so no one will notice me sitting in a beat-up old car.

But I'm glad I fight back. Even if I wish I could use words instead. My clenched fists echo with my mom's and dad's affirmative reminders that I am beautiful, and a result of their love—no matter what white boys think.

I never become a particularly successful brawler. No matter how much I windmill my little fists, I can't fend off those words and their way of getting under my skin. Words that have colonized my soul and trickled back out like poison ever since the first time I heard them. Words that make me hate my parents or myself one day and hate everyone else the next. Words that make me hate my teachers for never seeing what's going on or my classmates for never standing up for me.

The dad of one of my tormentors is a dentist at the state-run dental clinic in Lund. My fear of the dentist has nothing to do with oral hygiene. I never have any cavities. But I think the dentist himself is creepy. After all, his son is one of the kids who calls me those names in school.

Does the dentist know? Is it even something they talk about at home? I wonder every time I have to see him. When the dentist speaks to me, I look away and answer his questions quietly. I don't want to awaken his rage and hear my nicknames from a grown-up, bearded dentist. Especially not when he's sticking metal instruments in my mouth. What if he pokes me with that frightening hooklike tool he's scraping my teeth with?

"Would you like to come over and play with Magnus?" the dentist asks one day when my appointment is over and I'm about to leave the sterile room.

"OK, I guess so," I say, surprised.

Why does he want me to come over to their house? His son hates me. Doesn't the dad hate me too? I can't quite read his expression. He's smiling, but it's not entirely friendly.

"Bring that new record you have."

I'm supposed to bring my new record and come over to play? I've never been invited to so much as a birthday party at their place. Why this strange invitation, and why now? I don't get it.

A few months earlier, Mom had taken me and some other English-speaking kids to see the movie *Beat Street* at a theater in Malmö. The movie takes place in the South Bronx in the early 1980s, and it's about graffiti, breakdance, and rap. It was my first visual contact with hip-hop culture. I danced along in my seat in the theater.

Those cool actors in their Puma Clydes with fat laces, and one of the characters, Lee, even has ski goggles over his cap. It's the awesomest thing I've ever seen. The soundtrack is released in two vinyl editions—one with a yellow cover and one with a pink cover. I get the pink one.

I lie on the orangey-brown wall-to-wall carpeting in my boyhood room, listening to Cindy Mizelle's song "This Could Be the Night" and "Us Girls" by DJ Debbie D over and over. This is the record the dentist is talking about. No one else in my class has it.

A few days later, I hop off my bike outside Magnus's house and bravely approach the door and ring the bell. The dentist opens it with that same crooked, untrustworthy smile I saw during my appointment.

"Come in."

Magnus is standing behind his dad.

"Hi!"

"Hi, Magnus," I say.

"Why don't you go up and play in Magnus's room?" Dentist Dad asks. "You can leave the record here."

After an hour of forced, fumbling playtime up in Magnus's room, during which we pretend we're not schoolyard enemies, the dentist calls us back down.

"We're about to eat, Jason, so it's time for you to go home. Thanks for bringing the record. I copied it onto a cassette tape for Magnus."

It's a slap in the face. I realize the only reason I was invited over was so he could copy my album. This is the first and only time I ever visit Magnus's house. I understand the extent of the scam when I overhear Magnus bragging to Agge that he has the *Beat Street* album at home. I never say a word about how it all went down.

After four or five years of racist jeers, I finally complain to Mom.

"That's just awful, Jason," she says. "If they call you bad words, then call them bad words back. Your skin is much lovelier than theirs."

Mom gives me an encouraging look as we stand there in the kitchen. The linoleum floor, the counter tiles, and the wallpaper are the same brownish-orange hue as the carpet in my room. She strokes my cheek.

"Call them maggots. You can say that their skin is the color of disgusting, tiny worms that eat dead bodies, or that their faces are the same color as hospital sheets, as ghosts."

I want to tell Mom it's impossible to tease someone for being white. At school, white is better than any other shade of skin. It would be like standing around with empty pockets and trying to oppress someone because they have a pocket full of money. I want to be normal like everyone else, which means it's a crappy strategy to tease someone because he's so normal.

Instead, I say, "I'll try, Mom. I'll try to pretend the words don't hurt. But if it doesn't work, I'll hit back."

Magnus is a head taller than me, and ruddy and freckly. One day, in the hallway, when he thinks he should get to use the bathroom before me, he hurls his usual invective.

"You fucking nigger shit."

And I fire back in response.

"Salami head. Pepperoni face."

There! I gave my oppressor a taste of his own medicine. For the first time, I have managed to respond to a bully with words. They may be weak, but still . . . I did as Mom said, and after school I pedal home to her at full speed on my mint-green ten-speed Svalan bike with its white racing handlebars. I run up the stairs to the house and breathlessly report that I did it—I talked back to Magnus and Agge, just like she told me to. She hugs me and I feel like she was right all along. Everything is going to be OK.

"Good! Don't let those boys get to you."

She takes a step back, looks at me with pride, and says, "Sticks and stones may break my bones, but words will never hurt me."

I flash a huge smile. I'm like a dog who fetched a stick. But even so, somehow things aren't quite balanced. Even if I did manage to respond with more than small, clenched fists for the first time. Because what is a "pepperoni face" compared to a "nigger shit"?

The words *don't* just run off my back; the pain *doesn't* pass. I'm not aware of it, but in responding with silence, I allow the opinions of those around me to become reality—and I aim my hatred inward.

Very soon after this, Mom decides it's high time to contact my homeroom teacher to put a stop to the racist taunts. My teacher listens obligingly and makes a call to Magnus's parents, then calls Mom back.

"Apparently, Jason made fun of Magnus too, and called him 'salami.'"

I never tell Dad what recess at school is like for a boy with brown skin. Sometimes I wonder how he would react if he knew. He would probably storm into the teachers' lounge or into the bullies' parents' house and tell them a thing or two. Maybe I can't handle the thought of Dad making a big deal out of it. Or maybe I want to spare Dad from the reminder that racism exists even in the vaunted welfare state of Sweden?

When St. Lucia's Day approaches, the role of gingerbread boy is often mine. Only one year am I promoted to an elf. It's inconceivable that I might get to be a star boy, all in white. One year, Magnus and Agge sign up to be gingerbread boys alongside me.

Dad immortalizes the gingerbread trio in a photograph. My two tormentors and me. The two of them in some clueless form of blackface, and me, born for the role of a little man made of brown dough.

During these years, I often hear Dad and his friends talking about racism without making the connection between their experiences and my own. Many years later, when I read Amin Maalouf's book *In the Name of Identity*, I fall hard for his poetic lines about what he calls the genes of the soul. He writes that a person's identity "is like a pattern drawn on a tightly stretched parchment. Touch just one part of it . . . and the whole person will react, the whole drum will sound."

In 1987, Ariel joins my class. He has been labeled a "problem child." He lives in the same neighborhood as my dad, and his parents are from Argentina. His mother, a single mom and poet, is raising three boys, and Ariel learned to fend for himself early on.

He is creative, inventive, and strong. What's more, he knows all the tough guys from Djingis Khan and all the nearby neighborhoods.

Ariel, who will become one of my closest friends, does something that makes me love him for life. He notices what goes on at recess, and one fine day he comes wandering down from Tunaskolan's upper-grade buildings with Paul and Thomas. Paul has the same skin tone as me and is widely known as a cool dude no one fucks with. The trio walks up to the chorus of insult throwers. Paul, Ariel, and Thomas say that if the bullies don't stop chanting at me, they'll come back and beat the shit out of them.

From that day on, the racist choir is silent.

NEW GODS

"Brother, I can't believe it. Seriously, I just can't believe it."

So says Micke as he steps into my half-empty apartment in December of 2015.

"Here we are, meeting up to talk about my wedding just as you're about to head off and sign your divorce papers."

"Life, brother," I sigh in response. "With all this shit, it's quite the trip."

Our hug is a little longer than usual. I'm at the doorstep of a divorce whose seeds were planted a long time ago and started to sprout exactly one year ago. I can feel tears springing into the corners of my eyes.

"Fuck, I'm still feeling pretty depressed about it. Depressed and nervous."

"What do you think'll happen, brother?" Micke wonders.

"I guess, worst case, she doesn't call, or for whatever reason doesn't meet me at five thirty like we planned, and I have to start the new year with all this up in the air."

"Shiiit, brother. I mean, the stress. But it'll all be OK."

"We've got time for some coffee, Micke, have a seat."

I empty the electric kettle and fill it with fresh water, then sit down at the kitchen table, pick up my pack of Marlboro Golds, resolutely take out a cigarette, and light it. Micke laughs, and exclaims, "Did you start smoking again, you fool?"

The first time I ever see Micke is on an August morning in 1991 at Spyken in Lund, at orientation on the first day of my first year of *gymnasium*—upper secondary school—in a crowded classroom in the orange-red brick building.

I'd heard the rumors back in high school. That there was a black Nazi in the small town of Södra Sandby outside Lund. In those days, skinheads and Nazis weren't unusual in Sweden. But a black Nazi—how the fuck was that possible?

Everyone—and I seriously mean everyone—in Lund with skin even one shade darker than white knows that if you go to Södra Sandby you might run into Billen and Rosman—two extremely notorious skinheads who won't hesitate to beat up any fucking *blatte* whatsoever. Still, us Lund kids frequently brave our way to what we call "Killedisco," for dances at Killebäckskolan, the high school in Sandby.

Clashes are common. During these hormone-drenched years, most Lund boys find the pull of fighting stronger than the pull of the dance floor. Gangs meet and skirmish for no other reason than they don't know each other.

Skinhead culture is more widespread in the small towns around Lund, places like Genarp, Staffanstorp, and Södra Sandby. Those of us who live in Lund know it and consider ourselves to be better than the yokels out in the boonies.

There I am. The first day of my first year at Spyken. I'm sixteen. A few seats away from me is one of the three nonwhite people in the room. Wearing . . . yep, jeans and boots. With a shaved head. Shit, that's him all right. The black Nazi.

I'm wearing a hat I bought in Harlem—made of the black-, yellow-, and green-checked Ghanaian national fabric called kente—and my huge button with the picture of Malcolm X and Martin Luther King shaking hands is on my backpack. This is the very peak of my Black Power period. I've just turned an identity-related corner—after many years of wishing I could get rid of my black skin and my black dad, I am fully embracing my blackness.

One week earlier, Mom called me and my sister in for dinner. She was shuttling back and forth between the stove, the sink, and the dining room. Pots and platters brimming with our evening meal had been set out on the oblong oak table.

"Anja, Jason, wash your hands and come to the table," Mom said. "I've been cooking for an hour."

I stood at the threshold of the warm, bright room fidgeting. Mom looked at me.

"What are you standing there dreaming about? Sit down."

Anja was already seated, and she aimed a cheerful look in my direction.

"Mom, I can't," I began, a bit hesitant.

"What do you mean, you can't?" She laughed. "Did you break your hands? Did your fingers stop working?"

"No, I can't sit at the same table with you and Anja."

"What are you talking about, Jason? Why can't you sit with us, like you do every night?"

I gathered my courage and raised my voice a notch.

"Mom, you're white, and I don't want to sit at the same table as white people; you're the devil," I concluded coldly.

Mom's laugh seemed to get cut off halfway.

"Fine, then, if you don't like it, then you can go without dinner," she said, annoyed. "That's the silliest thing I've ever heard."

Anja followed our exchange as if she were watching a tennis match, and then her perplexed gaze landed on me. I couldn't bring myself to look at her or Mom; I just turned on my heel and went back to my room.

Now the black Nazi and I are sitting in the same room. I stare past the seatmates between me and Micke, a little anxious. He seems to be pretending I'm not there.

65

Rule number one is that black people greet each other. The brother nod. I've seen my father follow this rule since I was little. Everyone knows, and freely points out, that it's impossible to walk through downtown Lund with my dad because he has to stop and talk to so many people. And they're usually black.

So why won't this black guy say hello to me? Why don't I say hi to him?

Once we're outside for break, I complain to my black friend David.

"He's a Nazi," I mutter. "I mean, the dude didn't even say hello. A house nigger is all he is."

We've pieced together our identities from shards we've picked up from the hip-hop TV show *Yo! MTV Raps*, magazines like *The Source* and *Hip-Hop Connection*, and everything we've absorbed from Black Power literature. We've learned terms like "house nigger" and "field nigger." But it's confusing when we try to translate what we've seen on TV and in magazines directly into our reality in Lund.

Later that week, I'm sitting in my first history class of *gymnasium*, unshakably convinced that I know more than any of the other kids in this room about past world events. The teacher poses question after question, and the only ones who raise a hand are me and . . . well, Micke, who raises his hand for more questions than I do.

Apparently, he knows the answers to stuff I've never even heard of, I think grudgingly.

"The Triumvirate, it was called. It was a pact between Julius Caesar, Pompey, and Marcus Crassus."

Says the black brother from Södra Sandby, despite his Doc Martens. And so it goes, every single history class. His expansive knowledge of history outshines my own, time after time. I thought it would be so easy to show off during these eighty minutes every week, but I have to admit defeat. I reluctantly begin to respect the mysterious black guy. It's nuts how much Micke knows. But, I reassure myself, I'm sure he knows nothing about the Black Panthers, Malcolm X, civil rights, James Baldwin, or Frantz Fanon. Does he even know he's black?

Our relationship remains chilly during the year we spend in the same class. Even though both of us are black. Even though, up until then, I thought that was enough.

Despite everything David and I think we know about the world, we don't know that synth-pop music is popular in Sandby and that synthers and skinheads dress in similar ways. Doc Martens, short rolled-up jeans, and bomber jackets. In Lund, these clothes signal only one thing: racist. Little do we know that synthers wear black jeans and low Doc Martens, while the skinheads prefer blue jeans and tall boots.

Micke is a synther, not a Nazi. But that's one of many things I don't understand in Lund in 1991, when I still believe that blackness can only be expressed through hip-hop culture.

In the year 2000, Micke and I meet again. This time it's in a store-front in Årsta I just moved into with two homies from Lund, Simme and Måns. Simme and Micke are old friends, and one day Micke shows up at our place. I recognize him right away. The conversation is a little rocky at first, but we soon realize that both of us feel like going out to a nightclub. We begin to bond that night, at Biblos on Biblioteksgatan, while dancing to house music and doing shots. We have so much fun together that we go out again the next night, and the night after that. All my doubts about clothing styles and affiliations vanish into thin air.

But my fragile identity as a hip-hopper and a black person began long before *gymnasium*. My first contact with the music and culture that would come to define my life occurs in the spring of 1984.

My dad lives in a run-down apartment in southern Lund. I try to avoid being at his house. Sometimes I say I'm sick; sometimes I cry and use every method at my disposal to show that I don't want to go see him. I don't have a room of my own in his drafty apartment, and besides, my dad's crappy Swedish and—especially—the color of his skin are painful reminders that I'm not like everyone else. But I have no choice. He wants to see me, and I'm too little to have any say in how I spend my time.

Dad has just come back from New York, where he spent the first part of the spring driving a Yellow Cab in addition to visiting his sister and brother. He brought back the maxi-single with "Jesse" on it, a song the already-legendary rapper Melle Mel recorded as a marketing tool for Jesse Jackson's campaign to become the Democratic presidential candidate.

Dad takes the vinyl record out of its blue-and-white sleeve and places the black plastic disc on the turntable. He presses play and carefully lowers the needle. The first things I hear are Melle Mel's grunts.

The song is funky, but what captures my interest is when he starts to rap. Funk and singing I've heard before, but rap? It's another story entirely. The lyrics speak to me in a completely different way than those of my idol, Michael Jackson. With Michael, the lyrics don't matter—his music makes both Anja and me dance in front of the mirror in my mom's living room.

Rap becomes, for me, what cartoons once were. I listen to it every chance I get—I greedily consume every tiny hint of rap music I can get my hands on. Whether it's Mel Brooks's ironic "Hitler Rap" or Chaka Khan's "I Feel for You."

A few weeks later, Dad buys me Break Machine's new single, "Break Dance Party." With that, I own my first hip-hop record.

At this time, both of my parents are home-language teachers for the city of Lund, and even though I would prefer to skip the extra schoolwork, I'm a home-language student. That means that every Wednesday afternoon, I make my way to the basement of Vårfru School, where all the English home-language students have lessons. There I meet Isak and Nikolaj. I'm in third grade and they're in eighth; they're brown like me but ten times cooler. Isak's little brother, Paul, shows up sometimes too.

I'm allowed to hang out with them in exchange for helping them with their English homework.

They have a break-dance crew, and sometimes, after home-language class, I'm allowed to tag along and watch while they dance. Isak teaches me some moves, and I struggle to keep pace with their uprocking. I even try to land the perfect moonwalk.

After two semesters, Vårfru School gets rid of home-language classes, and my Wednesday break-dance hangouts end. I desperately try to cling to my dance skills by teaching Anja all the moves I know. When Mom, Anja, Roland, and I visit the US that summer, I bring my camouflage pants and my red beret: my break-dancing uniform. But once I've been forced to stand in front of my grandpa in my outfit and show him my moves, I'm so mortified that I never put on those clothes or dance like that again.

That fall, Aunt Jamie, my dad's sister, sends me a pile of records from the US. Among those vinyls are Shawn Brown's single "Rappin' Duke," where Shawn raps in a fake John Wayne voice about how he's so much better than any other rapper.

The music is so infectious that I can't help myself. My dancing shoes may be permanently shelved, but rap is not so easily forgotten.

In 1989, my cousin Joey moves in with my dad in Lund. Joey is two years older than me. He's tall and handsome and was popular with the girls where he lived in Fort Greene, Brooklyn. As a result, a few tough guys from the projects near his house attacked him. All to scare Joey off seeing a particular girl.

They sliced Joey with a box cutter, and he ended up with a scar on the back of his neck a centimeter thick. So my aunt sent him to live with her brother in Sweden.

Joey is like an early version of Will in *The Fresh Prince of Bel-Air*. He soon becomes very popular: both at Bladins International School in Malmö and in Djingis Khan, Dad's neighborhood at the time. He makes friends with all the cool kids in the neighborhood, which means they start talking to me too. When I walk around with him, I feel like one of the popular guys. Plus, he brought cassette tapes of LL Cool J, Eric B. & Rakim, and Jungle Brothers from home. Joey teaches me what words like "dope" and "fresh" mean, and he explains the meaning of the Jungle Brothers' song "Jimbrowski" to me.

"He's rapping about his dick, Jason. Jimbrowski is his dick."

Joey doubles over with laughter. He plays LL Cool J's dirty song "The Bristol Hotel" and knows the words by heart. He sings every line about the fat prostitute who frequents the Bristol Hotel, Room 515, in Jamaica, Queens. But I also get to hear the Jungle Brothers' song "Black Is Black."

Rap hits me full force. The brown rappers I see on the covers of Joey's cassette tapes look like me, but they seem so comfortable and sure of who they are.

Apparently, you can rap about anything from skin color to your dick. Joey plays Slick Rick's "Children's Story," and I'm spellbound. I listen to the fantastic story of Ty, who goes down the wrong path in life, and the plot of the song plays in my mind like a movie.

I watch as "Dave the Dope Fiend" hands Ty the shotgun just before the police shoot him dead and the song reaches its tragic conclusion. These are music and lyrics that paint pictures. Pictures from the streets and neighborhoods of New York. In *Hill Street Blues*, all you get to see is the police officers' stories, but thanks to this music, I finally get to hear about the effect Reaganomics has had on life in the inner-city ghettos of the United States.

The rhymes are as raw as the graffiti-covered brownstones, the abandoned buildings, and the sidewalks where blades of grass grow through the cracks. It's Harlem, the Bronx, and Brooklyn. It's the city I visited on so many summer vacations. But rap music helps me see New York through brand-new eyes. The things that draw me now aren't blueberry bubblegum and robot toys but the voices of the ghetto.

As far as cool factor, nothing comes close to Michael Jackson's moonwalk. But these rappers and their lyrics, their way of spitting words in time with the music, and their swagger captivates me. I, too, want to be that sure of what I'm doing. Of who I am.

Rap music radiates an attitude of *you may trample us down, but you can never shut us up*. It lights the same fire within me. I'm not going to fucking be quiet either. Above all, it's the words that draw me in, deeper than any other music has done before. The strength I feel when I hear Rakim rap about a master plan.

> Thinkin' 'f a master plan
> Cuz ain't nuthin but sweat inside my hand
> So I dig into my pocket, all my money is spent
> So I dig deeper but still comin' up with lint

Or KRS-One about Cedar Park.

I don't understand everything they're rapping about. But I want to know more. I don't know what comes first: Do I fall in love with the color of my skin and with hip-hop as a result, or is it the music I love first, and the color of my skin as a result?

Cousin Joey and this uber-cool music is the most awesome thing I've ever encountered. This is during the time when Michael Jackson, Prince, and Madonna reign supreme. They were unattainable, the gods of eighties pop culture, in contrast to the hip-hop stars who were accessible to me in a totally different way. Their pride in where they came from and the color of their skin; their cocky attitude toward the oppressive, racist system; their stories of the vulnerability experienced by citizens of American ghettos; their message of freeing yourself, resisting, holding your head high, waking up . . . and those rock-hard beats. Monotonous, naked drums, often accompanied by only a simple bass line and maybe a melody or two. Music that stood in stark contrast to Kool & The Gang or Earth, Wind & Fire's heavily orchestrated big-band sound. This was the music of the Reagan era's weak economic conditions experienced by black people in America. No sugary-sweet harmonies or big horn arrangements here. You might call Reagan the godfather of gangster rap. Under his rule the music made of hard drums and urgent voices was born. And by the late eighties, Public Enemy front man Chuck D epitomized the relentlessly revolutionary power of hip-hop culture.

Now I want nothing more than to hang at Dad's place. My father has moved back to the Courtyard E house at Djingis Khan he and Mom had shared, because Mom is now living in a big red brick house on Göingegatan 6, a much fancier part of Lund. I have my own room at my dad's, and the neighborhood is full of kids and teenagers. Plus, there's a skateboard ramp. I spend every spare minute skateboarding.

A new stage of my life begins. I'm in eighth grade and doing well in school. I'm still not one of the cool kids, but the upper grades of Tunaskolan accept students from Djingis Khan, so now Claudio is in the other class in my grade. Claudio is the most famous and coolest guy in the school, if not the city. He's the fastest at the sixty-meter race; he jumps the farthest in the long jump; he kills at both soccer and hand-ball. And he's black. His parents are from Peru.

No one would ever dream of dissing Cladde, as everyone calls him, for the color of his skin. Not even Magnus, who—thank God—isn't in my class anymore. The music, and the fact that I'm no longer a target, allow me to begin concentrating on figuring out who Jason really is.

That same year, Mom gives me *The Autobiography of Malcolm X*.

I enter my mom's house through a green wooden door at the front of the building, take eighteen steps up a set of stone stairs, and walk into a bright, welcoming kitchen that leads to an equally bright dining room. A dark oak table with six chairs and a crocheted white tablecloth. Every windowsill is crowded with potted plants, as they always have been at Mom's.

I am carrying the love of my life under my arm. My skateboard. I've only come inside to grab a glass of water and dry off my sweat, and then I'll head back out to skate some more. Mom hears me from her office and hurries into the room.

"Here, Jason, I think you should read this."

In her outstretched hand is a yellowed, dog-eared fat paperback. I take it from her. A black-and-white photo of a man adorns the cover, and stamped in red across the middle of the photo are the words "The Autobiography of Malcolm X." Above that, in smaller white text, it says, "He rose from hoodlum, thief, dope peddler, pimp . . . to become the most dynamic leader of the Black Revolution. He said he would be murdered before this book appeared."

Later that night, I crack open the book. This is my first encounter with a different sort of literature. Instead of Jules Verne or Arthur Conan Doyle, usually my favorite authors, I now have the words of a political revolutionary to fall asleep to. The book opens a door in my consciousness, and once I've stepped over that threshold, there can be no return.

My fourteen-year-old brain devours the book, and a rupture appears in my safe cocoon. My walls are about to be torn down, and fast. I start plowing my way through books by Bobby Seale, Angela Davis, W. E. B. Du Bois, Langston Hughes, George Jackson—everything I find on Mom's and Dad's bookshelves. I go from spending much of my time either on my skateboard or at Mom's house to spending more and more time reading at the library or seeking out Dad's kitchen.

"I bought that book in the late 1960s in New York," Mom says that afternoon in the dining room. "I didn't know about Malcolm X while he was alive; I only discovered the book after his death. I've always loved to read, and it's so well written. His eloquence combined with his tragic upbringing, his disgraceful downfall, his salvation, and his eventual awakening—it's such a sweeping saga. It's as if he lived four lifetimes in just thirty-nine years. Interesting that both he and Dr. King were murdered when they were thirty-nine. The US was so fucked up back then."

Mom puts an arm around my shoulders and looks me deep in the eyes.

"But I want you to be able to read about this man's transformation and how he finally embraced the knowledge that all races can come to an understanding and that whites and blacks can live in harmony, as he witnessed on his pilgrimage to Mecca."

Later that year, my big sister, Adadie—the child from my father's first marriage—makes the move from Jamaica, Queens, to stay with our dad in Djingis Khan. Adadie is nine years older than me and doesn't listen to hip-hop. But she talks just like my rapping idols. The same slang, the same cocky, street-smart confidence. Suddenly, I'm surrounded by cool black people.

Just before Christmas, 1989, my neighbor Ingrid asks what album I'd like for a Christmas present. I respond with a note sent through her letter slot: either Paula Abdul's *Forever Your Girl* or De La Soul's *3 Feet High and Rising*. The latter wish comes true.

So with rap music in my ears and with newfound pride in my black skin, the void in my soul is filled. Dad and his friends become my oracles, eternal founts of black information. I can ask them about Malcolm X, the Black Panthers, Booker T. Washington, Harlem, Chicago, Billie Holiday—anything I want to know. They welcome my awakening with open arms. I start to use the same slang as Dad's friends and the rappers I listen to. In the neighboring city of Malmö, I find Bro's Jazz Café, which is run by an older African American gentleman, Mr. Morgan. On the weekends, I take the bus to Malmö just to order a hot chocolate with marshmallows and sit at the café and dream I'm in New York. I decide to move to the US as soon as possible. I beg and plead with my parents to send me there for upper secondary school. I even manage to find a program in Switzerland where I can study for an International

Baccalaureate in English. But Dad doesn't think the school sounds rigorous enough, so they say no to this too.

"It costs money to live in the US or go to school in Switzerland. Anyway, we want to have you close to us," Dad always objects. "Here, you have access to the best education in the world, for free. Don't you realize what a godsend that is? A free education."

I was born with the silver spoon of the welfare state in my mouth, so I can't quite appreciate Dad's view on things. All I can see is that the grass is greener in the US or Switzerland, or anywhere that isn't Lund. I'm ready to take on the world.

I linger on each page, carefully reading about Malcolm X's life. Malcolm describes how he changed after visiting Roxbury, a black neighborhood of Boston, for the first time and realizing that there are places in the world where black people don't have to be on guard because they might be subjected to racism at any moment. That, he writes, is when he began to withdraw from white people.

I increasingly seek out the table where Dad and his friends sit around chatting. I want to hear everything they have to say about the world. An endless procession of characters and opinions pass by Dad's kitchen table: the enlightened and well-educated Don Clayborn; the clever, music-loving Don Franklin DeSasseur; the eccentric artist George Jones; the talkative and energetic Stanley Cummings; and the rebellious poet Jerry Harris. Together they work through how they feel about Sweden and the US and discuss how best to survive in the world.

"I'm telling you, brother, this country is going to the dogs," I hear Dad say about the 1986 assassination of Olof Palme. "I'm just gonna sit back and watch it happen. If they did that to their own prime minister, what do you think they'll do to us?"

"Can you believe what these motherfuckers at Arbetsförmedling told me the other day?" Don might say about the workforce center.

"I told them I ain't never going to no SFI class. Man, the whole world speaks English. I told them they should go to English class instead. Tryin' to tell me I need to learn Swedish."

"These Swedes, man, they just don't know."

"The white man is doing a job on all of us."

"Boy, I'm telling you Uncle Sam just never lets up, does he," a third one grumbles.

Suddenly, one of the uncles might turn to me and ask, "Jason, what do you think about this?"

Things have changed. I am now given a voice when I'm with them. These adults listen to me. They advise me. All I have to do is start asking questions about skin color and history, and I get a response in the form of stories and book recommendations. I get to hear about the murder of Black Panther Fred Hampton, the genius of activist Stokely Carmichael, the tragic fate of Black Panther co-founder Huey P. Newton; I learn that the battle for civil rights didn't manage to save the black ghettos of America from slipping ever deeper into drugs and violence in the 1970s and that the country essentially waged a war against Afro-America. I learn about slavery and the Ku Klux Klan. About the American Civil War, colonialism in Africa, South America, and Asia. I learn about cars, James Brown, Maya Angelou, Nina Simone, and how crazy the ghetto gets on payday.

They paint detailed, colorful pictures of lives lived with black skin around that brown, oval wooden table, which will end up in my kitchen in Södermalm many years later. The hip-hop I listen to echoes what's said around the table. Groups like A Tribe Called Quest, Jungle Brothers, and Brand Nubian teach me about Afrocentrism; groups like Gang Starr teach me about jazz.

These days I want to wear wooden necklaces from West Africa to school, and I spend hours, day and night, listening my way through Dad's jazz collection. When that's done, I bike down to the city library and listen to Ben Webster, Miles Davis, and Thelonious Monk as I devour books by black authors like Eldridge Cleaver, Ralph Ellison, Richard Wright, and James Baldwin—whose writing I try in vain to fully comprehend.

Among Dad's records, I find an old vinyl of Malcolm X's speeches. Just hearing his voice . . . his sense of humor and his clever formulations on everything from slavery to how best to win liberation for black citizens goes straight to my heart. Just as it did for millions of other people throughout the many years. My metamorphosis is unstoppable.

If Malcolm X hadn't undergone a transformation but had instead held fast to his racist Nation of Islam conviction that the white man is the devil, I'm sure I would have felt the same.

Dinnertime peace on Göingegatan is restored at last. In the years that follow, I may protest when Mom makes *kassler*, pork tenderloin, or bacon, but in the end, I always sit at the table with her and Anja and eat whatever is served.

I still spend hours in front of the mirror inside my tiny walk-in closet. It's like my own little room with a door to close behind me. I stand there pressing my nose down in the hope that it will look more African. I inspect my hair and wish it looked like Dad's so I could get a high-top fade like the trendsetting Brooklyn rapper Big Daddy Kane. I go all the way to Malmö to get a haircut from Comfy, a Nigerian woman who has a beauty salon on Södra Förstadsgatan. I explain to her that I want a rapper haircut.

"Why's your hair so straight?" she wonders, running her hand through it. "Didn't you say your dad is black?"

But she does her best to make my wish come true.

Afterward I look in the mirror and feel like, for the first time, I have managed to get a relatively hip-hop-like hairstyle.

I never miss a chance to affirm my blackness and show it to the world. I start to dress in baggy jeans, oversize T-shirts, and a cap like my idols in Brand Nubian and Gang Starr.

Dad is happy that his son wants to learn everything about blackness but horrified by my new style.

"Tuck your shirt in and pull those pants up. Don't walk around looking like a street nigger, Jason."

At the time, I don't understand Dad's views on his son's transformation. This guy came all the way from Harlem and settled down in a cold, unfamiliar country to live a more tolerable life so he could get an education and rent an apartment with no cockroaches and send his child to school without worrying that he might end up in the middle of a shooting. Now, as he watches his son begin to adopt the same aesthetic, slang, and appearance as the people who hung out on the corners in the city where he grew up, he must be experiencing the mindfuck of the century.

But I embrace the ghetto aesthetic as my own. It doesn't matter how often Dad reminds me that Lund is not New York.

One day, my new friend Max walks up to me in the schoolyard with a blonde girl who's one head taller and two years older than me. She's dressed head to toe in LA Raiders gear. A windbreaker and a cap with the Raiders logo. It's an outfit I'm familiar with. It's the exact same style of clothing the world-famous gangsta-rap group N.W.A. wears.

Max is clad in tapered jeans with Rasta-color piping down the seams, and he has a huge Mercedes hood ornament hanging around his neck from a fake gold chain. People who dress like Max in 1990s Lund are called "wannabe-wops." People who dress like Jenny aren't called anything because no one gets her style. But Max and I know. She's a hip-hopper. Exactly what we want to be. Jenny's a DJ and has tons of hip-hop records and seems to know all the hip-hoppers in Skåne.

"I'm looking for a rapper," Jenny says. "Someone to hold the mic and rap during my gigs. You look like a rapper, so you should start rapping."

She looks at me cheerfully.

"OK," I say without considering what this means or how it should be done.

That same night, I sit down at the desk in my bedroom at my mother's new house, with its sea-blue wall-to-wall carpet, my world map as a writing pad, and write my first rap lyrics. Spinning in the background is De La Soul's debut album *3 Feet High and Rising*. I spend hours putting together the rhymes and using as many cool English words as I can fit in. At last I'm sitting in front of my first page of rap lyrics.

That's all it takes for my new identity to become real. I write rap lyrics; thus, I am a rapper. *Rap ergo sum.*

The next evening, I do the same thing: sit down with my notebook and De La Soul on the record player and write another verse.

The lyrics are imitations of my heroes Chuck D, Q-Tip, Grand Puba, KRS-One, and Guru, but it doesn't matter in the least. I feel free. There are no limits when it comes to me and my rhyme book. I can pretend to be anyone I want. In my notebook, I become the coolest guy in Sweden. That feeling I get during those first few writing sessions in my childhood bedroom on Göingegatan 6 is irresistible, and it will come to define and shape the rest of my life.

I struggle to come up with a good stage name. A rapper has to have an awesome, unforgettable name, and acronyms are preferable. Like my idol KRS-One, whose name means "Knowledge Reigns Supreme Over Nearly Everyone," or Guru, "Gifted Unlimited Rhymes Universal."

I land on MC Shortstop. For the simple reason that I'm short. Plus, the baseball definition of "shortstop" suggests energy, which I have plenty of.

Then it happens. It's time for the Tunaskolan disco in the school cafeteria, and Jocke, a guy from Djingis Khan, is playing records. Since I'm now openly telling everyone I meet that I'm a rapper, Jocke asks if I want to perform. I say yes without a moment's hesitation and take out my little rap notebook, which I keep in the inner pocket of my black jacket.

Jocke puts on "Woodpeckers from Space." I stand beside his record player, behind the long, high bar counter in the small, dark room, clenching the notebook. Jocke hands me the plasticky microphone as I try to flip to my illest rhyme. The dance floor is full of people boogying down, unaware of what's about to happen. Then I find the text, grab the microphone, and start rapping with all the intensity I can muster. I read from my book and spit my rhymes hard into the mic. The bar counter is so high that people can only see the top of my head. But they hear me. The sound of my own voice coming from the loudspeakers and the knowledge that everyone's listening floats me right off the ground. I finish rapping that set of lyrics, but Jocke's disc is still spinning, so I just turn the page and start a new one. I stand on tiptoe and peer over the counter. I can see Christian, Jonas, and Ola, some of the cooler guys in school, looking at me. They're listening. I bring the microphone to my lips and try to rap from memory:

> I'm the best / fuck the rest
> Any other rapper can't protest
> The ladies love me / want to hug me /
> no other rapper is above me . . .

When the song is over and I head back out to the dance floor, people come up to me and pat me on the back. Even a few of the jocks from the handball team send appreciative nods toward me.

I am someone. After years of searching and being rootless, I'm on my way to creating my own unique—in my view—identity.

As far as I know, from 1989 to 1992, I'm the only rapper in Lund. I hold my head high as I saunter around Botulfsplatsen. No one can fuck with me now. I'm a rapper, coolest of the cool. In my mind, I'm surfing along on the awesomeness factor granted by the fact that my dad is from the tough streets of Harlem. So if I want to pretend that Stora Södergatan is Lenox Avenue, that's my prerogative.

Jenny introduces me to Ioannis, who works for Folk å Rock, the big record store in downtown Lund. Ioannis is a hip-hopper too, and a DJ—he was recently named the best DJ in Sweden for his superior scratch techniques. Plus, he's already a legendary graffiti artist under tags like "2 Cold" and "Ruze."

Ioannis makes music. He samples old funk, soul, and jazz records; puts the loops into his Atari computer; and adds drum samples. He makes hip-hop music. He's a beatsmith, a producer. The very first time we meet, we decide I'll rap on one of his songs. A few days later, we meet up by the bus stop in the residential neighborhood of Vildanden. We walk the three blocks to his buddy's studio, where we take a seat on the sofa and I get to hear the song. It's some sort of electronic, British Soul II Soul–inspired dance song. I take out my notebook, stand in front of the microphone, and start rapping along to the tune.

> When I'm on the mic I crush you like an ant
> So what you gonna do when you see me dance
> Flowin' that poetry like a scholar
> Want attention just holler
> Don't front on me I'm Goliath the giant
> And you are tiny the flea
> I be on every station I keep them comin'
> Without stagnation I'm here to stay . . .

I notice Ioannis and his buddy nodding along with the music and the rap, which puts even more air in my lungs as I rap on.

> On with the program Mr. DJ out with the positive notion
> Get out on the dance floor put bodies in motion

The year is 1990, and I've just recorded my first song: "Music is Hypnotizing." My voice is shaky, and the lines aren't delivered with the authority or rhythm of Grand Puba or Posdnuos on the records I idolize. But I'm the only rapper for miles, so to me and Ioannis and his friend, there's nothing strange about the song.

Dad, of course, tries every tactic to redirect me from my newfound passion. The infectious message of hip-hop culture is in direct opposition to the dreams he has for his son. The glorification of the ghetto and street culture, their style and slang, are not dignified for a black person. He thinks I should start dressing properly and excelling in academics if I want to make something of myself in the world.

"Appearances are everything," Dad reiterates. "You're going to be a lawyer. Education is power. Make yourself powerful. No one can take that from you. Stop fooling around with that music."

I choose the music.

RACE POETRY

I'm black, even though the color of my skin is brown. You don't have to get very close to me to notice that I'm short, or "vertically challenged," as I like to say. I get that from Mom and Dad both. As soon as I'm within sight, it's obvious: I'm not white. I get that from Dad. I'm lighter than he is and darker than Mom.

My blackness is inescapable. In the United States of the last century, I would have been called a Negro. And in modern-day Sweden, the word isn't so different: *neger*. It's taken time for me to learn to bear my color. I get better at it every day. Or so I tell myself.

Sometimes my eyes fixate on my hands, always visible at the ends of my arms. They're brown, but there's also something reddish in that brown, and a little yellow too, and the veins that weave across the backs of my hands create a web of green. But there's white in that color too. That spot just below my right index finger, for example, is still white. The spot I so fervently prayed would grow to cover my whole body back when I was eight. To make me white.

What is your heritage? Where are you from . . . really? Where are your parents from? Are you Indian? Are you from Thailand? You're Moroccan, aren't you? Latin American, right? Are you from Colombia? You must be . . . a mulatto?

Mulatto. A word I've never called myself. The word that means "mule." I have a hard time identifying with a word coined by those who owned my forefathers. Those who would have been happy to own me today, if humankind had found a cure for, an immunity to, that unavoidable force: change.

But we haven't; we can't. Today, my skin color does not automatically make me someone who can be bought and sold, like my grandfather's grandmother, Myla Miller, or her husband, Jack. When my grandfather was born, skin color was judged according to the "one-drop rule." The rule of "invisible blackness." In other words, you could be black long after your skin had stopped making it obvious. It took many generations to become white. According to this old-fashioned approach, my family tree might look like this:

My dad is a Negro.

Skin tone: coffee.

He had me with a white woman, which makes me a mulatto.

Skin tone: coffee with milk.

If I have a child with a white woman, the child will be classified as a quadroon.

Skin tone: 3 Musketeers nougat.

If that child grows up and falls in love with a white person and they decide to have a baby, my grandchild will be called an octoroon.

Skin tone: faded khakis.

When they look at their hands, that child will probably see something very different from what I do now. Say that one-eighth black person also has a child with a white person. My great-grandchild will be a mustefino, quinteroon, or hexadecaroon with one-sixteenth black blood in their veins.

Skin tone: butter.

If this mustefino, in turn, becomes a parent with a white person— will their child still be black?

In Louisiana, according to a law in place until 1983, a person was black if their blood was one-thirty-second or more black. This means that, from a racial-ethnicity point of view, former prime minister of

Sweden Fredrik Reinfeldt would have had to sit in the back of the bus thanks to his great-great-grandfather. But millions of other people all over the world, too, would be counted as black due to their invisible blackness.

Skin tone: parsnip.

At the next stage, when our blood is one-sixty-fourth black, the journey of my descendants will finally reach Destination: white. For divided sixty-four times, the drop of black blood my dad cast ahead into future generations will finally be erased by white blood. In other words, it takes six generations to become white.

Skin tone: wet cotton.

Thomas Jefferson had six children with his slave Sally Hemings. She was a quadroon. That is to say, a very light-skinned woman. Thomas Jefferson allowed two of these children to flee north from his plantation, Monticello. One of the most powerful men in the US didn't even dare to immediately free his own children, whom society considered black—slaves, even though they were octoroons.

I am fascinated that white men considered black blood to be so powerful that, in their pursuit of power over the world around them, they invented this race poetry.

Where did the deep-seated fear of blackness come from? Can one drop of white blood color the propagation of generations in the other direction? If a mulatto has a child with a black person, that child is called a griffe or sambo. But that's where the white blood loses its determination. The child of a griffe and a black person is just black.

Negro, mulatto, quadroon, octoroon, mustefino . . .

During long winters in Stockholm, you often encounter a warning sign that reads "Rasrisk." It means that you should look out for snow falling from roofs, but it could also be interpreted as "race warning." I smile to myself every time I see those signs. I think of them as a quiet warning to the white world that soon, soon the whole world will be brown.

STATUE FRANK

It's possible that my penchant for clutter is inherited. I don't know quite what it means, but my home is full of small statues, pictures, rocks, and other knickknacks from travels. It's like I've tried to dog-ear all the places I feel the need to bring home with me in the form of artifacts; I've placed these artifacts in special spots all around my apartment. The archaeology of a life, of stories.

Dad's apartment is also cluttered with small objects. He saved two little blocks I painted and gave him twenty-three years ago; they're in the place of honor on the bookshelves in the living room. To Dad's eyes, the threshold of originality is indisputable; the sentimental value in those chunks of wood is immeasurable.

I slept until eleven o'clock. Again. The roller blinds in the small guest room don't quite cover the window, and through the cracks at the edge, I can tell that this Malmö March day will have the same signature gray color as yesterday did. As usual, circadian arrhythmia is in full swing. The zombie apocalypse could have come and gone, and I wouldn't have noticed. I simply never wake up. The king of the snooze button, my kingdom for nine more minutes of sleep . . . the pullout couch creaks when I finally get up.

Dad has never judged me for sleeping in. For a long time, he has patiently accepted most of his son's shortcomings. My partying habits, sleep habits, food habits, bad habits. As long as I remain neatly dressed, wear a decent coat in the winter, and work a lot and save my money.

This morning, my thoughts are still revolving around the fact that our oldest living relative, Cousin Willie, has recently died, and that we missed his last birthday party.

Last night I lay down on the pullout bed with my laptop on my belly. I lay there until five in the morning reading through census information from South Carolina in the 1850s in the hopes of finding out which of the African American cemeteries in Allendale my grandfather's maternal grandfather, Jack Miller, was buried in.

I was so disappointed that I didn't even say good night to Dad. An extremely unusual and clear gesture, since Dad considers this sort of politeness and etiquette to be supremely important.

Anyway, I'm awake now. For me, life is at its hardest and most unbearable in those first two hours of every morning. Bitter as yesterday's coffee, I step into the cluttered living room, where a few daring spring rays of the sun have found their way in. Dad greets me, cheerful and friendly as usual. I try to muster all my mental energy to greet him back in a civilized manner. I sit down with a bowl of Oat Bran and lactose-free milk. I tell Dad that a buddy has sent me a really good YouTube clip of the American philosopher, activist, and author Cornel West, and ask if he wants to see it. He does.

We listen to Dr. West's passionate sermon on the bloody history of the US, and I make it almost the whole way through my bowl of cereal without losing my temper even once. Maybe my rage will subside before we fly at each other's throats. But then Dad mentions how pleased he is with himself for losing two pounds. Two!

"That's nothing, Dad, you need to lose at least ten. Your eating habits are awful. Greasy sauces, all those chicken wings and pork chops you gnaw on. It's so bad for you."

Here we go again. Dad defends himself as best he can while my pitch and volume get higher and higher. I truly become my worst self at his breakfast table.

"Stop. That's enough. Why do I always have to defend myself to you?" he pleads.

My anger is like a balloon that inflates and inflates until a comment like that punctures it and I calm down at last.

"I'm sorry, Dad. Shit, I'm sorry. It's not cool for me to lose my temper like this. I don't know why it always happens this way. In the morning, with you."

Although I always get on Dad's case when I feel like he doesn't take good care of himself, this time the underlying cause of my irritability is that he's refused to come with me to South Carolina. He, in turn, is increasingly upset with me for refusing to be talked out of going.

"You never listen to me, Jason. I'm gonna call Don. If you won't listen to me, I know you'll listen to him."

Don Franklin, also known as Statue Frank, once ran a market stall. He sold flags, posters, jewelry, and hats on Mårtenstorget in Lund every Saturday, and sometimes he traveled around the country to various markets, fairs, and festivals. When I was twelve, my dad told me I could work for Don on Saturdays. So every Saturday morning at seven, I turned up to help Don unpack his wares, put the stall in order, and sell things. The market ended at two o'clock, and I helped him pack up again. Then I would bike away cheerfully, a hundred-kronor bill or so in hand. Even back then, I knew that the true value of the experience wasn't in the opportunity to earn a little extra money but in the life wisdom I was able to absorb.

Don spoke to me in a much more direct way than my father did. I don't think Don even talked so openheartedly with his own sons. We had the perfect relationship. Don was a survivor, and it showed in the wisdom he shared. He was much less critical of Sweden than Dad was, and he remained in a good mood even during hard winds, hailstorms, and horizontal rain. There, in my early teen years, on the northeast corner of Mårtenstorget, I received a great deal of useful knowledge from this soulful uncle. Don's approach to life was grounded in reality rather than academics. He consumed the news as voraciously as Dad, but he always placed it in a more vivid street context.

"Always treat people with respect," Don might say. "Especially those you suspect don't agree with you, or even like you. You'll come out ahead in the long run. Conduct yourself with self-respect."

Or, out of nowhere, he might exclaim, "Never be silent, Jason. If someone says something you don't agree with, challenge them. You need to stand up for yourself. Always."

I never talked back to Don like I did with Dad. Instead, I filtered out the nuggets of wisdom I needed or thought sounded sensible and absorbed those.

As sociable as he was, people came from all over the city to talk to him about politics, Sweden, family troubles, health problems. I got to be a part of all these adult conversations. Above all, I got to meet other black people, which was priceless to me. I was given role models, testimony, inspiration, and cautionary tales for my budding identity.

A few years ago, Don had hip surgery, and the doctor accidentally destroyed a nerve. Now he has to use a walker and he definitely can't work. He's eighty-three, and the oldest African American man in Malmö. He speaks with a Southern accent, raspy, melodic, and cheerful—it's wonderful to listen to. He also has strong opinions on everything from how Obama is dealing with being in the White House to what the city of Malmö *really* wants to accomplish by reconstructing Amiralsgatan.

Dad dials Don's number and hands me the phone.

"Hey, Don. It's me, Jason."

"I know it's you, baby boy, I knew it was you before you even said anything, alright," Don says with his characteristic slow laugh.

"Alright" is like Don's personal jingle, a natural end to a sentence, signaling agreement or confirming that he can hear you. Sometimes he says it two or three times in a row. Alright, alright. His tone always rises on the second syllable, which makes his "alright" sound like things really are, in fact, all right.

"Well, Don, I'm in Malmö, and I thought maybe my dad and I could come by and see you today."

"Alright, baby boy, you just come on by. Pick me up two marinara pizzas and one of them big bottles of Coke, would you?"

"No problem, sir."

Don's house in Videdal on the outskirts of Malmö is the epicenter of clutter. My collection of knickknacks, and Mom's and Dad's, can't hold a candle to Don's. Here, everything is crowded on top of everything else. Wooden statues from West Africa, LPs, books, coffee cups . . . the living room is more like a workplace or some sort of warehouse. The incomparable trumpet tones of Miles Davis are the first thing that reaches our ears as the door opens, closely followed by the barking of Don's dog, Coco.

"Alright, alright, come on in," Don greets us.

He's wearing a thick, knitted blue-and-burgundy cardigan and a weather-beaten black cap with the former national coat of arms of Ethiopia, the Lion of Judah. On his feet, he's wearing a pair of leather slippers, and he doesn't appear to have shaved today. But he still manages to look much younger than his eighty-three years. "Black don't crack," as they say.

We each take a seat. Dad and Don exchange pleasantries and updates about who's done what and who was in attendance at whose funeral and who has fallen ill. The village news. But soon it comes up— the reason we're there. Don is from South Carolina, the very state I've been nagging my dad to visit so we can explore our roots.

"So your father tells me you wanna visit the Carolinas," Don says.

I twist in my seat and explain that partly I want to meet my relatives but that I also have a strong desire to just see South Carolina. To feel the atmosphere, smell the scents, look at the houses, the landscape. To measure with my own eyes the time that has passed since my grandfather left the state in the early 1920s.

Don's reply is lightning fast.

"You wanna see it? Man, look at television."

The old men laugh heartily. The room fills with the feeling that the little boy doesn't know what he's getting into.

"You don't know how people are there, Jason," the two men agree.

Hand slaps are exchanged.

"Those crackers down there are crazy, and the niggas still don't know nothin', man, I'm tellin' you. They'll eat you up, boy."

Laughter echoes again in the cramped living room, blending well with Miles's trumpet. But Don soon calms down and looks thoughtful.

"If you'd asked me in 1959 where South Africa was, I wouldn't have been able to tell you. But Scandinavia, I knew."

"Really?" I interject.

"Yeah, man. You know, I was in the army. Stationed in Germany, 1956, just when the Cold War was really startin' to wind up. I had a long leave and headed for Copenhagen. Man, that was a totally different world for me. Clean, white. Everyone was white. Maaan . . ."

He says this in his typical fashion. His slow laugh tumbles out of him as naturally as a large rock rolling down a hill.

"In Copenhagen, I ran into an older brother . . . this brother was walkin' around puttin' up posters for a performance. Turned out his name was Roland Hayes. A heavy brother. Opera singer. Man, I had never met a brother who sang opera, but Roland did, and he was huge. Just like Nat King Cole and lots of the entertainers back then, he sang in different languages. Brothers had to be talented to break through in those days."

The degree of urgency in Don's story is as keen as that in Miles's trumpet; he fixes his eyes on me as if to make sure I understand that this is important, serious information.

"You know, Roland's people were slaves. He was born dirt poor in Georgia. But there he was in Copenhagen, doin' his thing. He took me around and showed me the city, and I liked what I saw. The year before, Emmett Till had been murdered, so we talked about that, about the US and Europe."

Emmett Till was a fourteen-year-old boy who was visiting family in Mississippi when he was accused of flirting with a white woman who worked in a store—when, in fact, all he did was talk to her. The woman's husband and his brother beat Till up and poked out his eye before shooting him in the head. Then they tied a seventy-pound fan blade around his neck with barbed wire and threw him in the Tallahatchie River where his mangled, swollen corpse was found three days later. The attackers confessed to the newspapers what they'd done, but they were acquitted by the all-white jury.

"Roland was a beautiful brother."

This is Don's highest praise for a member of his tribe, and the very antithesis of a "nigga."

"I came back to the US as a veteran. But Uncle Sam sure as hell never showed me or any other one of us any love."

Don is constantly referring to "him," "he," or "the man." He means the white man or, simply, the American social structure and its protectors.

"Jason, you know it's nothing new in the States, we're still suffering. Even more than before, in fact."

Don leans forward and opens his eyes wide.

"The black man has been subjected to huge burdens. Man, I remember sitting in my car in Santa Monica in the early sixties. A blue Plymouth. I just wanted to dig the ocean and the sun, you know, California's beautiful. It must have been eight in the morning, and the Pacific Ocean is gorgeous at that hour. Out of nowhere, a patrol car rolled up and parked behind me. The officer knocked on my window. 'What are you doing here?' he asked. 'What do you think, I'm lookin' at the ocean and takin' it easy in my car. It's a free country, isn't it?' 'Oh, you think it's a free country, huh?' the cop replied. He went to get his partner, and they dragged me out of the car and beat me up. They hauled me into the station and held me for six hours. It was fucking afternoon by the time they let me out, and I had to walk all the way back to my car. But I learned my lesson. It sure as hell wasn't, *isn't*, a free country. Man, I'm tellin' you."

He smacks his lips in distaste. It occurs to me that it's not bitterness that makes him look down and speak more quietly but a sort of aching resignation.

"You know, as long as you kept to certain areas, it was OK to move around freely, but if we turned up in the wrong place, stuff like that happened. American society didn't treat black people as full citizens, and it still doesn't. Just look at the news recently. Look at what they did to Trayvon Martin, Michael Brown, or Tamir Rice. All three were murdered by the police. Why?"

Don throws up his hands and answers his own rhetorical question.

"Because they were black. And just like when I was young, the rule still applies: if you're black, your life is worth less than if you're white. That whole goddamn country is built on that rule."

Don's tone has risen again. He's echoing what African American Princeton professor Eddie S. Glaude Jr. calls "the value gap" in his book *Democracy in Black*: race relations in the US are built upon a chronic undervaluation of black bodies in comparison to white ones, and this disparity in value undermines all the civil-rights progress that was made in the last century.

"Cops still go on with that same bullshit, that same oppression. The people are still in a boiling rage. Imagine you go to the ocean, you're sitting at Ribersborg in your car, just taking in the beauty. Then you're assaulted by the state and thrown into a cell. Then imagine that this happens to you and your family, your friends, *all the time*. You would be boiling, y'all would've boiled over, dammit!"

Don's voice almost cracks with his outrage. The music is just as loud as it was when we first arrived, but it blends perfectly with Don's emphatic truths and sends powerful emotional impulses through my body. I feel the pain in what he's telling me.

"The game is rigged. Society is rigged with traps for black men, women, boys, and girls. You know my boy Sebastian . . ."

Don's voice trembles, and he takes a deep breath before he goes on to tell about his oldest son, who was born and raised in Sweden but now lives in the US; he's a few years older than me.

"Just a few years ago, he was stopped by the police in Georgia. He hadn't paid his car insurance. If you don't do that in Sweden, you get a few reminders first, and if you don't pay up, you can't drive your car. But Sebastian, they took him and threw him in jail. He had to spend ten days there. Not in a cell by himself, in some soft jail for traffic offenses, but in a fucking cage with hundreds of other people who are there for murder, drugs, and any other kind of shit you can imagine. It's pure fucking luck he wasn't injured or killed, or forced to resort to violence himself, which would have led to even more time inside. American society is a minefield for black people. There's a reason the US has the largest prison population in the world. Man, not even China has more incarcerated people than the US, and there are almost 1.4 billion Chinese. Boy, it's just sad, sad."

Once again, the old peddler's analyses are perfectly in line with what Professor Glaude expresses in his well-argued book: "We haven't reached any kind of promised land. We stand between lands, desperately holding on as we see so many people we love fall into poverty, go off to prison, or end up in the grave."

Don's sorrow is culture typical. Endemic.

From where I'm sitting now, on the periphery of a peripheral city in a country at the edge of Europe, looking at Don's wide, tear-filled eyes, I realize that he shares this very gaze with millions of African Americans. It's the sadness and rage that has been hammered into the eyes of those who live with black skin in a white world. His gaze sweeps the room until it finally meets my own again, and he starts over, noticeably calmer this time.

"In 1939, I moved with my parents from South Carolina to White Plains, just north of New York City. My mother worked as a maid. These days, black people don't get those jobs. The Mexicans take them. All that's left for blacks is prostitution and drugs. It ain't pretty, man."

Don sighs. Dad's eyes are on the worn blue carpet as he nudges the fringe back and forth.

"My mother earned five dollars a week. Dad, that bastard, he got mixed up in the numbers racket. You know, gambling—and liquor and abuse were always around."

The numbers was an illegal lottery run by the criminal elements in the black ghettos of America. For the most part, it resembled a regular lottery, with winnings and everything. According to Dad, my great-grandmother hit the numbers once, winning five thousand dollars, which was a fortune back then. Dad thought that would mean money for his school fees and food for his sister's kids. Instead, BM, as my great-grandmother was called, bought two mink coats. One for herself and the other for her daughter Madame. Typical ghetto mentality, as my dad resignedly calls it. He's of the opinion that this is why so many residents of the ghetto will never get out.

"And add to that the internalized self-hatred and hopelessness," Don goes on, "and it leads to what Bama the Village Poet sang about. 'Ghettos of the mind.' And besides that, we did live in the middle of an actual ghetto. Man, that was a fucked-up place, and my parents had a completely dysfunctional relationship. All along Brookfield Avenue, winos, alkies, stood around singing 'Drinkin' Wine Spo-Dee-O-Dee.' That was an early rock 'n' roll hit that opens with the lines: 'Now I've got a nickel, have you got a dime? Let's get together and get a little wine.' It was a race record. Music by and for black people. That's how it was back then. The white kids in my school listened to completely different music, dressed completely different, talked totally different from us black kids. In the 1950s, there were two parallel and definitely separate worlds in the US. Sometimes guys came from the city, from Harlem and the Bronx, and back then, the really tough boys had 'zip guns.' A sort of homemade pistol. If there was trouble, those came out and someone would end up in a bad way. It happened pretty often."

Don isn't laughing now; he just shakes his head slowly.

"Every day, you had to put on your gorilla suit before you walked out the door. I'm telling you, brother, you had to be strong. You put on your mental armor, you put your body and your mind on high alert. It wasn't even conscious; it was a reflex. Because you had been drilled since childhood to know that anything could happen at any time in the ghetto. Police, junkies, gangsters, or just folks who wanted to pick a fight. You had to be on a hair trigger, fully aware of every scenario at every moment. Not a day went by that you weren't reminded how bad things could go if you weren't vigilant and strong. That brings out the worst in lots of people, because everyone's fighting for the same thing. Survival at any . . . fucking . . . price."

Don rises from his chair; it's a struggle but he's determined. He rummages through some CDs and brings out a cover with a black-and-white picture of a stylish young man. Don smiles in triumph and holds up the small plastic square.

"Here it is, brothers. You're about to hear somethin' really great."

He inserts the disc into the ancient boom box and presses the play button. The song starts with a soft piano chord, and then comes a hopeful saxophone theme followed by a honey-smooth male voice singing about love and his sweetheart. Don lights up.

"What do you know about Johnny Hartman, boy? Man, this guy . . ."

"And Arthur Prysock," Dad offers.

"And Billy Eckstine," Don adds. "'The balladeers' . . . we black people also have such a tender, beautiful side, Jason. That side of our persona exists too. We can be beautiful and poetic—all the moods ever felt by humankind are personified in these descendants of slaves. From hatred, pure, intense hatred like you find in Aimé Césaire's poems, to the velvety-soft affection in Johnny Hartman, to the unrestrained, infectious happiness in Louis Jordan. It's in music and poetry that the most beautiful parts of us come out. Those feelings still echo today; I mean, just listen to Johnny singing here, maaan, it's beautiful."

Don is radiant with joy. Both old men close their eyes. It's as if the music gives them respite from the painful memories of their youth and the tragic conclusion that not much has gotten better in their homeland. Their heads sway back and forth to the unhurried beat of the song, and they smile from ear to ear. Once again, I'm filled with happiness as I witness the power of music in practice. In this, our kinship is complete. These old men and I are connected by the need to let music heal us when we feel our worst. Maybe I inherited that from them, even as they inherited it from their elders. I see it as my link all the way back to the roots of the music I love. All the way to the heart of the South, New Orleans, and the slaves' songs, which were transformed into blues, which gave rise to jazz and eventually hip-hop.

Don guides his walker from the stereo back to his black office chair.

"I was back in Copenhagen in 1966, and damn it was nice. I left my gorilla suit at home. I could breathe there. There was jazz there. I got to know the jazz saxophonist Ben Webster. I hung out with him at Montmartre, as one of the clubs was called. And that love. Maaan, I mean, that free love."

Dad hums in agreement, accompanied by Johnny Hartman pining after his sweetheart and the last few rays of the March sunshine slowly retreating from the cluttered living room on this Tuesday afternoon.

"Yeah, Copenhagen was alright. White women have always loved the brothers; they still do. And whitey just can't handle that."

Once again, their laughter tumbles through the room.

"You know, niggas talk a lot of shit, and women love it. Just look at Kanye West. He married a white woman at Versailles, maaan. I just about fell off my chair when I saw it on TV. Who the fuck would've thought? A black man at Versailles! They should have seen that back on Brookfield Avenue or in South Carolina. It's incredible. Whitey can't handle that!"

Don's smile fills his face, and he leans forward in his chair.

"You clean up your act, and he don't like you; you fuck up, and he hate you. You can't win, man. Whitey done a job on all of us."

Dad smiles in agreement, and the two gentlemen are united in the perspective they've gained from where they stand up on the mountain in the autumn of their lives. They've survived the trials that took the lives of many others where they came from, and soon they'll reach the last stop. These once confused, angry, sad, and defiant old men. But now they can laugh at how crazy the world is and just enjoy the fact that they have each other and that there are witnesses to how hellish, strange, and maybe wonderful life as a black person has been.

With the music tirelessly flooding out of Don's stereo and open pizza boxes strewn with leftover bits of tinned shrimp and crust on the table, next to an almost empty cola bottle, Dad pensively says, "You should stay in South Carolina for three months, Jason, so you really get a feel for the place."

"Hell no, more like three days," Don says cheerfully. "But whatever you do, baby boy, come back and tell us about the South."

GRANDPA AND MALCOLM

Thirty years after Grandpa and Madame died, Dad and I are sitting in an ivory Mercedes. He's driving. The woman at the car rental office asked if we wanted an upgrade. I saw the desire in Dad's eyes when she showed us the pictures of the cars in the fanciest category and thought, *What the hell, why not give him the chance to ride in style?*

In 2012, the summer heat lingers long into September on the East Coast. Dad and I are on our way north from a sparkling Manhattan to Westchester County, an hour's car ride away. Dad was a taxi driver in New York City for many years, and driving a car in the big city is as natural for him as walking. We take a ramp onto a larger highway that leads, in turn, to an even larger highway, and the hectic traffic on all sides on this delta of a road gives me the sense that we're in the midst of a herd of gnus spilling into an even bigger herd of gnus, all migrating north across the asphalt savanna.

Cold air streams from the vents in our roomy sedan, and jazz music leaps playfully from the speakers.

We're going to visit Grandpa. Dad is quiet. He's just enjoying the moment, the music, the city, the German steel, and the sunshine.

"I think it's here," he says cheerfully as he turns in through the large metal gates of the cemetery.

The place is enormous; it looks more like a park than a graveyard. Maybe that's because most of the graves are only marked by plaques on the ground, and you can gaze out over wide expanses of fertile green lawn with maple trees towering up here and there and casting their shadows over the ground. We step out into the burning sun. It only takes a second for me to miss the cool air-conditioning of the rental car.

"Now, let's see," Dad muses. "Follow me and we'll soon find Grandpa."

I don't remember ever having visited either of my grandparents' graves before. Dad ambles down the gray asphalt path that leads past a large chapel and down to the grave sites.

"Are white and black people buried next to each other here?" I ask, curious.

"Yes, I'm sure there're blacks, Irish, Italians, and Polish people here. But I imagine they're in different sections, that there's a black section and different white ones. That's how people live in New York. You pass each other on the street, ride in the same subway cars, and work in the same skyscrapers. But at night the whites go to the white neighborhoods and eat and sleep with their families and the blacks go to Harlem or Brooklyn. Culturally, the country is still divided by strict, invisible boundaries between races and classes. Even in death."

Sweat marches down our faces. I let my eyes sweep the ground to read the different names on the brass plaques sunk into the grass.

It takes us thirty minutes of wandering around this gravestone-free cemetery in the oppressive heat before we locate Grandpa's plaque out in the middle of a big lawn with unusually thick blades of grass.

Solomon Warren Robinson's grave. Dad kneels in silence before the plaque and places his hand on the hot brass plate. He bows his head and says a few inaudible words. In that moment, I am filled with a sense of relief and gratefulness that I stubbornly insisted Dad and I take this trip to the US together. Dad can talk to his father in peace, and I take a few steps back and squint into the sun.

After a few minutes, I approach Dad and the grave again. Dad tells me about his grief when Grandpa died. Just three weeks before that, his mother had passed away unexpectedly. As soon as he got back to Sweden after the funeral, the news reached him that Grandpa had passed as well. But he was out of money and couldn't make the trip back across the Atlantic to attend his father's funeral. He still carries the pain of that with him.

His face seems heavier and more furrowed than usual as he stands with his white panama hat in his hands. His half-closed eyes don't move from the plaque in the grass for even an instant. I think he feels guilty for leaving Harlem for Sweden.

A big piece of his heart remains on the cracked sidewalk slabs of 116th Street. When he left Harlem, he left it for good. He's only ever returned to his homeland to visit.

"I wish I could have stayed, but I had to leave you," he whispers to Grandpa. *I hated to leave, but I had to go.* It's like a song lyric.

We stand silently in the sunshine, the only sound the distant flood of cars rumbling somewhere beyond the trees of the leafy cemetery.

After a long silence, Dad asks if I want to see something cool. He squats down at his father's grave again, runs his seventy-two-year-old hand over the plaque in the grass one last time, rises again with great effort, and starts to zigzag his way among the graves. After forty yards, he stops, looks down, and shakes his head.

"Not here."

We walk back and take a left, then a right. Dad's eyes scan the ground, and he walks slowly so he can read the names. A little while later, he suddenly stops and exclaims, "Look, Jason. Come see!"

I rush the ten steps over to Dad, who's reading the name on the plaque: "Hajj-Malik El Shabazz."

"Wow, Grandpa is buried next to Malcolm X? How come you never told me?"

"It just occurred to me. I'd forgotten, but here it is—you can see for yourself."

As we stand before the grave, I clearly recall that day in Lund in 1989 when Mom gave me Malcolm X's autobiography, which so completely swallowed me up and flung me into a universe of black intellectuals. With my head bent over his grave, and with the burning sun on my back, I happen to think of a paragraph in the book that Malcolm wrote soon before he died:

> When I am dead—I say it that way because from the things I know, I do not expect to live long enough to read this book in its finished form—I want you to just watch and see if I'm not right in what I say: that the white man, in his press, is going to identify me with "hate." He will make use of me dead, as he has made use of me alive, as a convenient symbol, of "hatred"—and that will help him escape facing the truth that all I have been doing is holding up a mirror to reflect, to show, the history of unspeakable crimes that his race has committed against my race.

If only he knew how wrong he was. If he could understand what he would come to mean to me. To all of us. Dad, Mom, brown, white, and black people the world over have taken strength from his words, inspiration from his example, and power thanks to his lifework. Imagine if he had been able to know that his life hadn't been lived in vain, and if that had allowed him to rest in greater peace. I crouch down and place my hand on the brass plaque that bears his name. The plate is hot, just like at Grandpa's grave. I close my eyes and say to myself, *Thank you for showing me the way with your words, sir.*

Time is just like the air here at Grandpa's cemetery. It stands perfectly still. The thought is mind-boggling—that Grandpa and Malcolm X lie just a few yards from each other. When they were alive, they might have passed one another on Lenox Avenue without noticing each other, but now they're neighbors in eternal rest. Grandpa, the dedicated waiter who worked hard to put food on his family's table and who never made a fuss. And Malcolm X, who refused to stand by in silence, refused to remain within the fence white America had erected for blacks. The revolutionary who urged people like Grandpa not to live their lives in silence and subservience.

Without letting my fingers stray from the plaque, I look up at Dad, who's standing with his head bowed and his panama hat in his hand.

"Thanks, Dad, for showing me this. This is such an incredible revelation for me."

"You're welcome. You know, Paul Robeson is buried somewhere in this cemetery too. Your grandpa has finer neighbors in death than he ever did in life."

FORT CAMPBELL

"Did you know I was stationed at Fort Campbell in Kentucky?" my dad asks me.

"I had no idea."

"I was," Dad says. "All the way over in Kentucky. What a fucking place that was. I was in the army, and I was granted furlough when Uncle Richard died. I was on my way to New York on a Greyhound bus. I'm tellin' you, I would never voluntarily take the Greyhound across the US today. But in 1959, poor people had no other choice."

"How old was Uncle Richard when he died?" I wonder.

"Oh . . ."

Dad turns to Mom, who's sitting nearby on the sofa.

"Jason thinks black people had birth certificates back then. Ha! I have no idea."

"Right, you don't even have my grandfather's birth certificate, do you?" I interject.

"No, I don't. But Uncle Richard was old."

"How can we find out more about Grandpa and his father? Was my great-grandfather a slave?"

"We don't know, but I can promise you he almost definitely picked cotton. Like most poor folks in South Carolina in those days. By the way, do you want a cup of hot water? I'm drinking a lot of hot water these days. It's good."

He turns to Mom.

"Elaine, would you like some?"

"Of course, I love hot water," she replies.

"You should have five cups a day." Dad smiles.

Ever since two months ago when I told Dad I was planning to go to South Carolina, he keeps calling me up to tell me what a bad idea it is. He's recruited Don and Mom in his attempts to scare me off my travel plans. At the same time, though, my trip seems to have had a strange effect on Dad. Recently, more and more long-buried stories have been trickling out of him. With every passing day, he becomes increasingly convinced that it's madness to visit the South, but at the same time, he seems to find an odd sort of satisfaction in his very memories of what he experienced there. Or perhaps he wants to support his arguments against my trip with as much detail as possible.

In any case, I'm back in Dad's living room and hoping he will change his mind and come with me to the US.

Dad leans forward in the easy chair and fixes his eyes on me.

"But I can tell you that my auntie Sylvia—she was one of your grandfather's mother's sisters—was born a slave. We spent a lot of time at her house when I was little. She lived to be one hundred and two and died in 1966. She was a tough one. No one dared to speak up to her. She could quarter a chicken with her bare hands. I've never seen anyone else do that. When she spoke, you listened. People were strict back then. The adults didn't need to beat us, a look was enough. But if you talked back, you'd get a taste of the belt. Right, Elaine?"

Dad looks at Mom for support. She gives a nonchalant nod in response.

"Listen, though, I didn't finish my story about the bus trip from Fort Campbell," Dad says. "It was a slow journey. After driving for ages, we stopped for food in Roanoke, Virginia. For some reason, I just followed the line of people into the diner. I sat down at the counter like my fellow passengers. I ended up just sitting there a long time. The people next to me were already eating. "Excuse me, may I order now?" I asked the waitress. She wouldn't give me as much as a glance. It was like I didn't exist. Even though I was sitting there in my army uniform. An old black man was sweeping the floor—rescued again by an old man with a broom. He came closer and said in a low voice, 'If you're hungry, go out that door and around back.' 'Thank you, sir,' I said, and walked around the corner . . . and there was the sign: 'Colored.' All the black bus passengers were there. I was petrified with rage. Even though I was hungry, I couldn't bring myself to go in, so I turned around and got back on the bus."

Judging by Dad's dumbfounded expression, he still can't understand how the world can be so unjust.

"In one way, it was lucky that I saw with my own eyes what segregation truly meant, in the South," he continues. "Later, when I was stationed at Fort Benning in Georgia, I learned that blacks weren't even supposed to go to the white part of the city, unless you wanted them to find you floating in the Chattahoochee the next day. I swear, every week they pulled a dead black body out of that river. Uniform or no . . . you had to know your place. So when I was on furlough, I got off the bus in the black part of town, and my white fellow soldiers got off in the white part. Fuck!"

He runs his hand over his short graying hair and hunches over, tired, in his seat.

Mom's face is grim when she leans back on the sofa and looks at Dad. After a while, she turns to me with a cautious smile. I'm smiling back as if to say thanks when Dad wakes from his thoughts.

"I even recall the time there was a Ku Klux Klan meeting on the army base," he bursts out with a harsh laugh. "They were military and local men, the people who had gathered. On our base. Shit! We were reminded daily of our place in the world. The only rule that mattered in the South was 'Don't mess around with white folks.'"

THE RED SUITCASE

Boxes are stacked from floor to ceiling. Plastic bags and chairs, suitcases and fishing rods, crowd the small, crammed attic storage space. Dad saves everything—his motto is "it might be good to have around."

It's early summer of 2015 and the heat has gathered into an invisible, heavy mass on the seventh floor of the large apartment building on Föreningsgatan in Malmö. The air in the building's attic storage area is perfectly still; the sharp taste of dry wood and dust makes my throat feel thick. This is the sort of environment that triggers my allergies the most. The heat, the air, and the stacks of boxes make my patience shrink at a fierce rate. Dad is bent over a brown moving box, wondering aloud if he should keep the little portable charcoal grill that's inside. I just want to find what we're looking for, but everything is happening in slow motion. Dad must have noticed my growing irritation, because he looks up from the box.

"Jason, take it easy, we have to be methodical about this. Everything is organized into a system you don't understand," he says.

"Yeah, yeah," I say, dropping a box with a thud to indicate I'm not entirely pleased with this tempo.

"Take that one down," he commands me, pointing at a shelf.

"Which one? The garbage bag?"

"No, that gray plastic bin at the top. Take that down first. Then you can move the boxes."

I move box after box. The air fills with more dust, and it's getting harder for me to breathe. The cramped hallway between the storage lockers quickly fills with junk.

"Careful, you might hurt yourself if you try to lift something too heavy."

"Dad, I'm fine. I can handle this."

"That's what you think. One day you'll learn."

I've participated in this ritual ever since I can remember. When I was a kid, Dad and I cleaned up his storage unit every Saturday. We would move everything onto the lawn outside the oblong building. Once that was done, Dad would stand there taking in the piles of boxes, lamps, carpets, suitcases, fabric, grills, and tennis rackets. Then he would go through them all. Only occasionally did he throw out some small item. After that, we would move all the belongings back inside again. This never led to increased storage space in the unit, not in any of the places he's lived since I was born. But the taking of inventory brought him some sort of satisfaction, as if having an overview of his stuff gave him control over the chaos.

"Dad, why is this here?"

I've come to the bottom of an unusually high pile of boxes; underneath it all is an old toilet.

"It was removed when we renovated the bathroom," he replies, as if this is perfectly natural.

"Yeah, but that was years ago. Why didn't you get rid of it?"

I remind myself to take deep breaths, even though the air is so dusty I can feel every last mote in my lungs. I know the process will only be protracted if I let my irritation win out, if I start an argument with my old man.

"That toilet might be good to have around. Don't you worry about what I keep in my storage area. Now, we're here to find that suitcase. Where could I have put it?"

Dad scratches his head.

"Are you sure it's up here, and not in your basement storage locker?"

"This is the only place it could be. You need to have a little patience. I'm the only one who knows what's up here. If you'd visited a little more often, you could have helped me organize the boxes and my belongings so it would have been easier to move around in here. But you're never around, and I'm too old to lift things."

Dad eyes me as if he hopes I'm going to come to my senses and move back to Malmö.

"Why don't you throw this crap out? It's mostly junk," I say, my tone harsher than I intend.

"Junk? What do you know about junk? This is my life, Jason. These are the things I've collected in a lifetime in Sweden. You have no idea what's in these boxes."

Dad gives me the same challenging look I've gotten so many times, the one I know so well. It's a look that says, *You think you know it all, but I will always know more, so take it easy.*

"I stayed in Sweden for you. So you wouldn't have to grow up without a dad and become just like the other confused black boys in this country, the ones who don't know where they come from. So don't come around here talking about my 'junk.'"

After nearly reaching maximum volume, Dad's voice falls back to normal and his eyes turn sad. *You don't seem to understand the amount of effort life has demanded,* his look seems to say. Once again, my chest is full of a nagging conscience, that familiar feeling that I'm not grateful enough, not a good son.

We dig further through the brown boxes and the black bags without saying a word to each other. After a few long minutes of silence, I find a small red suitcase made of fake leather, with a large belt buckle on the front, and take it down off the shelf.

"Is this it?"

Dad's face lights up.

"I told you I knew it was here," he says triumphantly.

I place the suitcase on the floor, undo the buckle, and open it.

In the suitcase are four gigantic brown envelopes. I pick one up. They're all bursting with folded letters.

"These must be the letters, Dad."

"Yes, give them to me," he says curtly. "That's my history. I want to be very careful with them."

A few weeks earlier, Dad had told me he'd saved all his correspondence with his parents from the years 1957 to 1982. From the time he returned to New York from Nigeria until my grandparents died within three weeks of each other. I jumped up off the chair in his living room, eager to head straight up to the attic to retrieve the letters.

Dad wasn't very enthusiastic. No doubt the letters are under or behind a ton of other stuff in the "*ferrowd.*"

The *ferrowd,* as he calls the storage unit, is so frequently used that he always says it in Swedish—the *förråd.* Another word he likes, which always pops up in Swedish in the middle of all his English, is "*Stadsbibbliyoteckit*"—Stadsbiblioteket, the city library. He and Mom and their English-speaking friends have invented a new form of English-Swedish that only the initiated can understand completely.

When I insisted that we go get the letters, Dad sighed in resignation.

"If you want to get them, we'll have to plan a time when you can bring a strong friend to help us move all the boxes and furniture that's in the way. But it's going to take some time."

He looked at me thoughtfully and went on. "I don't know why you want to see these letters. But I can tell you they're not leaving this building. Not a chance."

I expect Dad is afraid of what's in the letters. All the mistakes and sorrows of a life are probably hidden there in the lines that were written almost fifty years ago and are now tucked into the bursting envelopes.

But at least Dad didn't refuse to let me read them. I think he's as curious as I am about what might be hiding among the folded sheets of paper in that suitcase. His parents' words to him, completely unfiltered by his memory. Since I never got to know them, I hope I can find some clues as to who they were, what and how they thought, how they expressed themselves, and what they were driven by. But maybe most of all, I want to know more about the young man my father once was. What sorts of conversations did he have with those closest to him?

We carry the red suitcase down to the apartment. Dad looks a little grim as I set it down in the hall. He lowers his head and walks past me.

Later that same day, I'm sitting around the rectangular black dining table in the bright living room on Värnhemstorget in Malmö with Dad; his wife, Monique; and their friend Enid. The turkey legs and sweet potatoes are all gone. The plates have been scraped clean.

"Who wants dessert?" Monique asks cheerfully.

"I could definitely manage a little something sweet," Dad says with a broad smile.

"Can't we read some of the letters, Dad?"

"God, this boy is making me jump through burning hoops," Dad says, turning to Enid. "We had to spend an hour tracking down those old letters in the attic."

I go to the hall, get the red suitcase, and take out one of the large envelopes full of letters. I gently remove a small bundle of delicate paper and start scanning the pages.

"That one," Dad suddenly says. "That looks like a letter from my father."

It's a thin blue Air Mail letter dated 1978. So in my hand I'm holding one of the few things I've ever seen that belonged to my grandfather. His hand carefully wrote the address on the outside of the letter. The foreign Swedish words "Uardavägen E:181." The address where my father lived back then. Now, almost forty years later, I'm holding Grandpa's words and thoughts in my own hand. A wave of gratefulness toward Dad for saving these letters washes over me, and excitement rises in my chest. I turn the letter over and slowly begin to read. Dad's gaze is fixed on the blue paper.

> *Dear son,*
> *I hope you and Jason are doing well . . .*

"I can't quite read Grandpa's handwriting," I say.

"Give it to me, I'm old and I bet I can make out these chicken scratches," Enid says with an indulgent laugh.

I hand the letter to Enid, who's eighty-three years old. Her once brown eyes have turned ice blue, just like Dad's. She doesn't look a day over sixty. She has short hair that's almost snow white, and her eyes are alert and filled with happiness, unlike Dad's—too often, he looks tired and distant.

As Enid tilts her head back to focus on the writing, I am struck by the diametrical difference between the ways she and Dad have aged. Like my mom and other older women in our family's circle of friendship, Enid is still full of burning curiosity. She is physically active, makes new friends, and dares to be adventurous and open. Don, Hilmi, and Dad are examples of aging people whose lives seem to coagulate instead. They're not much interested in anything new, think they know most of what's worth knowing, and they seldom take any risks. The old men seem pretty convinced that the world is populated with idiots. They share an almost cynical weariness of life, while the older women around me are as vivid and thirsty for discovery as could be.

Dad squirms in his chair as Enid begins to read the forty-year-old words, and silently eats a spoonful of ice cream from the bowl Monique has just set before him.

According to Enid, Grandpa writes that he's doing fine and prays to God that Dad and I are too, but he's so alone in Harlem and isn't doing well.

> *Come home right away, I miss you so much. Why*
> *can't you and Jason live in Harlem, near me?*

Grandpa states more than once in this letter that he wants Dad to return home. Dad hangs his head over his bowl of dessert. It's as if Grandpa's pleading carries him back to the past, to feelings he purposefully forgot and hid away long ago.

This must have been what Dad was dreading.

When Enid finishes reading, all is quiet around the table. I look at Dad, whose chin has sunk to his chest.

"Your grandpa's letters were always the same," he says, lifting his head to look at me. "He wrote about how lonely he was and how he wanted me to come home to Harlem and take care of him."

His voice grows pensive and his eyes moisten. This doesn't happen often. The last time I recall seeing Dad cry was in 1997 when we saw *Amistad* in the theater. In one of the scenes, you see how tightly the slaves are packed belowdecks on the ship, crammed in like firewood. They're drenched in urine and feces. Surrounded by dampness, stench, and bacteria, illnesses spread like wildfire, and as a remedy, the crew drags a group of slaves up on deck.

In the next scene, twenty slaves, chained together, are standing in line on the deck. One of the sailors opens the gate in the railing and shoves the woman at the end through the opening. She drags another woman with her. One by one, the chained slaves are yanked into the depths of the sea.

I recall turning to Dad in the dark theater in Lund. Tears were pouring from his eyes. I don't recall seeing that happen before or since.

Dad stares intently down at the black tabletop as Enid places Grandpa's old letters back in the envelope. Normally he would have been shoveling down his ice cream, but it's almost untouched. Silence grips the table; it feels like it lasts forever.

I'm overwhelmed with sympathy for him, and it strikes me that the guilt-trip is an inherited sin. As far back as I can remember, my dad has called, emailed, and texted the very same sentence to me: *Come home. I'm lonely and I miss you.* He must have inherited it from Grandpa. We're linked together by an invisible chain of behavior that's been hammered into us by our parents.

The letters have been found, and the suitcase, with its cracked red leather, stands in the guest room, where I'm sleeping on the sofa bed. Now that I've heard one of the letters read out loud—one of what must be hundreds, judging by the bulging case—and seen Dad's reaction, I realize I have to make sure we read through all the letters together.

As soon as possible.

But what if Dad's pain is too great? What if he changes his mind? What if he decides to hide the suitcase in the attic again before I make it back to Malmö?

DON'T LEAVE ME

It's eleven o'clock in the morning on September 3, and I'm waking up gradually when Mom calls up the stairs.

"Jason, that was Monique. She and Madubuko were just at the clinic, and they were sent straight to the ER. I told them we'd meet them there—get dressed right away, we have to go to Malmö."

The evening before, Mom was sitting at her kitchen table telling me in worried tones that Dad wasn't feeling well and had been extremely out of sorts for the past few days. I had just arrived in Lund to visit my family before my upcoming trips to the Congo and then the United States, including South Carolina.

I throw on my clothes, then dash down the stairs and toss back a glass of grapefruit juice. Maybe it's the adrenaline, or maybe my brain isn't quite awake yet, but I can't form a single word as we drive down the super-straight highway to Malmö.

Mom makes no attempt to break my silence. This is a considerable sacrifice for someone who likes to chat as much as she does. As far back as I can remember, she's talked nonstop from morning to night—with her friends on the phone, with her family at home, with strangers on the street.

It's an unusually gray September morning, and Malmö couldn't look less charming. A little preview of autumn, which will be upon us soon.

We hurry into the ER. The woman behind the first desk directs us to a waiting room farther in to find Dad. The room is full of people. The average age must be at least sixty. Monique and Madubuko—M&M, as we call them—are sitting in a corner. Dad is slumping, his head drooping.

"Hi, Dad, I'm here now," I try to say as cheerfully as possible.

He barely looks up, just keeps staring at the gray hospital floor. As if he doesn't see or recognize me.

"How are you, Dad?"

Dad remains motionless and silent. His face is gray and furrowed, and he looks a decade older than when I saw him in early August. His head is hanging like a vulture's.

"Dad, how are you feeling?" I ask him again.

"Tired . . . I'm tired . . ." Dad responds, making an effort to look up. "Can I lie down?" he manages to say, but he can't seem to raise his eyes to look at me.

His voice is feeble and his gaze sluggish. I place one hand on his shoulder and the other on his arm. He's cold as ice.

"Monique, Mom, feel how cold he is."

My pulse and breathing quicken. I run over to the nearest nurse.

"Excuse me, you have to help us. My dad, he's sitting over there, he needs to lie down. Can you bring a stretcher? And also, he's really cold."

"Cold, you said?" I have the nurse's attention. "OK, I'll take care of it."

The nurse bends down in front of Dad's chair and tries to make eye contact with him, but he just stares vacantly at the ice-cold floor of the waiting room. She feels his arm.

"This isn't good," she says with a quick glance around the room.

She signals for help, and in an instant, two more nurses show up. They transfer Dad onto a stretcher. Two doctors rush in. They ignore us but briskly issue a string of orders to the nurses. Suddenly five people are hovering around Dad. They're hooking up cords, taking his blood pressure, and asking him questions all the while.

"Hi, Madubuko, how are you feeling?" the nurses ask him one after the next.

He doesn't respond; he looks completely blank, like someone who was just woken up and can't place where he is or what day it is.

"Shit, what's going on?" I think—a little too out loud.

I see Monique's teary eyes. *This can't be happening right now . . . not already,* I have time to think. *Fuck, I'm not prepared for this.* They roll Dad's stretcher into a smaller room.

"I'm sorry, only one family member may stay in here with him," one of the doctors says over his shoulder.

"I'll go," Monique offers.

"OK. Mom and I will wait outside."

Mom's eyes are alert, searching. It's like she's looking for a solution but can't find one. There are very few times I've seen her at a loss for words. But she remains perfectly silent—just as she was during our car ride.

The door is open, and the walls are made of glass, so we are witnesses to all the action in the room. The nurses try to start an IV in Dad's arm but can't find a vein. He's too cold.

"His blood pressure is falling," one of the doctors says.

Machines are arranged, carts rolled up, curt commands exchanged. It's obvious that this is an emergency situation. Even though it's good to know that Dad is receiving care now, my fear owns me. He'll be seventy-five in December. He doesn't smoke and he's never been a drinker, but he's overweight and basically never exercises.

What if he dies today? What if his final moment comes so suddenly, on a gray Thursday afternoon in Malmö?

I learned about how unexpectedly death can arrive when my friend Petar died in a car accident in 2004. We humans may have endless plans, schedules, ideas, and desires, but death can step right in and put an end to everything. In the middle of a sentence.

As the doctors work feverishly around Dad's metal stretcher, Mom and I sit in silence, squirming nervously in the waiting room. There's so much I haven't had a chance to ask Dad about. I've never managed to apologize for the irritation and lack of patience I've had toward him. I want to ask his forgiveness as soon as he wakes up. I've also never thanked him for staying in Sweden and being a good father to me. I've never thanked him for allowing me to grow up with a mom and a dad, unlike so many of my friends who grew up without their fathers around.

My thoughts are whirling like a centrifuge in my lowered head, coming out equal parts prayer and incantation: *Dad, don't leave me. I won't be able to finish building the bridge from Skåne to Harlem without your help. If you disappear now, my link to Africa, to the United States, to my black skin, will be forever severed. And part of me will disappear too. Don't sentence me to wander forever rootless in this place I haven't managed to make my home. How am I supposed to fill in all the gaps in my history without you, without your memories and experiences, your stories, your thoughts, your wisdom? Dad, I need you. How will I explain to my future children where we come from? How am I supposed to explain how stubbornly you fought all these years, so far from your homeland? How am I supposed to keep growing if you die?*

Tears spring into my eyes. But I have to hold it together. If I open the floodgates, I'll lose control and become overwhelmed with sadness. My throat is dry, but no matter how much I try to swallow, the parched feeling won't go away. I put my arm around Mom's shoulder, and she rests her head against me. I can only imagine what's going on inside her. She was the one who followed Dad to Sweden.

It's like Mom has read my thoughts when she lifts her head and straightens her back.

"He can't leave me here. He can't leave me alone in this country, he promised me he wouldn't."

Suddenly I catch a glimpse of the love that once flourished between Mom and Dad. Once upon a time, they loved each other so passionately that they ignored all conventions, taboos, their own families' wishes about marrying within your own race. They loved each other across the massive wall between black and white in 1960s America. So deep was their love that Mom gave up her job, her life, her friends, and her family and moved to Sweden—to be with Dad. To support him as he chased his dreams. If it hadn't been for Mom's courage, I never would have existed. If it hadn't been for my parents' intrepid love, I never would have been born.

The level of activity in the small room is so intense that Monique isn't allowed to stay. She joins us and takes my mother's arm. I've never seen her so emotional before. I once saw her eyes fill with tears, but I've never seen her and my mom holding each other.

Just a few weeks earlier, Dad had emailed the following lines to me and some of my cousins:

> *Another one of our heroes is gone. For those of you who are under 50, who grew up in Sweden with limited insight into the civil rights movement, the riots, the fighting in the streets, the bombings, the arson, being shot and sometimes shooting back, being refused hotel rooms, being refused a seat in restaurants, being refused a place in schools, perhaps the name Julian Bond doesn't mean much. Maybe names like John A. Williams or Amiri Baraka or the dozens of other heroes of my generation, from the 1960s in America, don't mean much either. Certainly a name like Martin Luther King rings a bell,*

but you can't truly understand the passion with which they fought. And then we have Malcolm X, whom some try to understand.

This week has been tough for many of us veterans. First John A. Williams died, and now Julian Bond. What weighs most heavily on me is that I can't be there in the US with friends, family, veterans like myself, to grieve for our departed heroes and remind each other of the experiences we shared and the demonstrations we walked in. It pains me so much and begs the question again and again: what am I doing here?

But the struggle continues—doesn't it?

Madubuko

That email, which I brushed off as resulting from Dad's fear of his own death, almost seems macabre now that I'm convinced I'm about to lose him.

But Dad survived. He had to spend all of September and half of October in the hospital. Slowly but surely, as Monique reported by phone, Dad was regaining the spark in his eyes and the energy in his body. The doctors said he had an advanced infection due to blood poisoning that had come from a bleeding ulcer. It was curable. But healing would take time.

Every time I talk to Dad on Skype or on the phone, I notice his spark has waned and his will to live seems considerably dampened. He speaks slowly and distantly, and it's clear that the infection has taken a great deal out of him, that his body has been aging at double speed. I can't escape the jarring thought that Dad might leave me before I'm ready, yet I remind him often that everything's going to be fine. He responds, "I'm old and I'm sick."

ALLENDALE

The waiter tells us that the pigs' ears are the chef's specialty. We order them. They're about three times crunchier than bacon, wrapped in lettuce, and drowned in a sweet and spicy sauce. Simme struggles to spill as little sauce as possible each time he brings an ear to his mouth.

"This is fucking delicious," he keeps saying between crackling bites. The ears taste like bacon but have the consistency of a Skor bar.

With great amusement, I watch my travel companion, who's also one of my closest friends—documentary filmmaker Simon Klose, who everyone calls Simme. No one else I know has such a great love for anything edible. I rest my hands on the armrests of the wicker chair and give my jaw a break between bites.

We're sitting on one of the spacious verandas that wraps around a big old wooden house in the American South. It's early October, but there's none of the autumn chill that's hit Lund, where we just came from. It's still seventy-three degrees and humid in Charleston, South Carolina. Stately trees tower just beyond the veranda; above them the sky is bluish black, sucking up the day's last rays of sun.

The brilliant-white eighteenth-century house is swarming with people. All the guests—the ones on the wooden veranda that looks out over old Charleston, and those in the large dining room inside—are white. As the white-clad waiters dart between the tables and the grand doors that lead to the brightly lit dining room, I wonder silently: *How many descendants of slave owners are sitting here beside us right now?*

We're at Husk, the flagship restaurant of celebrity chef Sean Brock.

Simme shovels down the last of the saucy pigs' ears. As usual, I'm skeptical when it comes to trying new foods, and I'm satisfied to have eaten even a small piece of the odd cut of meat.

Items that were once slave food are now served as expensive delicacies in this splendid house, which evokes a plantation from the days of slavery with its great wooden columns and colored glass panes. The slave owners ate only the better parts of the animals. Whatever was left went to the slaves, who became so adept at preparing delicious food from the scanty bits rejected by their owners that their food culture, to this day, is called soul food.

Soul food is the pillar of American home cooking. The term began to be widely used in the 1960s, when pride in African American culture reached its peak. "Say it loud, I'm black and I'm proud," sang James Brown in 1968, and that line was like rocket fuel for black people in the US and all over the world. Actual slave food largely consisted of various porridges: dishes that could be made of simple ingredients, that could simmer away during the many hours slaves worked in the fields. But the dishes that survived into modern times are the slaves' celebratory foods: fried chicken, green beans and pork, macaroni and cheese, pecan pie, candied sweet potatoes . . . dishes swimming in cream, oil, fat, and sugar, ingredients slaves could only treat themselves to on special occasions.

Slaves were usually not allowed to learn to read and write, so the black cooks couldn't jot down recipes or write cookbooks. As a result, the authorship of their culture was taken over by the slave owners, and today these foods are embraced by everyone, no matter their skin color. It seems to me that the unmistakable feeling in hip-hop, blues, and jazz—that unpredictable, cocky, rule-breaking swing; those thick, sweet harmonies; or the hard, subdivided beats—might be reflected in soul food.

Maybe that's what the soul *is*. "I know you got soul," Bobby Byrd sang in 1971, over a drumbeat so infectious it's been sampled over and over again by hip-hop producers. Soul is the same as feeling, and the feeling has to be right, or else neither music nor food will work. It's as if African American culture must rely upon an abstract ingredient in all its forms of expression in order to be complete.

The waiter returns a few minutes later and puts down a large bowl of fried chicken skin, a platter of oysters in chicken fat, and a bowl of slow-smoked ribs. There is contented nibbling and lip-smacking from all the small tables on the veranda, which is lit by candles now that the sun has gone down. It's symbolic of the romantic South.

"My, my, gentri-fried chicken," Simme cries with a satisfied smile as he reaches across the table and starts helping himself. The food has a Creole vibe, as I imagine the food in New Orleans must have, but there's still something different about this. Like Caribbean meets Atlantic.

Simme is innately enthusiastic, which makes him the best travel buddy. Our banter is mostly made up of puns and mash-up words. His eyes shine with the joy of having combined "gentrified" and "fried" into one word.

"Haven't you ever had authentic Southern soul food before?" I ask Simme.

"Obviously I've had a poor little fried chicken or two before, but I've never had the real deal," he responds as he passionately gulps down oysters and crackly fried chicken skin. "It's so fucking sick that we're here. We're going to eat and explore our way through South Carolina!"

We shovel down the rich soul food as night embraces the lovely wooden building; our conversation peters out as our stomachs fill, and I think of Dad.

He's still recovering at home in Malmö. Time and again, he's tried to dissuade me from traveling through the American South to look for my roots. Yet he calls and emails to tell me what I should make sure to see and what I must avoid at all costs in the Southern states. I've got detailed instructions about which relatives I have to see and who I can't forget to call. It's like he can't help coming on this trip with me—but he prefers to follow along from his easy chair on Föreningsgatan in Malmö.

An hour late, Alluette Jones steps into the restaurant. She is undeniably elegant. She looks like a movie star, and her glamour is only emphasized by the gracious way she ignores her own late arrival. She's sixty-five years old but doesn't look a day over fifty. She has high, prominent cheekbones and is tall with impressive posture; her hair is short and gray and styled in tiny, tiny curls. She wears a black suit and has a gaze that scans and takes in the whole scene. Although it's ten at night, her steel-rimmed sunglasses don't come off even once.

She used to run the successful vegetarian soul food restaurant Alluette's Café in the heart of Charleston—one of the last restaurants in the city to be under African American ownership, she tells us. It was a popular place, and soul-food chefs from all over the country flocked there, but when the property owner decided to renovate the place to luxury levels, she had to close up shop.

"We were well known, and a destination for foodies from all over the country," she says, bringing her glass of wine to her lips for a nonchalant sip. "But now they're going to build a luxury hotel, so there's no room for black-owned businesses."

Her cheeks rise as if she's going to smile, but instead her expression is one of loathing and bitterness. Alluette straightens her back, taps her chest, and goes on. "We made healthy soul food. Who in the US has ever done that?"

I don't even have time to move a muscle in response before she answers her own question.

"No one! My people eat nothing but crap these days. We're stuffed with sugar, trans fats, and meat full of antibiotics, all from huge factories."

A few days earlier, I was at the home of my friend, the restaurateur Marcus Samuelsson, in Harlem, telling him about Simme's and my upcoming trip to South Carolina. He cut me off midsentence and started messing with his phone, exclaiming after a few seconds, "Alluette Jones! You have to call her. She knows everything about South Carolina. I'll text her and let her know you're coming."

When I called Alluette a few hours later and introduced myself, she said she'd be happy to guide us around Allendale.

"Anyone who's interested in black history is a friend of mine," she said.

Now, as we're sitting in the fancy restaurant on King Street, the picturesque main street that runs through downtown Charleston, I tell Alluette that I've hardly seen any black faces in the city. She rolls her eyes and says, as if it should have been obvious, that the black people live in North Charleston. It is its own city, with its own mayor, own budget, and own problems.

"How many of the hundreds of thousands of tourists who come to Charleston each year do you think go to North Charleston?" Alluette asks, her voice cutting. "At least one thing was better during segregation: black neighborhoods were left alone, economically. You had black people who owned restaurants, bakeries, stores, bars. Hardly anything in Charleston and North Charleston is owned by African Americans these days. Segregation and racism are not only part of the economy— they're even in our food. We eat nutrient-poor, chemical-filled food. No wonder we get diabetes, ADHD, ADD, and high blood pressure at higher rates. No wonder we become overweight and drained of energy."

It's impossible not to notice how passionate she is when it comes to food and the civil rights of African Americans. Or how furious she is. Alluette speaks loudly without taking notice of the other guests on the veranda. She gesticulates and concludes her comments by staring deeply into my eyes over the rims of her sunglasses. She waits for her words to sink in, and when I respond with a "That's really tragic," she punctuates it with a loud, "Who you tellin'!" Not like a question, more like an *amen* or a *now you get what I mean*. She speaks in headlines.

The poorer you are, the worse nutrition you get. Like their forefathers, the descendants of slaves are at the bottom of the food hierarchy. The lack of nutritious food in the ghettos of certain American megacities is so serious that the phenomenon was given a name: food desert. A food desert is any area where it's impossible to buy fresh fruits or vegetables within a one-mile radius. In certain cities in the United States, the radius is as large as ten miles. The limited access residents of the ghetto have to cars and public transportation makes access to nutritious, wholesome food even more difficult. If you add in the proliferation of fast-food chains in these areas, the spread of conditions like obesity and diabetes is unavoidable. A lemon at Whole Foods costs more than a hamburger at a fast-food restaurant. These food deserts are found in Chicago, New Orleans, Memphis, Detroit, Camden, and dozens of other cities around the country.

By the next day, we've exchanged the brilliant-white dining room and lovely veranda of the lavish Charleston restaurant for a room with red-tiled walls and plastic tables and benches that are bolted to the floor. We've taken a two-hour car trip through subtropical forests and ramshackle villages, straight into the heart of South Carolina. The scenery flashing past our windows was more than just abandoned houses, wide-open fields, and thick woods; we've gone from an America of prosperity and freedom to a part of the country seldom seen in the movies: the poor, forgotten America.

Alluette observes me with curiosity as I grasp the chicken sandwich between my thumb and index finger. The bun is thick, rubbery, white, and greasy. I put the sandwich down and rub my fingers frantically with my napkin to get rid of the grease. I lift the top of the bun to reveal a bit of fried chicken that's blackish green at the edges and most closely resembles a malignant tumor.

"You can't eat that," Alluette says. She's sitting across from me and Simme, and her face wrinkles with distaste.

The pockmarked Indian woman behind the counter doesn't say a word when an indignant Alluette asks for a new sandwich. The clientele at Krispy Krunchy Chicken in the small town of Allendale in South Carolina is 100 percent black.

"Look at her thighs . . ."

Alluette points at a woman in her twenties who's wearing denim short-shorts that are stretched to the limit. Each of the woman's legs on its own is easily bigger around than my torso.

"It's all the steroids and hormones she gets from what she eats. You don't get that fat otherwise."

"Alluette, have you seen Chris Rock's film *Good Hair*?" I ask.

"Of course, I have," Alluette responds, looking at me like I'm stupid. "But I'd rather see the movie *Fat Asses*. There's a film that needs to be made. My people shouldn't look like this."

Krispy Krunchy is next to the only open gas station in Allendale. The rest of the gas stations, and every third building we've driven past so far, appear to have been long abandoned, with the junglelike foliage of South Carolina sprouting through the cracks of the concrete. Nature is slowly reclaiming large parts of the city. Deserted restaurants, motels, gas stations, and houses are the first and most haunting sight we see in the poorest district of South Carolina.

In his book *Deep South: Four Seasons on Back Roads*, American travel writer Paul Theroux describes Allendale as a ghost town: "Poor, neglected, hopeless-looking, a vivid failure."

I wonder what southwestern South Carolina looked like in 1907, when my grandfather Silas was born. Back then, the cotton industry was still bringing great riches to the local landowners—those who originally built all these now abandoned buildings. The fact that this community is one of the poorest in the state means that it's also one of the poorest in the United States. Almost the entire population is African American, and almost half live under the poverty level. If you take a closer look at the poorest places in the US, it's clear that they are primarily inhabited by people with black skin.

Allendale is where "the one percent" live. Not the richest one percent, who prompted Occupy Wall Street to besiege Zuccotti Park in New York City in September 2011. No, those who live here are on the opposite end of the economic spectrum: the poorest one percent in the nation. The number of people living in extreme poverty in the US—that is, those who live on under two dollars per day—has doubled in recent years, and Allendale is far from alone in being like a ghost town: abandoned, hopeless, poor, and black. Camden, Ferguson, Flint, and Gary are a few of the many cities that are slowly, bit by bit, being reduced to ruins.

South Carolina was one of the first states to be colonized by Englishmen in the 1600s. Here they built stately houses and enormous fortunes. The fertile earth was perfect for cultivating cotton, rice, and indigo, which was prized for the blue dye that could be extracted from it.

Here, the earth was colored red by black blood.

An early black activist and leader by the name of Denmark Vesey was hanged in this state in 1822, accused of plotting a slave revolt. He was born on the island of Saint Thomas in the Caribbean, a slave on Danish land, and took his first name from the nation that owned the island. Scandinavian colonialism and its involvement in the transatlantic slave trade is basically never discussed in Sweden, Norway, or Denmark. Least of all in the countries' schoolbooks. How many slaves changed owners in the Swedish Saint Barthélemy? How many suffered on the journey across the Atlantic in shackles made of Swedish iron? How many were born in the Danish Caribbean or kidnapped to be shipped on Danish vessels? How many slaves were fed rations of dried Norwegian cod in the New World?

Before he was murdered, Denmark Vesey founded the distinguished Emanuel African Methodist Episcopal Church in Charleston, a congregation intended to give black worshippers a place of refuge from the threatening treatment they had to endure if they tried to pray to Jesus in white churches.

The question is, how long could a person with Denmark Vesey's insubordinate, progressive convictions survive in the South Carolina of today? How much has changed since he dangled to death on the rope of racism?

Simme, Alluette, and I spend the day in Allendale looking for traces of my grandfather Silas.

None of his children or grandchildren have set foot in Allendale since he left the place in the early 1920s. It's as if the small town would have had a Medusa effect on them, and they would have been petrified, eternally damned to the same poor, oppressed fate as their forefathers.

I haven't been able to trace my ancestors on my dad's side any further back than this. Was Allendale the first place they arrived from the slave ship? If Silas hadn't left this backwoods place, I never would have existed, and my parents never would have set foot in Sweden. Silas has been popping up in my thoughts more and more often in the past few years. I have to see Allendale to understand the prospects my grandfather faced when he was young.

Is Allendale, this village of origin, the last missing piece of my mosaic? Will I ever finish reconstructing my fragile identity? My mind is reeling when Simme suddenly gives a shout.

"Stop the car!"

Before the wheels have stopped turning, he's dashing through the ditch and into a sea of white clouds to the right of our gray Hyundai.

A cotton field.

I allow my eyes to take in the whole scene. It's like I've stepped out of a time machine. As if the bloody past of South Carolina never ceased but continues to flourish in the form of small white tufts of cotton in endless fields. Was this where my forefathers slaved? Did their calloused hands harvest this very field?

"We have to film this," Simme cries, sweeping his hand to encompass the wide expanses.

The cotton is high. The white bolls sit on their brown branches among green leaves and half-dried grayish-brown ones. I assume it will be time for harvest soon. I am my father's and grandfather's son, so I've got a pair of handmade, shiny British leather shoes on my feet. As gingerly as I can, I walk through the muddy ditch and to the field. In my hand, I hold an empty paper bag that, a little earlier, had been filled with snacks from the last gas station.

I gently pick one tuft. The cotton rests in a hard, brown, crown-shaped shell, like a flower that has dried out and split, offering up its white innards. To get the cotton out, I have to stick my fingers in a little and tug. It's so soft. If it weren't for the seeds in the fluff, you could have used the cotton straightaway.

In my grandfather's day, one hundred pounds of cotton would bring about fifty cents. A really good picker could pick three or four times their weight in cotton, but one hundred pounds was the average. It takes about seventy bolls like the one I just picked to make a pound. So Grandpa and his fellow pickers had to pick around seven thousand bolls a day.

> The hands got cramped from the repetitive motion of picking, the fingers fairly locked in place and callused from the pricks of the barbed, five-pointed cockleburs that cupped each precious boll. The work was not so much hazardous as it was mind-numbing and endless, requiring them to pick from the moment the sun peeked over the tree line to the moment it fell behind the horizon and they could no longer see. After ten or twelve hours, the pickers could barely stand up straight for all the stooping.

This is how Isabel Wilkerson describes an average day in the fields in her epic book *The Warmth of Other Suns*.

The soft tuft between my fingers feels unreal.

In the 1840s, cotton made up a large portion of American exports. Millions of people were tormented, tortured, raped, and killed for the sake of these soft, strong fibers. Over the course of almost four hundred years, between twelve and twenty million people were taken from Africa and transported across the Atlantic; millions of them died on the passage across the ocean.

How could this innocent, soft, beautiful plant in my palm rouse such greediness in people? How could we take these gifts from nature and be so quick to enslave and kill because of them? Cotton, diamonds, oil, gold . . .

In 1860, when Jack Miller, my grandfather's maternal grandfather, lived in Allendale, the collective value of all the slaves in the United States was estimated to be greater than the value of all the railroads, factories, and means of production combined.

Cotton. What a gift to the white American South—and what a hell for its black majority. It contributed to the industrial revolution in Europe. Cotton picked by my forefathers' hands was spun in the textile factories of central Sweden and worn on Swedish bodies. More than half of the cotton imported to Sweden in the 1800s came from this very place. Slave-picked bolls became the frills adorning Swedish kings.

My shoes have sunk into the muddy field. Ten yards to my left, Simme is filming a panorama of the landscape. As I roll the cotton into a ball between my fingers, my slave ancestors and their descendants— my grandpa Silas, his grandfather Jack and grandmother Myla, his aunts Sylvia and Esther—appear before me. They sing their work songs under the broiling sun, dutifully bent over the thigh-high plants. I can see them stop, now and then, hoping that the foreman on horseback won't notice, gazing across the field and wiping sweat from their brows.

I have never seen or stepped into a cotton field before. But here, in a field in need of hands to harvest the tufts of gold, I think of how my ancestors' backs must have ached. How, day after day, they were forced to endure the hard work of plucking the clouds loose and filling the sacks over their shoulders. How they were whipped bloody if they didn't pick enough, how they were careful not to pick too much so that the next day's quota wouldn't be greater than today's. How their African backs must have bent from year after year under the whip. How perhaps the songs they sang were the only vent, the only way to recover strength, they were allowed.

Maybe the foreman used the notorious cat-o'-nine-tails, with each of its nine straps studded with knots. It was just one of many whips, all designed to cause maximum pain and injury. The rough leather tore the skin from slaves' backs, and it wasn't unusual for a whip to destroy the eyes of the person they were punishing.

It's October now, a sunny and comfortable seventy degrees. I try to imagine the days when the sun shone stronger and Jack and Myla picked cotton from sunup to sundown. If they were lucky, they could avoid the whip, and all they had to deal with were mosquito bites and backaches.

My ancestors' lives were measured in burlap sacks stuffed with cotton. I can hear their voices. I can hear what might be the highest art of longing and lament: the blues.

In "Cotton Picking Blues," Big Mama Thornton sings about the physical pain involved in picking cotton all day in the hot sun, the straps of the bags digging into flesh.

This is one of the strangest and most powerful experiences of my life. It's like I'm communicating with my genetic memory. I have found another shard for my mosaic, a vital link to my history. This is the feeling I came to Allendale to find. An ounce of understanding for what my forefathers suffered.

I hear your blues.

My little paper bag is full of the white cloud tufts when I return to the road. My shoes are covered in mud, but this small, symbolic moment spent picking is my only way to contact my ancestors. I will put the cotton clouds in a jar and place it on my desk as a constant reminder of where my family's journey to Sweden once began.

In the middle of Allendale, near the train tracks and in the shadow of three gigantic, abandoned silos, is a row of deserted shops in what must have been the heart of the town, once upon a time.

"Have you ever heard of Roy C.?" Alluette wonders. "Never? Well, this is his record store. It's world famous."

She points at the only shop on the whole street that doesn't have a boarded- or bricked-up front window.

By "world famous," she must mean "famous in South Carolina." The shop looks more like a flea market than a record store. Everything from wigs and hair extensions to black Barbie dolls and a ton of CDs is strewn haphazardly on the worn brown shelves and the glass counters, gathering dust. The shop window reads, "CD-R varieties."

Roy C. Hammond is at least six foot three, and despite his seventy-six years, he doesn't look any older than sixty. He's wearing a short-sleeved gray-and-blue shirt that must have been tailored to his specifications; it looks like some sort of cross between a 1960s pilot shirt full of pockets and darts, and a retro-futuristic *Star Trek* garment. A gigantic smartphone is clipped to the center of his shirt. He's balding on top, but the hair around his ears is still black as ebony.

He extends a palm that swallows my own hand entirely. His back is straight, and his eyes are friendly, if a little tired.

I ask Roy C. how he ended up in Allendale.

"Well, when I was sixteen, I dreamed of becoming a professional boxer. I got in touch with the same folks who had trained Joe Frazier and Hurricane Jackson. The first day I was supposed to train in their gym, Hurricane was there. He asked if I wanted to spar. Spar with a full-grown man who just one year later would challenge Floyd Patterson for the title of heavyweight world champion? Of course, I wanted to. Hurricane told me to hit him as hard as I could. He promised not to hit back, so I socked him with a right hook that got him in the cheek. He looked honestly surprised."

Roy C.'s voice is raspy, and it strikes me how proudly he carries himself. It makes me think more than once about how saggy my own posture is, even though my shoulders have only been weighed down by privileges. During our conversation, his big cell phone starts ringing. His annoyance grows, and at last he asks the short woman working in the store to take his telephone to the back.

"I don't know who's calling, but I ain't got time right now."

I'm surprised at how seriously he's taking this opportunity to tell his story to me and to Simme's camera.

"I was sixteen, but I punched like a man. So Hurricane responded with a straight left that hit me right in the mouth. I was inexperienced and unprepared besides, since he had promised not to hit back, so I didn't have my guard up. Everything went black, and when I woke up, I decided I'd never box again. So there my first dream went to hell. While I was on the platform, waiting for the train home, I sang. A man came up to me and asked if I wanted to come into his music studio and record a song. *Sure, why not,* I thought. The song we recorded is called 'Who's That Knockin',' as The Genies, and it was a big hit. Since then, I've been living my second dream."

Who's that knocking on my door
all last night and the night before . . .
I can't stand that awful thing
Who's that knocking on my door

Sings Roy C. in a deep voice.

Now the old man is sitting on a wooden crate in a secondhand store in one of the poorest towns in the country. A man who wrote several big hits in his life and toured all over the world.

"How do you like Allendale?" I ask.

"Well, you know, we got a problem here."

"What's that?"

"These black people just hate each other. They'll sit next to each other in church on Sunday, but come Monday, they got no love, no

134

love for their neighbor. Poverty's eaten up their morals and minds. All they think about is how everyone else has got it better, and they hate each other for it."

I tell Mr. Roy that my grandpa was born here, and that I'm here partly to visit the place where he was born but also to ask around and see if I can find any relatives.

"Well"—he nods—"best you ask Reverend Cave. He's eighty-nine, and besides preaching on Sundays, he runs one of the two funeral homes in town. He knows everything. He's buried just about everyone around here."

There's no hospital in Allendale, much less a grocery store, as far as I can tell. But here, as everywhere, life and death run their course. Death might even be greedier here among the poor and hopeless ruins of Allendale. Although the town is situated in the midst of fertile fields, I don't see a single place to buy fruits or vegetables. Aside from the pecan trees that line the roads, there's no sign of "real food," as Alluette calls it.

Just as we're about to leave, Roy says, "You said you do hip-hop, right?"

"Yes, sir," I reply.

"Well, you know the song 'Impeach the President.'"

"Of course, I do, sir. It's one of the five most sampled songs in hip-hop."

"I know. I made that record, that's my song."

In 1973, Roy C. Hammond wrote and produced the song "Impeach the President" for the band The Honey Drippers from Jamaica, Queens, a notorious but vibrant neighborhood of New York City.

"You know that President Nixon was a bad man, the way he broke into that building. The man just wasn't fit to be president. So I wrote this song. Well, it went on to become mighty popular in the late eighties and the nineties."

That song has been sampled thousands of times.

"You know Nas?" he asks.

Do I know Nas? I grew up with his music.

"Biggie Smalls?"

"Of course. They're my heroes," I tell Roy. "I have hip-hop to thank for who I am."

Roy nods placidly.

"Well, they all sampled my song."

Goddamn! Here, in a forgotten, destitute corner of the world, I have found a man whose songwriting formed one of the pillars of the music that has guided me through life. And he doesn't seem to have received a cent for it either. What he has is the memory, the story, and this secondhand store. I suppose it's always the case that the people who lay the groundwork for a culture do so without expecting anything in return. Roy C. Hammond wrote and created music because he had to, not just to survive financially but because his soul demanded it. The guitar picking and trumpeting of innumerable other descendants of slaves created global movements like jazz and blues and later rock and hip-hop, and Roy C.'s creativity made waves that reached as far as the gray hills and tree-lined streets of Lund.

I can hardly comprehend that I have found a legend of hip-hop here in Grandpa's old town. Is this a sign from my ancestors? Are they trying to tell me I made the right decision in coming here and searching for my roots? That's how I choose to interpret it.

We get back in the car and drive on, down streets flanked by one burned-out, dilapidated house after the next. We're supposed to take a right on Razor Road to find Reverend Cave's funeral home, but every other street sign seems to be missing. Huge trees veiled with Spanish moss line the roads. People wander along street corners and outside the sad, rickety little houses—I can't imagine they're on their way anywhere, but they still wake up in the morning, get dressed, and go out. All of Allendale is like some sort of institutional waiting room populated by invisible spirits.

The people on the streets are a seldom-seen reminder of the injustices America is built on. They echo with the despair that caused

Denmark Vesey, Harriet Tubman, Malcolm X, Kendrick Lamar, my grandmother, and Dad to raise their voices and dedicate their lives to talking about the struggle for something better.

Most of them bear the same dark pigment that their forefathers brought over the Atlantic. Skin tones have not blended to the same extent here as they have in New York or Washington, DC, where the African American population comes in countless shades, from black to light brown. In just eighteen hours, we've gone from eating dinner among the descendants of slave owners to standing among descendants of slaves.

"Stop the car!" Alluette commands, pointing at a man in his thirties who's sauntering down the street in a white T-shirt three sizes too big that's full of holes and covered in stains.

She leans over me with easy authority and yells through the open window.

"Where is Cave's funeral home?"

"Aw, wul, ma'am, is juss down the road here, you juss pass on down, you can't miss it."

His dialect is gooey with diphthongs.

"What do you think it does to a person, living in an environment like this day in and day out?" Alluette says to Simme and me. "Walking around in all this decay and witnessing the proof that hope was abandoned long before the buildings?"

I observe this ghost town with the distant gaze of a visitor. One that says, *Wow, this is so far from my reality, and it's so nice to know that I can leave this place whenever I like.* I nod vaguely at Alluette.

Majestic oak trees with thick trunks and long branches crooked with age make the run-down shacks look even more fragile and tumbledown. *Black men have been hanged on some of these branches,* I think as we travel down the pitted, cracked road. A police car is parked in front of one house, and the officer is standing in the driveway, talking to two women who are sitting on a rickety veranda.

"Ask them if we're headed the right way," Alluette urges me.

Just as I'm about to stop, the officer hops into his car and drives off. Alluette shouts as loud as a street preacher at the women on the veranda, asking them if this is the way to Cave's funeral home. The response is hardly recognizable as English, but I manage to understand that we're on the right path.

There it is, up ahead. The four white limousines don't lie. There's no Mafia meeting in the little house. It's the funeral home. It seems that, no matter how poor they were in life, citizens of Allendale take their final journey in a white limo.

The cicadas are noticeably raucous, as if nature wants to prevent us from ignoring its pulse. The man who approaches our car is called Kevin Price. He works for the pastor, who unfortunately has had to travel to a nearby city for a doctor's visit.

Kevin, who is also wearing a threadbare, overlarge T-shirt that was once white, tells us that Allendale has a gang problem. The picture on his giant cotton shirt is of a woman sitting in front of a birthday cake. "Rest in peace," reads the text above the image; underneath is "never forgotten."

"The pastor is eighty-nine, so he knows everything about this area," Kevin says in his heavy Carolina accent. "More young people than old ones are buried here these days. Drugs and guns. Generations of inherited poverty and hopelessness have destroyed people's souls. Their ability to love themselves and their neighbors has been seriously compromised. We keep very busy; every Saturday and Sunday, we bury someone. Must be three or four funerals a week."

Allendale, which has no shop that sells fruits or vegetables, no grocery store, and no hospital, does have two funeral homes, where business is booming. "All you gotta do in life is stay black and die," as my great-grandmother used to say. Those are two things you can never get away from. Down here in the South, there's a lot of blackness and death, something that's clear even to a genealogy tourist like me.

I tell Kevin about my grandfather. His last name was Robinson, and his maternal grandfather was a Miller.

"Ya-ow, we have lots of Millers and Robinsons here," he drawls in the affirmative, and starts reciting names. "Ned Miller, James Robinson, Clive Robinson, Dexter Miller . . ."

Well, maybe they're my relatives. People were given last names by their slave owners, and that means that large groups of African Americans have the same last name even if they aren't necessarily related. In medieval England and Scotland, you were called Miller if you were a miller; Baker if you were a baker. During slavery in the South, you were called Miller if you were black and owned by someone of that name.

Kevin gives us Pastor Cave's number, but there's no answer when we call.

Just a few miles outside of the tiny ghost town, Alluette gives a shout.

"What? Check out that house."

A big white house with a pale-green roof and a grandiose veranda supported by glossy white columns rests in the center of a large yard. This is Erwinton, one of the region's most famous plantations. Simme googled "plantations Allendale" before we left our hotel room in Charleston this morning and found around fifteen in the vicinity. Cotton was to the South what oil is to Saudi Arabia.

We step out of the car. At least, Simme and I do—Alluette firmly declares that she refuses to tread on this ground.

"There's blood on this land," she says. "And besides, surely members of the Erwin family still live in that house. Those crazy people might shoot us."

The house is flanked by two oak trees, their trunks thick. William Robinson Erwin built this house in 1828. Robinson? I wonder, could my family have worked here? It can't be ruled out. In any case, I can't escape the thought that it might have been so. Perhaps I'm standing on the land of those who owned my ancestors. Could my relatives have been whipped here when their cotton harvest didn't live up to the day's goal as set by the slave driver? Presumably.

What did they do to keep from living their lives in despair? What did they tell their children? How do humans survive that frozen state where each hopeless day turns into the next until life is over?

But they made it through. Through the sun, the whip, the humiliation, the burden of work, the malaria, the poor food, the wooden benches they stretched their aching bodies out on at night, the trauma of having their children sold away, the systematic rapes, the lynchings, the lack of rights, the hopelessness. No wonder the stories of the Bible spoke to them, drilled their way into the depths of their souls. The stories of the people of Israel were tales of an enslaved people. They must have identified completely. Faith and songs, prayers and cries.

Although the slaves made up the majority of the population in the South, they hardly ever revolted against their white oppressors. The whip kept them in check. Can a person be systematically frightened into submission? Is that the root of the hopelessness that, still today, grows side by side with the cotton here? A long-ago violently injected submission that continues to hold these citizens in a stranglehold of invisible oppression?

Cornel West, in his formidable book *Race Matters*, describes this poverty and oppression:

> Nihilism is to be understood here not as a philosophical doctrine that there are no rational grounds for legitimate standards or authority; it is, far more, the lived experience of coping with a life of horrifying meaninglessness, hopelessness, and (most important) lovelessness. The frightening result is a numbing detachment from others and a self-destructive disposition toward the world. Life without meaning, hope, and love breeds a coldhearted, mean-spirited outlook that destroys both the individual and others.

Double oppression: from the outside, in the form of poverty and structural obstacles, as well as from the inside: the incessant self-contempt that turns one's gaze to the ground and serves as a constant reminder to be submissive.

Imagine that everyone around you is born into and eventually dies silently in poverty. Can the effects of being surrounded by such hardship be so strong that, ever since the first slave set foot here, black people in South Carolina have associated the color of their skin with submission and pain?

And here I am, having never felt what it is to be hungry. At least not a hunger that I know can't be satisfied whenever I want. I've never been cold without knowing where I can find warmth; I've never felt what it is to be poor. Even as these thoughts crowd in my mind, I think of the seriously obese teens sitting on simple porches on the back streets of Allendale. Perhaps suffering isn't just a fate; maybe it's an identity. Maybe you're in greater social danger if you read books and dream of getting an education than if you just stand around a street corner all day in a size-XXXL T-shirt, without any plans or any hope for a brighter tomorrow.

Poverty isn't just an economic reality in Allendale. Poverty is part of the psychocultural spine that holds the whole place up. I try to imagine my way into one of these souls. What it would have been like to be born into not questioning the situation I find myself in, the world around me. But I can't.

I don't know what it's like to be them. I just want to shout out loud that they're blind, that they have to wake up. That it's time to demand justice. After four hundred years. I want to go back to Charleston and walk into Sean Brock's fancy restaurant and spit in the eclectically garnished pigs' ears. I want to scream that all of South Carolina is still built on blood. Blood from black bodies that turns to gold in white pockets.

Frederick Douglass wrote in his 1845 autobiography, *Narrative of the Life of Frederick Douglass*, that both the enslaved and the enslavers were ruined by this cruel system. Blacks were treated like animals and whites turned into animals.

My mind is racing as Simme and I walk up the white-painted steps of Erwinton, heading for the large glass doors.

No one seems to be home in the two-story wooden house. A wide, pillared veranda surrounds the whole place; it, in turn, is framed by a neat hedge. The leafy yard with its ancient oaks, cypresses, pecan trees, and sycamores is perfectly still and deserted under the gray clouds, and it occurs to me that maybe this building, too, is frozen in time.

Up on the veranda, Simme takes photographs through the large living room windows and out across the grounds. Unlike Kevin, Alluette, and Roy, we've never had segregation imprinted upon us. We're steeped in social-democratic egalitarianism and the Swedish right to roam on private property, dammit. Of course, we can move about freely. Of course, we are allowed to be here—the world has been ours from birth. Who's going to tell us otherwise?

In plantation houses like this one, the ladies sat in their dresses of imported silk with lace crinolines and blinding-white collars. Carefree days—the elegant ladies and gentlemen amused themselves with tea from Ceylon, wine from France, and card games in the shade of generous verandas or dances in well-lit ballrooms.

Each of life's joys was just a snap of the fingers away. The slaves prepared the food, played the music, constructed the buildings, plowed and sowed the fields. The plantation owners calmly raked in the profits. The tyranny and terror that made their lifestyle possible was the basis of an entire economy. So distant the slaves' anguished screams must have been for the daughters of plantation owners. How their pain must have been held at arm's length to protect those clueless little dears.

How much mental gymnastics did it take to paint a picture of a reality where it was morally justified to kill and rape for your daily bread and your lifestyle and then pray piously to Jesus every Sunday? Here, on the blood-nourished lawn in front of Erwinton, the ruthless cycle of suffering comes alive in my mind.

Alluette honks. She wants us to return to the vehicle. We meander back across the fertile grass, and when we get to the car, we're met by Alluette's pained expression.

"I guess they had to take that goddamn statue down," she snaps. "At least that's some kind of progress. Let's get the hell outta here."

Revolution happens slowly in South Carolina. On the internet, you can see a picture of Erwinton from a few years back, with a statue of a small black boy dressed as a jockey standing on the lawn in front of the house. The caricature has only recently been removed.

A few miles on down the country road, we spot a worn old wooden sign. "Antioch Christian Church." That's where we're headed—to the oldest cemetery in the area. The gravel road is overgrown and pitted, but soon we come to an eerie abandoned church. It looks like a white barn with large windows along its sides. This church was founded by the same Erwin who built the plantation, back when my great-great-great-great-grandfather was alive. Although I've spent many hours looking at old census records online, my genealogy research is pretty foggy so far back in time. He might have been called Handy Miller, born around 1800.

"Watch out for snakes," Alluette warns just before we get out of the car.

The grass is tall, and the sky is dim and gray. A chill runs through me. Over time, weather and soil have left some gravestones standing, while others have overturned, soon to be overgrown by foliage. Erwin, Flowers, Box, Calhoun. The names on the stones are those of people whose morals allowed them to own people the same way a dairy farmer in Löberöd owns cows. Although that farmer would never get it into his head to whip a cow who didn't give enough milk. Or hang a cow from a tree to set an example for the other cows. Or rape the calves.

Adam Hochschild writes in his book *Bury the Chains* that the idea that it was wrong to own slaves was about as foreign in the early 1800s as if someone today claimed it was morally reprehensible to own a car. African American author and journalist Ta-Nehisi Coates writes in his article "The Case for Reparations" that in the United States in the nineteenth century, aspiring to be able to afford slaves was as natural as saving up for a house or a condo today.

Smaller stones stick up around the large gray ones—only a bit bigger than the cobblestones in Lund. Some are inscribed with a letter or two. Initials. MK. JR. AG.

Alluette shudders.

"Those are the graves of slaves. Keep in mind that those buried here were relatively privileged slaves. Probably lighter skinned than those who worked outside the home. House slaves, servant slaves. The few who were given the right to be buried with their owners. Just like someone who wants to be buried with their pets."

I walk over to the largest grave in the churchyard—a large obelisk. On the front is an inscribed text: "Here lie the mortal remains of Robert Martin, Lieutenant Colonel of the Confederate States of America, born in Charleston February 12, 1835, died in Augusta, Georgia, in 1874. A loyal gentleman, a devoted patriot, and a true Christian."

This man fought for what he believed in. The right to own other humans, the right to own slaves. A loyal gentleman . . . a true Christian . . . ? It turns my stomach. I want to spit on his grave. I want to piss on his name. I don't want his descendants to be able to exonerate their family's history and defend the systematic murders that the so often glorified Confederate states upheld, sponsored, and represented.

Even the very slim chance that the men and women buried here oppressed my ancestors and their contemporaries, in particular, makes me want to throw up. It's more than I can handle right now, that people who raped, whipped, and killed black men, women, and children for hundreds of years don't end up with their gravestones pulverized into sand. It's like my back is starting to develop stigmata, inherited wounds that sting and itch just from standing here. As if the whip against Myla Miller's back still burns—but now on the back of her great-great-grandchild. My own presence here offends me. Why have I even honored this place with a visit?

Alluette calls out from across the cemetery.

"That's enough of this. There might be snakes here. Besides, I don't want to walk around the graves of people I didn't know and wouldn't have wanted to know."

Rage aches inside of her too; it's obvious from her strident, sharp voice. This place is clearly haunted by the bloody past. Simme is the last one in the car. He, too, has been affected by the cold chill that permeates the deserted graveyard.

"Shit, what a creepy place," he says, slamming the car door.

One summer evening in downtown Charleston in 2015, twenty-one-year-old white man Dylann Roof walked into the Emanuel AME Church, the same church that was founded by the revolutionary Denmark Vesey. He spent an hour praying with a small group of people and then shot and killed nine of them in cold blood.

Because they were black.

Another outbreak of the hatred that's been tradition in the South for hundreds of years. The same hatred that kept my grandfather and father in check. The same hatred that makes my dad say to this day that he never wants to set foot in South Carolina again.

It's not over; it hasn't stopped. Hate dies hard here in the South, and it doesn't seem to want to become part of the past. I am the most privileged of my grandfather's lineage, which means that I am granted the luxury of the rich and the free: the ability to be a tourist in this landscape of pain and hopelessness. Maybe the fact is that my dad doesn't want the floodgates of our family history—slavery, subservience, dysfunction, poverty, and hopelessness—to open and come back to haunt him.

It's as if history freezes in the moment. History is what hurts. If you open it up for a closer look, you risk your own destruction.

When I get home from my trip and enthusiastically hand a glass jar to Dad in his apartment in Malmö, he will ask, "What is this?"

"It's cotton I picked in Allendale; it could be from a field where your forefathers slaved."

"God dammit," he responds with disgust, "why don't you throw that shit out? Would you bring back a piece of Auschwitz and give it to the family of a Holocaust survivor?"

In the wake of the mass murder at the AME Church in Charleston, a public debate arose about the fact that the Confederate flag still flew over the South Carolina statehouse.

"It's not about a fucking flag," Alluette exclaims when the topic comes up. "Technically, the slaves were freed a hundred and fifty years ago, but the injustice is still with us today. The structures that were created to keep black people on the outside of society are stronger than ever."

White gold. King cotton. Bloody black backs constituted the basis for the economy of the United States, boll by boll. The suffering of slaves became songs that ended up belonging to everyone; their food became home cooking. Their fingers, vocal cords, and minds have participated in building this country. The white man brought nothing to the table but the whip, the rifle, and the Bible.

But the Confederate flag no longer flies over the South Carolina statehouse, and the statue of the little black boy no longer stands on the lawn at Erwinton Plantation. Micro-steps of progress.

As a few last rays of the sun manage to penetrate the gray clouds, Alluette reads aloud to me and Simme from her leather-bound notebook full of recipes. The green South Carolina foliage flies past the car window, and I send up a silent thank-you to my grandfather Solomon Warren Robinson for leaving Allendale for Harlem over ninety years earlier, and for being strong enough to survive the life he was given. Everything I am and have been allowed to become can be traced back to the fact that he gathered his courage, as a thirteen-year-old black boy, and broke out of his cage in the poorest of poor places. I may bear scars from what I've experienced because of my skin color, but my grandfather freed not only his own body but those of future generations.

"He was smart and he was lucky." Alluette smiles when I tell her how grateful I am. "He knew better."

To be young, black, gifted, and broke. Two generations later, I, his grandson, was born freer, with lighter skin and straighter hair. If Dad lived here, he never could have gotten the life-prolonging angioplasty he had last year. He never would have met a white woman like my mom, much less had a child with her.

Before we leave Allendale, Simme wants to take a few pictures of the gigantic silos in the center of town. As he's out photographing, Alluette says, "You know, I'd like to make a movie called *Being Black in America Is Hazardous to Your Health*."

I laugh.

"Shit, now there's a film I'd like to see, Alluette. Someone needs to tell that story."

"I mean, can you imagine what it must have been like for a young, pregnant black girl in South Carolina a hundred and fifty years ago? You had absolutely no rights. You don't know if your child is going to be strung up in a tree, sold, or just worn out in a cotton field. Now, that's trauma. And now, my government spends billions of dollars a day fighting terrorism on the other side of the world. Well, fuck, we've been terrorized all along. Who's fighting the terrorism African Americans have been dealing with in this country for four centuries?"

Her voice rises in tone and volume.

"What psychologist gives *us* therapy? PTSD, my ass. We're all suffering from it. It's become part of our DNA."

Later that day, in Room 611 at the brand-new Hyatt Place hotel in Charleston, I'm watching a 2012 BBC documentary in which fundamentalists armed with axes are chopping away at legendary buildings in Timbuktu. The medieval sand structures crumble bit by bit. Images of burned books from Timbuktu's historical library flash by. So removed from history humans are, foolishly ignorant of whatever happened before their own lifetimes. If only these so-called Islamists knew what they were burning. Some of Africa's, and Islam's, oldest texts, from the continent's oldest library.

My grandpa's grandfather, Jack Miller, who was born in the mid-1800s in Allendale, married Myla at the age of eighteen. They say she was a slave from Mali, where Timbuktu is.

I'll never forget the day—an afternoon in the early 2000s—when I was sitting at Dad's house and paging through a dog-eared photo album. On the inside cover, I found a family tree that had been hand-drawn in marker. At the very top were written two names: "Jack Miller and Myla Miller, 'Timbuktu.'"

"Why does it say 'Timbuktu' next to Myla's name?" I asked Dad.

"That's what she was called. She's your relative."

"But that's incredible, I mean, I call myself Timbuktu, and I had no idea that's what she was called, back when I chose that name."

"Well, maybe she's talking to you."

JIMMY, JUANETTA & JOAQUIN

Simme and I wake up early on our last morning in Charleston. We're on the coast of the South Carolina Lowcountry, a large, fertile area that is home to the Gullah people (or Geechee, as they're also called). Their language, food, culture, and traditions are almost identical to what the slaves brought over to this green coast several hundred years ago. Their word for "peanut," for example, is "*guber*"—basically the same as the Kikongo people's word, "*n'guba*." The sweetgrass baskets the Geechee people are known for are woven with the very same techniques as those used by the Wolof people of Senegal.

The rain whips down onto the picturesque street outside our hotel window. Large, heavy raindrops pelt the tops of our heads as we run to our little white South Korean rental car.

Our destination is Manning, where my aunt Juanetta lives. Yet another little backwater town in the green inland areas of South Carolina.

I call Dad, who answers on the second ring.

"Son, what's this guilt-trip talk?" he says slowly from the other side of the Atlantic.

He's referring to a text conversation we had the other day. He wrote that he is slowly getting better but that, as his only son, I ought to be in Sweden to support him in his recovery. I texted back that I don't want any guilt-tripping from him, and that he knows why I'm not there with him.

This exchange is so typical of my dad and me. Simme always says I'm too tough and impatient with Dad. My response is that I think he is too demanding and too quick to blame me. A wave of irritation wells up in me when Dad brings up our texts before even saying "hi."

"Dad, this reminds me of the letters Grandpa sent to you in the seventies."

Our styles of communication have been passed down through the generations. I have promised myself countless times that no way in hell will I subject my own children to this kind of talk.

"Your grandpa didn't guilt me at all," Dad says, defending himself. "But your grandmother was a master manipulator. Grandpa was kind. He was just lonely. He wrote the way he did out of love."

"Sure, but it still must have made you feel awful to read about how lonesome your dad was. Was that really right of him?"

"Jason, quit that now, I'm perfectly at peace about my relationship with my father. Don't come around forty years later and judge who he was or what he did."

"OK, Dad. Let's not argue anymore, I just called to see how you're doing."

Dad's reasoning and defense of Grandpa makes me even more irritated. I don't understand his need to revise the truth and his history, his tendency to sanitize things that happened. It makes me doubt the honesty with which he talks about himself and his emotions. What scares me most is the idea that I could be like that when I'm older, whether I am doomed to continue living out a drama that started with Grandpa, or even earlier than that.

My conversation with Dad shifts into a more conciliatory tone. That's how it usually goes. First the conflict, which we soon put aside; then we go on as if nothing has happened.

"OK, Dad. We're heading to see Aunt Juanetta now."

"Good. I'm very glad you're making connections with family on your own. But just so you know: she's very poor. Just so you're prepared."

"I know, I know. She seemed really nice on the phone. I'm sure it will be fine."

The windshield wipers are waving back and forth like the arms of the audience at a hip-hop concert, but we can barely see the road. It's like trying to rake leaves in a stiff gale. The little rental car plows its way through puddles the size of soccer fields. I hardly dare to blink.

After a long, focused journey through the rains of Hurricane Joaquin, I call my aunt to let her know we'll be in Manning in about an hour.

"How do we find your place?"

"I'll come meet you by the Piggly Wiggly."

"What's that?"

"Just head right into town and drive past the two stoplights and you're there. You can't miss the Piggly Wiggly—it's a grocery store. I'll be in a silver minivan."

The rainy gray countryside whizzing past the windows of our car makes me forget we're in the American South. This looks like the southern Sweden I grew up in, which makes me think that the cotton fields are oddly misplaced. There are no sunny yellow rapeseed fields under the heavy, low-hanging clouds. Instead, fields of ivory berries stretch toward the horizon, the cotton whiter than Jesus in a Bible. White as blood, white as gold. "White is right," as they said in Grandpa's time. Always let anyone white pass.

If Simme and I hadn't just been in Allendale, I'm sure we would react more strongly to the sights on the road that leads us into tiny Manning.

We pass dilapidated shacks among stately poplars. The gray clouds and endless rain of Joaquin lends a melancholy look to the landscape. We're traveling back into the invisible America. It's a poor area, but I don't see as many ghost houses as in Allendale. Only a third of the people in Manning live below the poverty line.

I veer into the parking lot of the Piggly Wiggly and pull in next to a silvery-gray car. Sitting inside it is Dad's youngest sister, Juanetta, who cheerfully tells us to follow her.

We drive through town and out between the cotton fields, which are sometimes broken up by bits of thick forest. By the time we turn off the county highway and pull onto the grass in front of Auntie's mobile home, it has stopped raining. A banana tree and a few young fruit trees grow in the large yard; the rectangular trailer with its corrugated plastic roof stands in the middle. It looks like a long camper without wheels that has been stretched out a little and decorated as if it were a house. The home seems freshly painted in gray and white, and there are a lot of potted plants by the door. It's simple, but it looks cozy and welcoming.

I sigh with relief; after Dad's warnings, I had a mental image of my aunt living in total squalor. I thought I would be met with burned-out cars, piles of trash, and down-and-out zombielike relatives who could hardly speak properly.

What's more, I thought she would have no interest whatsoever in meeting me, since we haven't met in person since 1981 and haven't been in contact a single time since. But, in fact, I am met with friendly chestnut-brown eyes and a warm hug. She opens the screen door to the porch, and we walk into the narrow trailer. It's dark inside. The blinds are down, and the timeworn curtains are pulled as well. Two large sofas covered in white sheets stand next to each other along one wall. The room can't be more than ten feet wide. The wall-to-wall beige carpet has outlived its life expectancy by a decade or two.

"This is your uncle Jimmy," says Juanetta.

"Heeey, Jason man, welcome."

The eighty-three-year-old man stiffly rises from his easy chair and embraces me. He has short gray hair and a pair of thick eyeglasses. He moves with difficulty, in a manner that speaks of the pains of old age, but his eyes flash with life. Everything about the man, aside from his body, seems spry and alert.

"When was the last time . . . was it in Philly or New York?"

"I think it was in Philadelphia, Uncle."

The round Juanetta stands beside him, beaming with warmth. She looks so much like my dad. A few shades lighter, but the same round face, the same eyes, the same height and broad nose.

"It was in Philly," Jimmy says with certainty.

"It sure was, Uncle, in 1981."

I was only six years old. I'll never forget it. Apparently, there was some sort of toy factory on the outskirts of Philadelphia, where toys with minor defects were sold at a discount. My dad bought a big dark-blue robot action figure for me. A Mazinga Shogun Warrior. It was beyond awesome. Mazinga was sixteen inches tall and could shoot missiles from his left hand. The missiles were stored on the robot's shoulders. Mazinga appears in every family photo from those days. That was the last time I saw Juanetta, Jimmy, and their children, Tony, Michael, and Sean.

Simme and I take a seat on one of the sheet-covered sofas. My fear that things might be tense between me and family members I haven't seen in over thirty years has vanished. Juanetta takes out a leather photo album, pointing at pictures of relatives and telling us about them.

A dozen or so books and a ton of framed photos compete for space on the small shelf in the corner. The walls are decorated solely with pictures of the family and their relatives. The largest picture is of Jimmy and Juanetta and their three children. It's a typical studio portrait, the kind you find in any yearbook or photography studio. Juanetta is standing on the left while one son sits in front of Jimmy; the other two sons flank their parents. Everyone is smiling.

The most noticeable feature is that Jimmy is wearing a pair of large aviator sunglasses. They've booked an appointment with a professional photographer and agreed to be posed in a studio, but that doesn't keep Jimmy from wearing his shades. He looks a little out of place in his Hawaiian shirt and sunglasses—like he's dressed for a press shoot for the 1980s TV show *Magnum, P.I.*

Jimmy and Juanetta lived the better part of their lives in the Germantown neighborhood of Philadelphia. But rising rents and a crumbling job market forced them to leave the city ten years ago. It's ironic that the South Carolina Grandpa found so hopeless is now, a century later, the place that offers his daughter her hopes and dreams. In the early 1900s, black people migrated from the plantations of the South to the industrialization of the northern states. In the 2000s, more and more African Americans are moving back south.

This is the first time I have seen the other side of gentrification with my own eyes. Sure, it's great that crime is down in Brooklyn and trendy clothing stores and restaurants are opening there. But where can they go, those who lived there long before economic interests moved in, when rents are driven up and they can no longer afford to stay?

I wonder if Grandpa would have chosen to move back to South Carolina now, or if the suffering he associated with this state would have meant he would rather live dirt poor in New York than go back home. I expect many people who flee their homes and are forced to live the rest of their lives in unfamiliar places never manage to get over the desire to return, while someone who migrates in the hopes of finding a better life never wants to go back.

Depending on what happens in your home, it may be the only spot on earth where you are at peace, or it may be the very place that has the power to destroy you.

"We like to go loud," Jimmy says. "That's just how we roll. There are no neighbors to disturb here. It's not like in Philly. I've always played music loud, but now we can do it around the clock with no need to worry who we're bothering."

The heavy raindrops of the hurricane whip the plastic roof of the trailer with such force that Jimmy turns up the jazz that's flowing from the TV in an attempt to drown out Joaquin's incredible precipitation.

"Check this out," Jimmy says, opening a photo album he's retrieved from a shelf under the table.

He holds it open to a page that contains one photo. It's an old picture of Grandpa. Daddy Robinson, as Jimmy calls him, is standing next to twenty-year-old Juanetta.

"I was really pretty back then," Juanetta says with a hearty chuckle. "Now I'm just fat."

"Daddy Robinson was as smooth as they come," Jimmy says.

In the picture, Grandpa is dressed casually. No tie. He only dressed like that when he was chilling. I do notice his shiny shoes and blinding-white spats, though.

"Look at those shoes."

"He was a stylish man," Juanetta interjects. "That's how he managed to meet my mom. His shoes were always shiny."

Then Juanetta shows me another old photo: a beautiful woman in some sort of flight-attendant uniform sitting coquettishly with her legs crossed and talking on an old-fashioned phone. It's a 1940s studio portrait of Grandpa's second wife, Juanetta's mother, Mary, the same woman my grandmother despised for her light skin. I suppose it looked cool to be talking on the phone, as if you had things to do and people to speak to. The photograph reminds me of the pictures in Dad's magazine *The Lundian*, which often show someone at a keyboard or, indeed, on the phone. Dad thinks it looks more professional to photograph people who appear to be working.

Jimmy's gaze is alert and friendly, always seeking a pair of eyes to lock on to so he can tell a long anecdote that's broken by his own laughter. It's as if the ability to find humor in sadness has immunized him against becoming bitter. Here is an eighty-three-year-old man sitting in a worn brown easy chair in a tiny trailer home, smiling at life. No matter how much the system of structural racism has tried to bring him down, it hasn't taken away his ability to laugh.

Uncle Jimmy leans toward me with a loud whisper: "Do you smoke reefer? You know, weed?"

I laugh, out of surprise and because of his use of the dated slang "reefer"—I've only ever read that word in books and seen it in some old movie or another.

"I need it for my arthritis and cataracts," Jimmy says. "It's one of the secrets that's kept me alive."

"I quit smoking weed," I say, "but Simme would be happy to smoke with you."

"Definitely," he says with a wink.

Jimmy takes a small metal box from a drawer in the small chest next to his big plush easy chair. He opens the box and shows it to us, nodding eagerly, with a big smile.

He quickly rolls a joint without mixing in any tobacco, as people often do in Sweden. Of course. I have no problem being the only one in the room who isn't smoking up. Years in music studios have taught me to deal. At least for the first few hours, I'm fine; after a while, weed smokers can get a little too zoned out, which makes it hard to have any sort of meaningful exchange.

"This is loud," Jimmy says, offering the joint to Simme.

Jimmy smiles contentedly and blows out the drag he just took. Then he chuckles to himself and watches Simme as if he's thinking, *Let's see how this Swedish boy handles the strength of this grass.*

"Loud, you know, this is some loud shit," he repeats, his face serious, pointing at the metal box, which is open on the table in front of us.

Jimmy watches carefully to make sure the joint makes it around the room, to everyone but me. Each time it lands in his possession, he becomes quiet, focuses on the glow at the tip of the thin white paper cylinder, and takes a deep, reverent drag. Then he deftly hands it on to the next person, nodding, blowing out smoke, and laughing. The old man's feeling good now.

Jimmy tells us that during the 1970s, he and Juanetta used to have reefer parties. They would invite a bunch of friends over, and the guests would bring a lot of pot and set it out so everyone could roll joints and smoke as much as they wanted all night. Originally, the use of weed spread from Mexican immigrants to African Americans, and nowadays people from all social classes and ethnicities smoke up.

The pot makes Aunt Juanetta and Uncle Jimmy even chattier, and the jazz from the TV is turned up another notch or two. Loud weed and loud music.

I ask Jimmy about a picture on the wall where he's dressed in a uniform.

"Yes, I was a soldier. The Korean War. I was there in 1950. We were shipped out to Yokohama from San Francisco. The voyage took eighteen days, man, you should have seen it. People got sick as hell. There was always a long line for the latrine."

The music is screaming from the television, but Jimmy has no trouble being heard over it. He watches us over the edge of his large glasses as if to make sure we're listening.

"One thing's for sure. We fought for our country, and several of my friends died for these United States. In 1952, I was back in the States on a military base in South Carolina. Some of my friends and I were gonna go to Georgia. We drove, in uniform, of course. Then we stopped at some diner somewhere on the border between South Carolina and Georgia. No sooner did we set foot in the restaurant than a woman came up to the highest-ranking man in our group and said, 'White in front, black around back.' 'You cannot be serious,' said the sergeant.

'Are you telling me these soldiers who just got back from defending this country can't sit here?' 'White in front, black around back,' she repeated. 'I can't believe it,' was all he could say. Over and over again. 'I can't believe this is what we fought for.'"

Jimmy's cheerful mood has vanished. His face twists with rage, and he lowers his gaze to the floor. No one says anything. Juanetta is still sitting with her hands folded in her lap, her smile intact. Jimmy looks at Simme and me, his expression meaningful and sad. We eagerly wait for him to continue. Then the old man grunts as if he's been awoken from a dream state and goes on.

"Our sergeant was white. He was more upset than any of us black folks. We were used to it, of course. But then and there, I decided to leave the army. There's no point in sacrificing your life for a country that isn't grateful. I might as well just keep living my own life instead. I was twenty years old; I had my whole life ahead of me."

The food that was served to the whites had been made by black hands, I think. Essentially, all the food served in the South was prepared by black cooks. How come it was fine to eat a fish fried by a black person, but you couldn't eat it next to a black person?

My musings are interrupted by Juanetta: "Have some more snacks, boys."

She points at the plates of bread, cold cuts, cheese, chips, cookies, and soda. Alluette would not like this. Processed foods bursting with chemicals, sugars, and trans fats. We eat our food on paper plates.

"We're good at surviving," Juanetta says. "Otherwise we would have died out like the Native Americans. Just take the Geechee language. Geechee was a way of communicating so the slave driver couldn't understand what you were saying. The slave driver thought the slaves were singing in the cotton fields to make the work go faster. But the songs were communication. People were sending messages to each other."

Juanetta looks around, fixing her eyes on each one of us, and then she says, "If you constantly tell a child it's good-for-nothing, lazy, thieving, and ugly. If you hit that child and treat it without respect its whole life. What kind of person will it become? What do you think that child will do? We are that child. Four hundred years of abuse, pain, and murder have made us what we are today. Beautiful, terrible, dysfunctional, and strong."

This is the first time Juanetta's face has been without a smile since we stepped into the trailer home. Simme and I look at each other and nod. No one says anything. The only sound is the jazz from the TV and the rain that's still pattering on the roof.

These are the people I missed building a relationship with. This is my family, these are my people. I am eternally linked to the folks in this simple mobile home, in a big field in the middle of inland South Carolina—a universe away, culturally, from Sweden and my daily life in Stockholm.

A smile spreads across Juanetta's face once again, and as if she wants to lighten the mood, she gestures at the snacks and cookies and says, "Now, now, boys, you've hardly eaten a thing. Help yourselves . . ."

Simme and I thank her but decline. It's time for us to start the long car ride back to Charleston. Jimmy eagerly tries to convince us to sleep over in the trailer home.

"Uncle, it's time for us to go," I repeat.

Jimmy watches me with a happy face and a quick retort: "Time hasn't even started yet."

UNCLE OBI

The next morning, Simme flies out of bed.

"C'mon, bro. Up and at 'em. Our flight leaves soon."

I lean toward the nightstand and turn on the TV in the hopes that it might wake my brain enough that I'll have the energy to stand up.

A reporter is standing in the pouring rain in the otherwise picturesque heart of Charleston, just a few blocks from where we are. Images flash by on the screen: flooded streets, people wading in water that comes to their waists, cars almost completely covered. "There's a two hundred percent chance of rain in Charleston today," the reporter says. One hundred is a definite chance—so what's two hundred? *There is no limit to superlatives in the United States* is my first bleary thought of the day. I get up.

The lawn outside our hotel has literally been transformed into a lake, and the rain is still whipping down. How the hell is our Kia supposed to manage the twenty-minute trip to the airport? Every ten yards, we have to ease our way through another giant, deep puddle. The highway is practically empty.

One drenched half hour later, we're surrounded by lightning strikes, but that doesn't seem to keep the small airport from remaining open. One banana and a bathroom break later, we're in our seats at the very back of the small plane.

Simme is talking nonstop. It's only nine o'clock, and we didn't get back last night until three, so my brain is still just crawling.

"Simme, I can't talk right now."

"What are you talking about, man? We have to talk, or else we'll just sit here being terrified."

The atmosphere on this plane is tense. He's right. So we talk about our experiences in Allendale and Manning over the past few days.

We keep talking all through the bumpy ascent. But at last I can no longer keep my exhaustion at bay. Hurricane-level turbulence or no—I pass out and sleep with my head drooping like a swan's.

A bang wakes me up. In my dreams, I was far from seat 28D. We have landed in Baltimore. The home of the loveable, homeless heroin addict Bubbles on *The Wire*.

My thoughts jump from Bubbles to Dad's friend George Jones. George was an African American man who came to Sweden in the early 1970s and ended up in Lund. Most people in town knew who he was. To some, he was the black drunk who hung around Mårtenstorget or Central Station. For those of us in Djingis Khan, he was the funny, kind man who always stopped his bike and told us a thing or two about life.

Many people would say he was crazy. But in my eyes, he was an eccentric, an artistic soul, imported straight from the tough streets of Pittsburgh to the rounded cobblestones of Lund. George stopped by Dad's place at least twice a week, mostly to share the local gossip and just chat. George swore like a sailor and was constantly laughing and telling jokes.

"He was the best poet I've ever known," Dad always says when George's name comes up. "It's just a pity that he drank away two kids, two wives, and a whole life. But he was happier than just about anyone."

In the South, they eat grits, a corn-based porridge that works as well for lunch or supper as it does for breakfast. They don't really taste like anything, but you can either add spices and shrimp, or serve it as is with eggs, meat, or vegetables. It's the potato of the black South, a soul food staple.

Dad used to bring containers of grits back from the US. So when George or one of his other African American friends was visiting, grits were always on the menu. I remember Dad and George having earnest conversations over plates of herring and grits. The perfect combination of the new and the old. Sweden and the US. As usual, they were raining down complaints about Sweden, about why the country was so backward. Swedes were too quiet, Sweden was too strictly organized, Sweden was too boring, Sweden was too far behind the US, Sweden was . . . not home.

George was 100 percent ghetto. He had enough charisma to fill a whole gymnasium and the table manners of a three-year-old.

One day, when Dad and George were sitting around the oval kitchen table eating grits, something black fell onto George's plate.

"What was that, George?" Dad asked.

"Oh, it's just a stone," George responded as if it this were a perfectly natural occurrence, then continued to shovel down his fish and grits.

"Lemme see that . . ."

Dad leaned over to inspect George's plate, and, his face twisted— half in disgust and half in laughter—he exclaimed, teasing, "That ain't no stone, it's a tooth! George, what the fuck!"

"No, that ain't no motherfuckin' tooth, man," George protested. "It's a stone, and tomorrow I'm gonna take it up with Ingvar down at the store. He can't be sellin' herring with stones in it."

"George, it's your tooth and it's totally black," Dad insisted, upset, throwing up his arms. "When was the last time you went to the dentist?"

George didn't stop chewing, but he protested with spirit, his mouth full of food: "Aw, fuck, man! I ain't gon' to see no fuckin' dentist. Them motherfuckers take all you got, leave you with nothing but an aching jaw and a hole in your pocket. How come my mouth hurt more after I visit the motherfucker than before? Fuck that."

George was the antithesis of what Dad had learned from his father: "Always look sharp and never let the white man see you drunk." George generally looked like he had come from outer space and plunked down in a landfill wearing clothing that was eccentric, to say the least. He was drunk more often than sober and always very visible in lily-white downtown Lund. He might show up dressed in a bath mat with a large belt around his middle to hold it up, a fisherman's cap, and a pair of gigantic sunglasses. He looked like some sort of hip-hop version of Obi-Wan Kenobi.

George and Dad were two different ghetto stories. One industrious and ambitious, the other willful and shameless. To my dad, that black tooth was nothing but a painful reminder of the saying: "You can take a nigga out the ghetto, but you can't take the ghetto out the nigga."

On our way to the rental car in Baltimore, I realize I miss George an awful lot. I should have appreciated his peculiar presence and creative sayings more back when he was still biking around the tree-lined streets of Lund. Once I ran into George on Spexarevägen, where he pointed up at the white contrails of a passing plane and said, "Look, you see that? I can control that motherfucker. Mind control. I got it. Do you?"

Or the time he jumped off his bike outside the Gräddhyllan coffee shop in downtown Lund and said, "Jason, you're a Capricorn. Never forget that. You're in the crown."

Another time he walked up to me and a group of teenagers outside our local ICA grocery store in Djingis Khan and exclaimed, "Trust me, high-speed digital evolution. That's what the world is going to be about."

This was in 1989. The dude predicted the internet.

I love *The Wire* so much it feels like I've already visited Baltimore. Like I know the city and its history. From a booming port city to one plagued by unemployment, population decline, and notoriously bad crime statistics. The city's history was sort of like Malmö's.

Randy Newman wrote about the city in his song "Baltimore" in 1977, detailing the harshness of life in the city. When Nina Simone's version of the song hit my ears in the early 2000s, I'd even tried to translate it into Swedish.

Baltimore is the city where my cousin Obedike Jr. worked as a police officer until he was shot in the line of duty for the third time and his family convinced him to quit. For him, there was no other option than to leave the city for York, Pennsylvania. These days, he owns a restaurant there that sells soul food burritos. But his dad, my uncle Obedike, still lives in a small suburb called Catonsville. Everyone who can afford it has fled the inner city.

The GPS in our upgraded rental—a Japanese sedan this time—takes us on our tour of the monotonous suburban streets of Baltimore. Yet, compared to our hurricane morning in Charleston, this feels like a walk in the park. It's difficult to navigate through residential neighborhoods of single-family homes under these thick gray clouds, but at last the GPS voice guides us to a cluster of brown apartment buildings across the street from an equally brown, equally shabby high school.

Uncle Obi is a loud man. He opens the door and thunders, *"Nephew, Welcome!"*

I receive a bear hug, then introduce Simme to Obi and his wife, Evelyn. The front door opens straight into their small living room. Across from the door is a worn black sofa. There's just enough space for it to fold out into a bed when it's time for Obi and Evelyn to turn in. The once white walls are covered in photographs of smiling faces in graduation gowns. My cousins' university educations are Uncle Obi's greatest achievement in life. In spite of devastating statistics, none of their four children have become drug addicts or landed in jail. Instead, each of them has a college degree. Both Obi and Evelyn worked as bus drivers almost their whole lives to save for their children's expensive educations.

The furniture in the small apartment is black. The sofa, the bookcase, the table, the desk, the picture frames. It's all black—even the tile in the kitchen, which is no larger than a closet. We view a tiny bathroom, and with that, our home tour is finished. The whole apartment smells like some indeterminable food or spice.

"He's been making his Nigerian food again," Evelyn says with a weary expression. "Something with shellfish."

Uncle Obi's laughter could move mountains, and right now it nearly shakes the carefully hung graduation pictures off the wall.

"It's just some *egusi* soup. No one else in the family is brave enough to eat the food I prepare."

My uncle identifies primarily as Nigerian—more specifically, he belongs to the Igbo people. When asked if he listens to Fela Kuti, he rolls his eyes and responds, "No, I don't listen to no Yoruba man sing."

Uncle Obi is six feet tall and almost as wide.

"You look like you lost some weight, Uncle," I tease.

"Yeah, you tease me, boy, go ahead."

Evelyn sighs pointedly. "He won't listen to me, anyway."

As long as I've known my uncle, he and his wife and his four children have eaten a lot, and between meals, they basically talk nonstop about what to eat for their next meal. McDonald's has always been a family favorite. On Sundays, Eve and Obi gather all the kids and grandkids in town and invite them out to breakfast, often to an all-you-can-eat brunch buffet. This gang could eat their way through the best-stocked pantry in one sitting.

Obi was only eighteen months old when my grandmother put him and his big sister, Nana, on a boat in New York. Their destination was Enugu, Nigeria. Their father, Balfour Linton, the Pan-Africanist who was my grandmother's second husband, had died just six months earlier from complications after an illness. This was in 1951, around the same time Uncle Jimmy was sent onboard another boat—to war in Korea.

"I don't know whose titty I was sucking on, but it must have been someone's," Uncle Obi says, with a meaningful look at me.

"What kind of mom would do that?" I ask.

"I don't know. Madame was never much of a mother. But she had her reasons. To your grandmother, the struggle was always more important than anything else."

Even Obi refers to her as Madame.

The Igbo capital of Enugu in southeastern Nigeria remained Uncle Obi's home until he was seventeen, and his sister Nana stayed in Nigeria until just before she died.

"When I came back to New York, shit . . . things moved quickly there; it was loud, dirty, dangerous. I was a boy from rural Nigeria. What did I know? If it wasn't for your dad and your aunt Chinyelu, I don't know what I would have done."

Uncle Obi shakes his head firmly. "I remember the first time I saw Madame," he continues. "I was sitting in an office with your dad, and I saw someone in the hall on my way in. *That person looks just like Nana,* I thought. *What is she doing here?* Then the woman came into the room, and I realized she was older than Nana. And I knew who she was right away, even though I hadn't seen her in so long. I was seventeen, Jason. That woman was my mother. She asked how I was. And that was all. No tearful mother-and-son reunion—not a chance, with that woman. She was hardcore, Madame."

The pain on Obi's face is so clear that it's like it happened yesterday.

"I guess that's why her kids all turned out the way we did," he says with his roaring laugh. "Shit, she did the same thing to me as she'd done to Madubuko ten years earlier. Drove me down to the army recruiting office in Times Square. Difference was, I was sent to war. She abandoned me again."

"What? I didn't know that, Uncle. Were you in Vietnam? What was it like? Tell me!"

"It was hell. Bloody. I don't want to talk about it. Those memories are best left in Vietnam."

"But, Uncle, weren't you—"

"I ain't saying another word about it," he cuts me off, nailing me with his most commanding look.

I understand a little better, now, where my uncle's natural authority and severity comes from. Images from movies like *Platoon* and *Apocalypse Now* flash through my mind. Only I exchange one of the green-clad soldier's faces for my uncle's. A man who watched friends blown to bits; perhaps he even shot women and children.

We trudge out to the cracked parking lot outside Obi's apartment building and hop into his old black Nissan SUV, which is crammed with stuff. Piles of CDs, books, and loose pieces of paper crowd the beat-up passenger compartment, and I feel like I'm in Dad's attic storage area, but on wheels. Obi, Simme, and I are on our way downtown. Uncle wants to show us the University of Baltimore, where he's about to earn his second master's degree, this one in conflict management.

Obi chats cheerfully about everything from sorrow to joy. Just as I realize we're approaching the storied center of Baltimore, I catch sight of a few blocks of two-story row houses. Half of the gray buildings, which haven't been touched by a paintbrush since the eighties, are boarded up. They radiate hopelessness. The small alleys behind and the narrow streets in front of them are full of trash. Allendale has hardened me to witnessing urban decay to some extent, but still: How can people live like this? I don't know if it's the cold air Hurricane Joaquin has blown all the way up into the state of Maryland, or if it's just too early in the day, but there's no sign of life on these streets. Maybe the residents feel it's better to stay inside as much as possible, to avoid seeing how hopeless and abandoned their neighborhood is. This is *The Wire*.

"Aw, that ain't nothing, Nephew," Obi says. "If we kept going straight here, instead of turning off, you wouldn't have seen nothing but boarded-up houses and a bunch of crazy niggers. This city is outta control, I tell you."

I don't doubt it for a second.

In April 2015, twenty-five-year-old Freddie Gray died one week after being assaulted by six police officers. Freddie Gray's death was just one in a series of cases in the past year in which the police killed young African Americans. From twelve-year-old Tamir Rice, who was shot while playing outside his home, to twenty-eight-year-old Sandra Bland, who was pulled over for changing lanes without signaling and found dead in jail a few hours later.

Baltimore exploded in riots. It's almost an American tradition: rioting in black neighborhoods. The African American population puts up with structural obstacles, racism, poverty, and oppression, but then something happens—often police violence—and it's the last straw. This sort of unrest has occurred with such frequency in the country's history that there's even a name for it: "race riots." It sounds so harsh to my ear. Especially considering that it's always the same race rioting, and always for similar reasons: rage at the incessant pressure people are forced to endure, brought forth by slavery, government oppression, and systematic terror that continues century after century. American society is eternally locked into the fight between black and white, rich and poor.

Obi parks across from a twelve-story concrete building and points south down the avenue.

"It happened here, a little farther down. The riots. Crazy motherfuckers!"

The air is raw. We walk briskly into the university. The building is nicer on the inside than you'd expect from its exterior. There's a large atrium where students are sitting on benches along the walls, chatting by the coffee machine, rushing down corridors and up gray stone staircases with yellow metal railings. We could be in Lund or Jakarta, but now we're in the main character of *The Wire*: the city of Baltimore. I wonder, as I scan the atrium, how people in here reacted while the riots raged on outside. What did they talk about? Did any of the students leave the safety of their school and join the despairing masses in the streets?

Opposite a large bulletin board full of flyers advertising apartments, used cars, and study groups, we wait for a yellow elevator.

"They just destroyed the city," Uncle Obi says, swaying his way into the elevator. "We were afraid of what might happen; there were curfews and violent confrontations between the police and the rioters. They were all just criminals taking advantage of the situation so they could steal new TVs."

"But, Uncle, you don't really mean that, do you? People were mostly angry because their rights weren't respected, especially by the police."

"They were criminals," Obi says firmly. "If you want rights, you don't go out breaking shop windows, looting stores, and setting the cars of hardworking people on fire."

We get out on the tenth floor and walk up to the glass wall at the end of a long corridor. The eastern, western, and southern parts of the city stretch out beneath our feet. The grayish-black sky hangs low over the forest of houses that extends toward the horizon. From up here, you can't see the poverty and frustration that tread those sidewalks.

Uncle Obi leans against the wall and says, "I was never much for the civil rights movement. Partly because I was a little too young and didn't know much, and I wasn't very emotionally invested in the American struggle because I'd just returned home from Nigeria. Plus, I became a soldier. We were taught not to question authority. We were trained to be killers, not thinkers. Malcolm X was already dead by the time I got back, and anyway, he was an extremist who first preached separatism and later did a one-eighty. I just wanted to go back to Africa. Being black in Africa is more natural to me than being black in the US. Here, your black skin is based on too many compromises and concessions. No, I gave up hope for this system a long time ago. I'll go back to Nigeria the first chance I get."

"But, Uncle, things didn't go so well last time you were in Nigeria."

"You're right about that. My sister is crazy."

He smacks his hand against the concrete wall.

Uncle Obi has strong opinions on most things, and he's not much for subtlety or nuance. But despite his blunt and sometimes rude ways, he manages to be a warm man, and very likeable.

"I mean, my sister . . ."

Obi lets out a long, loud sigh. The creases on his forehead furrow harder and his eyes narrow.

"I went to Nigeria a few years ago when my stepfather, Ajuluchuku, died," he says, turning to Simme. "I wanted to receive my rightful share of the inheritance. He owned a lot of land in Enugu. But he has a bunch of other kids too. The man had three or four wives, so, you know, I wasn't the only one wanting his land. But the strangest thing of all was that the person who fought hardest against my demands was my own biological sister Nana. She was chief of police in Abuja, and suddenly she showed up in Enugu with several officers. Can you believe, my own sister put me in jail so I wouldn't get a couple acres of land. Who does that? To their own family? We could have shared it, like brother and sister. But not Nana, oh no."

Obi's voice has become markedly louder. The students in the library and the group study rooms around us, on the tenth floor of the law school building at the University of Baltimore, are noticeably bothered by the bombastic voice in the corridor.

"Let's go get something to eat, Uncle."

To Uncle Obi, food is always a good idea.

"OK. Let's get pizza," he responds, pleased.

At the sports bar half a block from the school, Obi orders two hot dogs and a bag of chips.

"That goddamn doctor says I'm not allowed to eat bread," he says, spearing one of the hot dogs with his fork. "No simple carbs and no shellfish. Can you believe it? I love shellfish, and I'm not supposed to eat them because my doctor said so? What does he know?"

"But you have to take care of your health."

"Fuck, I have to live too. Speaking of which . . ."

Uncle Obi leans toward me with a grave expression.

"Your dad is very sick right now. His body will heal, we know that, but the real problem is in his soul. He's dying. If you don't give him a grandbaby now, he's gonna die. I'm serious, Jason. You better give him a kid, don't wait. It's not that he has too much sickness or too little intelligence—it's family that's the problem. We're old and we're all spread out. The loneliness is gonna kill him."

Uncle could have punched me in the gut with one of his brick-size fists and it would have hurt less than his words do. I wasn't prepared for him to drop such a guilt bomb on me. For him to lay the responsibility for Dad's survival at my feet.

I suddenly realize that Dad's bleeding ulcer, which almost killed him a few weeks ago, might have been caused by his worrying about me. Could it really be my fault that Dad got sick? Should I even entertain such a horrible thought? My closest friends say I am way too prone to guilt. That I bring a ton of anguish upon myself for no reason. But how the fuck do you avoid it? Simme's good at that. I'm not. Everything fills me with dread and regret. As if the only thing that will keep me on the right path is constantly reminding myself of my own mistakes.

Simme sits beside us, filming our conversation.

"Your dad should live here." Obi nods. "Close to his family. Either that, or you have to give him a grandbaby. Make him a kid. Remember what I'm telling you. Loneliness is a killer."

He utters these words between great mouthfuls of chips and hot dog.

The server approaches our table.

"Excuse me, what are you guys filming for?" he asks, pointing at Simme.

"What?" Obi exclaims.

"I'm just wondering if he has permission to film here. Otherwise, you have to ask the manager."

"The manager?" Obi blusters back. "We're only taking video for our family. For private use. Tell your manager he needs to shut up and mind his own business."

My uncle stares resolutely at the server, who takes a step back.

"OK, sir, I'm sorry, I just need to know. We have a policy."

"I don't care about your policy," Obi interrupts the shaken server. "Now let us finish our meal. Get lost!"

Uncle Obi does not have my fear of conflict. He faces the world with his hand in a fist, and in this case, it seems to have worked well. The server leaves and we don't see him again.

"Who are you going to vote for in the election?" I ask, hoping to change the subject to something less serious.

"Trump, who else?" Obi responds, looking at me defiantly.

"Trump?" I repeat with a laugh. "You're kidding, right?"

"Of course not," Uncle says, straightening his back.

"But I thought you were a Democrat?"

"Democrat, Republican, who cares. I'm voting for Trump because he's willing to actually do something about a group of people that needs to be dealt with in this country."

"What? Uncle . . . are you talking about the Mexicans?"

"That's all I'm going to say about it, Jason. Trump's got my vote."

I sigh inwardly. To base your view of the world on misinformation, racism, and ignorance—but, right now, I don't have the energy to try to pull off my uncle's Bible-size blinders.

Obi pushes his plates away. He's eaten everything but the two hot-dog buns.

"We gotta pick up Evelyn and head to Olivia's house," he says. "I promised we would be there for dinner at five."

"Uncle, it's four now. Will we manage to eat dinner in an hour?"

"Of course you will."

"I eat like a bird, you know that."

My uncle gives me a big smile and exclaims, "My Puerto Rican nephew. You sure are a special little bird."

Obi has always called me Puerto Rico due to my light skin and straight hair.

Each time we stop for a traffic light, white and black men move among the cars. They're homeless men wandering down the white-painted lanes. Most of them appear to be between thirty and forty. This is something you no longer see in New York or Los Angeles. But you do in Addis Ababa and Johannesburg, and possibly also Cincinnati and Detroit. The downside of the Land of the Free.

The reality Simme and I witnessed in Allendale exists here in Baltimore too, but on a much greater scale. In some neighborhoods of this once proud city, a third of the buildings are abandoned, and just as many of its inhabitants live below the poverty line. In fifteen of the city's most vulnerable neighborhoods, average life expectancy is lower than in 229 of the countries on earth. Someone born in one of these neighborhoods can expect to die on average nineteen years earlier than someone in the richer parts of town.

"Iraq Vet Needs Money For Food," reads one creased cardboard sign held up by a white guy in front of Uncle Obi's windshield. I think of Uncle Jimmy, who fought in Korea and came home to a country where he wasn't even allowed to sit wherever he wanted on the bus or eat in the front of a restaurant.

How much money does this guy bring in by begging between the lanes of cars? Does he have enough to pay rent—if he even has anywhere to live? He's wearing a threadbare blue flannel shirt and what once must have been a green knitted hat and a pair of sand-colored boots, the kind you see on soldiers when the news shows images from the American war in Iraq. His whole body is covered in dark flecks from oil and exhaust.

How the hell does he stand it? A Lund guy like me surely would have just laid down to die. Have I ever had to fight so hard for something? I imagine that, just a year ago, bullets were whizzing past the ears of this veteran. That he saw friends blown to bits—and now he is forced to humiliate himself in the cold between the cars on a four-lane road in Baltimore.

Gratefulness is not something this country offers all its citizens. It brings to mind a passage from African American author Zora Neale Hurston's autobiography *Dust Tracks on a Road*:

> There is something about poverty that smells like death. Dead dreams dropping off the heart like leaves in a dry season and rotting around the feet; impulses smothered too long in the fetid air of underground caves. The soul lives in sickly air. People can be slave-ships in shoes.

We park at the very end of an idyllic street of single-family homes, in front of an astonishingly large blue house with a glassed-in front porch. We hardly have time to turn off the engine before my cousin Olivia rushes out with a huge smile. She opens my car door and gestures at me to give her a hug.

"Woow, it's been years, Jason. I listen to your music all the time."

Her sons, Jaleel and Kevin, run in circles around us.

"Say hello to your cousin now, boys," she urges.

They look up at me shyly for a split second, then continue to chase each other around in front of the house.

Olivia and her husband bought a big house in a nicer neighborhood than the one where her parents live.

"It hasn't been renovated since the 1920s. It's an antique, by American standards. But we're slowly working on getting it in order. By the way, why wasn't I allowed to make dinner for you?"

"That would have been really nice—" I respond, shrugging apologetically.

"If you'd cooked, your brother's wife, Cherise, would've been jealous," Uncle Obi interrupts brusquely. "I can't deal with no more family politics, so we're going out for pizza instead."

"Pizza," Olivia snorts. "You're not even supposed to eat bread."

"And I don't, just ask Jason," he says, nodding at me. "Did I eat the hot-dog buns at the restaurant?"

I shake my head.

"But you ate quite a few of the chips, Uncle."

"Why are you tattling on me?" he says, and then continues, triumphantly, "Chips ain't bread, they're potatoes. I can eat those, can't I?"

"You're incorrigible, Dad." Olivia sighs, kissing him on the cheek.

I see what Obi was talking about before, when he said that loneliness kills. He runs the risk of eating himself to death, but at least he won't die of loneliness. He's got the most generous of loves, the unconditional kind a person can basically only get from family. The love that lives on despite our faults and downsides. The same love that means I am welcomed with open arms by these people I so seldom see and don't really know. Uncle Obi's pronouncement that loneliness is killing Dad is tearing me apart.

"If I get my PhD, I'm going to write my dissertation on the relationship between Dad and Cherise," Olivia says, laughing.

"Wow, you're getting a doctorate?" I ask.

"I'm thinking about it. But if I do, I won't be able to work as a social worker anymore. I'll be overqualified, and there are too few faculty positions at the universities, so I might be doing myself a disservice. But my master's thesis was about Dad."

"What did you write about?"

"It's about his PTSD," she says, casting a loving glance across the room toward the sofa where Uncle Obi is playing with his two grandchildren. "He's also been diagnosed as bipolar, but without psychosis."

Shit, Olivia is saying all of this openly, in front of both her parents. But Uncle Obi's eyes glow with pride as he listens to his daughter.

"Dad can hardly bear to talk about his PTSD, but I've noticed it in him all my life. Although it wasn't until I started college that I realized what it really was. I think his condition stems from both his upbringing in Nigeria and his experiences in Vietnam. The PTSD, that is. The bipolar disorder was either inherited from his mother or arose during his difficult childhood far away from his immediate family, in a foreign country where he was constantly subjected to a lot of physical and mental violence."

I remember Dad's stories of being beaten by the other wives of Ajuluchuku, my grandmother's husband at the time. They were not merciful. Suddenly, four American children showed up in need of feeding and raising; their mother wasn't there, so they ended up at the bottom of the pecking order. It was worse for the girls. If they were perceived to be impudent, if they didn't wash the dishes or clean up properly, they received strict punishment. "Only a sadist would rub chili pepper on the genitals of an eight-year-old girl," Dad told me once. *No fucking wonder you'd end up with some sort of diagnosis after that,* I think now as Olivia talks about her father.

I don't believe for a second that I could sit around and drop these kinds of diagnoses about my dad in front of other people without wild protests from his direction.

Suddenly four-year-old Jaleel runs up to Olivia.

"Mom, I need a meal," he says.

"That's a fancy way to say he's hungry," I say, smiling at him.

"He has type 1 diabetes," Olivia says seriously. "I have to teach him to be aware of his illness at all times. It's really important to hammer it into him now, while he's little, so that it's automatic when he gets older. If he isn't careful about what and when he eats, there could be dire consequences."

"He's lucky to have such a good mom," I say.

Olivia smiles.

"Dad has type 2 diabetes."

"He does?" Another thing I didn't know.

"That's right," Obi interjects.

"I've told him time and again, you can actually get rid of that form of diabetes if you just change your diet. But he won't listen."

Uncle Obi turns away and pretends to be absorbed in a discussion between Jaleel and his brother, Kevin, who's two years older.

"You see?" Olivia says, pointing at her father. "He just doesn't listen."

"I do listen, Olivia, but the thing is, you also have to be able to live a little," he protests.

"Yeah, live until you die."

I am reminded of a quote from Blur bassist Alex James, who says he celebrated his twenties with drugs, his thirties with alcohol, and his forties with food. Not that Uncle Obi's life seems to have revolved around sex, drugs, and alcohol in any way, but food—yes. That can be just as much a drug as anything.

"Come on, good people," urges Evelyn, who's been sitting quietly on the sofa and observing her family with a contented expression. "Time to head to the restaurant and eat."

It's dusk, and we drive a few blocks through Catonsville to a typical Italian American family restaurant. There are brownish-orange vinyl booths along the walls, and the center of the spacious dining room is filled with large tables. We're far from the only big family there for Saturday dinner. The restaurant is loud, and the pizzas are the size of SUV rims. This place alone must be responsible for a considerable percentage of the cheese consumption in the state of Maryland. We sit at a long table in the center of the dining room. Uncle Obi stands there high-fiving the staff and tries to order his food without interference from his daughter or wife.

"I'll take care of this," he says, pointing at the table. "Sit down, y'all."

"Always the same thing," Evelyn whispers, rolling her eyes.

Uncle Obi's family has always accepted his food obsession, if reluctantly. Even as they gently scold him, trying to get him to do better. Olivia takes out her phone as we eagerly wait for whatever Obi has ordered for us.

"The riots were awful. Look at this."

Olivia holds up her phone to show me. It's a picture of a street full of young people. Some are standing on the roofs of cars, others are holding up signs that say, "Fuck the police," and some are smashing shop windows.

"Where did you take this?"

"From the window at work. They were like animals."

"But don't you think the frustration that caused them to burn down their own streets was justified?" I ask. "I mean, it was totally sick what the police did to Freddie Gray."

"I don't know," Olivia responds. "All I know is that they looted so many pharmacies that my clients couldn't fill their prescriptions for weeks. I have clients who have depression, who are bipolar, bordering on psychotic, and things get awfully dark for them when they don't get their medicine."

"But do you think any of these guys were thinking of that when they burned these places down?"

Olivia just throws her hands up.

The romantic sense of the revolution that swelled in my chest as I sat in my office in Södermalm watching the live feeds from the Baltimore riots last April is cast in a whole different light in the present moment. I thought my family would talk about Kendrick Lamar's groundbreaking political album *To Pimp a Butterfly*, about how the US is undergoing yet another phase of the struggle for equality, and that the country is at the start of a new civil rights movement. That they would analyze the causes of systematic police violence directed at African Americans and explain the emergence of Black Lives Matter, which started as a hashtag on Twitter and later grew into an organized movement during the demonstrations in Ferguson after the police killing of Michael Brown. Black Lives Matter has succeeded in turning the world's attention to the social, legal, and economic injustices that still affect black America. The movement is gaining momentum, and six months from now, I will meet one of its prominent figures, DeRay McKesson, at a dimly lit bar in Brooklyn. He'll tell me about how he was so appalled at the news that yet another black man had been murdered at the hands of the police that he got in his car and drove from his hometown of Baltimore halfway across the country to little Ferguson. Since then he's traveled tirelessly around the country to organize demonstrations, and he even ran for mayor of Baltimore.

But instead of a discussion about the struggle for black rights, my Baltimore family has only condemnations to offer. There must be at least four sides to this coin. The police, the human rights activists, the criminals, and the plain old nine-to-fivers—and none of the groups seem to have much empathy or understanding for the views of the others.

But they all live in Baltimore and have to share crumbs from the same decaying inner-city cookie. Since the riots, the crime statistics—for homicide in particular—have shot up. This, some citizens say, is because the police don't dare to or want to do their jobs, in protest for being slandered after the Freddie Gray case. Others say that Baltimore is Baltimore, and crime and murder are as natural there as the world-famous crab cakes or the Patapsco River that flows majestically through the city.

The discussion is interrupted when the server places a twenty-inch pepperoni pizza in the center of our table and a bowl in front of Uncle Obi.

"What's that?" Olivia wonders.

"It's soup," Obi replies with a sly look on his face.

"Soup? That's shellfish."

"Do you see any shells?" he responds, throwing out his hands.

She just shakes her head.

"Uncle, those are oysters," I say. "Simme, look, a whole bowl of oysters without their shells. Have you ever seen anything like that?"

Simme laughs.

Watching Uncle Obi shovel the oysters onto his fork with a slice of pepperoni pizza is priceless. Oysters and pizza. It reminds me of the herring and grits Dad and George ate. High and low. After a while, the server places a gigantic plate of salad in front of Obi.

"This is what I ordered," my uncle says contentedly.

Then another bowl is delivered. This one does actually appear to contain soup. It all goes down the hatch, even as Obi tells us about how shocked he and Evelyn were last time they were in Atlanta to visit my aunt Chinyelu and her husband, Oggi, for Thanksgiving dinner.

Obi calls him an Igbo thief.

"He ate more than I've ever seen anyone eat. It wasn't a plate, it was a platter. Man, I've never in my life seen anything like it. He finished two huge turkey thighs on his own. You know how big a turkey thigh on one of them Georgia turkeys is? Big as your arm, Jason . . ."

Once again, all eyes are on our table. I imagine that the other guests must be wondering what the big, loud black man finds so amusing.

Pizza, soup, oysters. It's all eaten up cheerfully but without ceremony. I see how the dinner table is the magnet that brings everyone in this family together; perhaps it's also a prerequisite for the affection I have been marveling at all afternoon.

Although I know it will be met with fierce protest, I eventually find myself forced to say that it's time for Simme and me to head for New York. We have a long trip ahead of us.

"I don't understand why you can't stay," Uncle Obi says. "You just got here. We have so much to talk about, and it's family brunch tomorrow and your cousins are going to be there."

On our way out the door, he asks us to wait a moment. A few seconds later, Uncle Obi is standing behind the counter discussing something with the owner.

"Here we go. One for you, and one for you."

Simme and I each receive a bottle of wine. The old gray-haired Italian leans across the counter and explains that the corkscrew is a gift from him, but the bottles are from my uncle.

"But promise you won't drink them in the car," he admonishes us.

"I promise."

"I'll give you a ride to your car, but there's something I want to show you on the way," Uncle Obi says.

A little bit later, we stop in front of a high-rise along the highway.

"See the sixth floor?" Obi asks, pointing up at the building.

"Yes. It looks completely empty."

"That's right!"

A satisfied smile spreads across his round face. He shoots me a cunning look over the edge of his wire-rimmed glasses.

"If you help me out with five thousand dollars, we can get our Nigerian radio and TV channel off the ground. We need it. As well-off as you are, Jason. Think about it. It would be a big help to your family."

All I can do in response is smile. For the past few years, toward the end of each Skype session or phone call to Uncle Obi, this question has popped up. Money.

"I know you've got it. When are you going to share? Family has to stick together."

THE RABBIT'S FOOT

A few days ago, as I sat in a dark sports bar with Uncle Obi in down-town Baltimore, listening to his memories of Harlem in the sixties, he cut himself off in the middle of a diatribe on how much cheaper food was back then and raised his voice and said, "Jason, your great-grand-mother . . . she was a hell of a character. BM, we called her. Big Mama, she was about a head shorter than you. It was one of those opposite nicknames. Like if you're fat, people might call you 'Tiny.' I'm tall, so I would be Little Obedike . . ."

Uncle Obi wiped a smear of ketchup from his lips and scratched his chin.

"Boy, she was mean," he said. "No one messed with her. All the gangsters, pimps, everyone on the streets of Harlem knew who BM was, and she got respect. If you crossed her, she wouldn't hesitate to cut you. She may only have come up to here"—he pointed at his large belly—"but she definitely would have stabbed you in the ass."

In the few photos I've seen of BM, she's always wearing a fur. As if she never allowed her picture to be taken in the summer. Wearing a fur was important to BM. It signaled her status, showed that she was someone. It's all the more important for someone without social stand-ing to bear status symbols. My equally poor grandfather did the same, after all. Wide-brimmed hats, shiny shoes, razor-sharp creases pressed into his pants, ironed shirts. Each time I see a picture of my grandfather or great-grandmother, I think of my own vanity and proclivity to wear what I consider to be nice clothes.

My only memory of Big Mama is from 1981 in Harlem. We met in the small park with green benches in the center of the square in the projects where she lived. The many projects of America are solid clusters of buildings. Ten or twenty of them, about twelve floors each, all built in the same style, with the same brownish-red brick walls.

I was six years old then, and I recall Dad pacing restlessly back and forth on the street outside Great-Grandma's front door.

"BM won't let us in—so typical," he says anxiously.

We've been standing there for five minutes, ringing the bell outside the building. Dad snorts with impatience.

"She probably saw I've got a white woman with me. You know, the only white woman BM ever accepted into her apartment was your mother."

In 1981, Pat is my dad's girlfriend. A round, friendly white woman from Pittsburgh, Pennsylvania. She has a daughter with brown skin named Margaret, who's a year younger than I am.

At last, my dad gets hold of BM from the phone booth down on the corner. She asks us to wait for her near the benches in the small square. When the barely five-foot woman finally meets us on the street, Dad's tone suddenly changes from annoyed to servile and humble.

"Yes, Mama, we have a car. Yes, Mama, I have a good job. No, Mama, I'm not moving back to Harlem. No, Elaine and I got divorced several years ago. Yes, Mama, I have money. No, Mama, the car isn't old and rusty."

BM approaches the bench where I'm dangling my legs in boredom.

"Here you go, sugar." My great-grandmother smiles, stroking my head and placing something in my hand. "You go ahead and listen to this."

It's a radio shaped and painted like a can of 7UP.

"Wow, awesome, thanks," is all I manage to say, and I frantically start twisting the knobs, trying to find a cool radio station.

Now, on a hot day in late October of 2015, I'm approaching the spot where the wide streets called St. Nicholas Avenue and Adam Clayton Powell Jr. Boulevard intersect 116th Street in Harlem. The small triangular area is called A. Philip Randolph Square. Named for the African American socialist civil rights activist who became the first black union leader in 1925. He led the Pullman porters' union.

As I reach the square, it occurs to me that my grandfather Silas spent years working for the Pullman Company, which dominated American railway traffic for over a century. He was a proud member of the Brotherhood of Sleeping Car Porters, although I doubt he would have cared much for the union founder's socialist ideology.

The park benches form a circle around the square in the shadows of some spindly maples. It's clear that the winos and regulars own the benches, but I find an empty spot on a splintery seat, and suddenly I'm in their living room. An older black woman and the two white children she's watching are sitting on the bench across from mine.

I'm alone and invisible in the bustle of this megalopolis. I open my backpack and take out my paperback copy of *Invisible Man*—Ralph Ellison's milestone in the African American canon. The book describes a young black man whose ambition and conviction drive him to travel from the South to Harlem. He becomes politically active there but also encounters a different sort of racism than that in the South. In the end, the hardships he must endure make him question everything around and inside him. At last, the main character realizes that the invisibility he suffers from comes not only from his surroundings but also from within.

Ellison lived only a few blocks from here. A member of the Communist Party for a number of years, he was politically to the left of A. Philip Randolph. On the other side of the boulevard stands the imposing beige-gray building called Graham Court, which was built in 1899 by order of the same man who was behind the famed, lavish Waldorf Astoria Hotel. The building was intended for wealthy white families. It was never the plan that servants like my great-grandmother BM would live on these streets, but the wave of black migrants, like Grandpa and Great-Grandmother, changed the demographics of Harlem. In 1910, only 10 percent of the inhabitants around here were black, but by 1930, that number had risen to 70 percent.

BM—or Bethalia Davis, which was BM's real name—was born in North Carolina in 1904. Her mother was Cherokee, and her dad was Geechee. She lived in this very part of Harlem long before she was sent off to the brutal projects where Dad and I visited her. Each morning that tough, tiny giant of a woman traveled to Queens to clean the train cars in the rail yard, and then she went to Manhattan to clean the homes of rich families.

I look around and wonder if she ever sat on these benches, speaking her mind about the day's hardships, getting an update on the neighborhood gossip, resting her tired feet. For BM and my grandfather Silas, free time and amusements and recreation weren't something proper people spent time on. Life on the streets of Harlem was like life in the wide-open fields of the South and involved dutifully doing your work. How pleasant it must have been to sit on a park bench for a moment and take a break.

Last year, the city removed all the benches from this square to keep people from smoking, drinking, or pissing there. But the regulars showed up anyway. They brought in chairs, boxes, and crates and continued to use the square as a living room out in the fresh air. At last, the city gave in and brought the benches back.

In 1994, Mom sent me to live in New York. She was wrapped up in sorrow after the death of my stepfather, Roland, had her hands full with Anja, and was at her wits' end with me. I had been going through one of the darkest periods of my life. Among other things, I had spent a weekend at Kronoberg Jail, smoked heroin, and found myself locked up in a room at Malmö Hospital one night after overdosing on LSD and alcohol. I was nineteen years old and going downhill at full speed, and paradoxically enough, New York offered a much-needed sense of calm in my life.

In New York, I had to get up at six thirty every day to eat breakfast and squeeze myself into a crammed subway car during the morning rush hour in order to get to my job as a receptionist at a small telecom company on the Upper East Side. Illness, snowstorms, traffic disruptions— none of these were valid excuses to miss work. My time card had to be stamped by eight o'clock, five days a week. I was also expected to work one weekend per month. New York wasn't like Lund, where I could laze about with friends, hang in the studio, smoke grass, and dream of conquering the world. I found myself in the real world, where I was expected to hold down a job, grow up, become an adult.

My big sister, Adadie, who had gotten me the office job, was generous with her New York wisdom.

"Jason, you have to be tough. Don't take shit from nobody."

Aside from putting in my hours at the brown plastic desk across from the entrance to S'il Vous Plait, as the company was called, I learned all about my boss Mr. Brunel's dietary preferences—I was sent to buy his lunch every day. I became an expert at filing papers and answering the phone. But I secretly nurtured a dream of becoming a full-fledged rapper.

Through a friend in Malmö, I came in contact with Tyrone, an impresario and talent scout who lived in the Bronx. He was enthusiastic from the start. In true American style, he thought the sky was the limit when it came to how high I might soar in the world of hip-hop. It was like a dream to me. Ever since I had put those first rhymes to paper in my childhood bedroom with the sea-blue wall-to-wall carpet on Göingegatan in Lund, I had dreamed of the chance to try out my rap chops in New York. I was cocky and arrogant. Of *course*, I was a rapper— the only one in Lund between 1990 and 1992. When I met other rappers on my expeditions to Malmö, Copenhagen, and Stockholm, we always spoke English. During my first big solo performance at Kulturmejeriet in Lund in 1992, I spoke English between songs.

That was how you talked if you were a hip-hopper. Even though most of the people in the audience knew me from school and from around town and were well aware that I was a Scanian-Swedish-speaking Lund kid just like them.

I called Tyrone from a graffiti-covered phone booth outside my workplace on Eighty-Sixth Street on the Upper East Side.

"Come to the Bronx. Hop on the D train after work and head up to 167th and Grand Concourse. I want you to meet Akil. He's a producer, and he makes good beats. You two are gonna make magic together."

To me, the endless days in the office were just a stop on my way. This was it. I would show up in the Bronx, captivate everyone with my rap skills, and then conquer the world.

It was just before seven in the evening when I headed up Eighty-Sixth Street to the subway station. The stiff wind that sweeps down the broad corridor of the Hudson River in wintertime—the locals call it The Hawk—cut right through my brown cotton jacket until I could feel it in my bones. Before I walked down the stairs toward the train, I lit the little stump of a spliff I had in a tin. The marijuana helped me relax; it was an unfailing crutch in my youth. I inhaled the damp, herbal smoke and headed for the turnstiles.

The shaky train carried me farther and farther north, and at each station, more white people got off. The effects of the sweet joint pulled my thoughts in tighter and tighter circles around the hip-hop meeting I was about to attend.

When the silver car rolled into 167th Street, the only people left onboard were me and a collection of sleepy, benumbed black and Puerto Rican men with construction helmets and worn briefcases. I zigzagged through the crowds on the platform and found the stairs up to the turnstiles, navigating past loud kids with wide sweatbands and baggy down jackets, old ladies with shopping carts, and huge Puerto Rican guys eyeing everyone on the platform with a glare.

That culture shock. So far from Lund and the organized throngs around the buses at Botulfsplatsen. My whole dream life boiled down to these burning moments. I had spent all my waking time these past few years scrutinizing borrowed and stolen hip-hop magazines like *The Source* and *Hip-Hop Connection*. I had watched every episode of *Yo! MTV Raps* and gone over and over every album cover I could get my hands on so I could feel like a part of hip-hop culture. I believed that if I wore the right jeans that hung just low enough, walked around in the right shoes, and had my cap turned backward just right, I would become part of this massive movement. But as I walked across the crowded gray platform, I began to doubt that I truly belonged there. I was scared. How was I supposed to act? What if I was robbed? Or got beat up?

With my eyes on my untied beige Timberland boots, I climbed the stairs toward the turnstiles. I couldn't bring myself to walk through them. I didn't know what was out there. I stopped at a dented phone booth just before the guard booth.

"Hey, Tyrone. It's me, Timbuktu," I said tentatively. "Can you come down to the subway station and pick me up?"

"Too scared to walk by yourself?" he responded with a roar of laughter. "I'll be there in a minute, my man."

One minute can mean thirty in the US; I waited a long time for him. My stomach roiled, half with shame over my lack of street smarts and half with butterflies because this was the moment I had been aiming for and dreaming of for so long. It was already dark when Tyrone and I walked up the steps to Grand Concourse, the multilane artery that runs through the Bronx. We turned onto a dim little side street where only one in three streetlights worked. Huge guys with pit bulls called out the day's crack prices from the wide doorways on either side of the street.

"Yellow tops, two for five, two for five. White tops, two for four. Come get it while it's hot."

I stared at my own shoes as I followed close behind Tyrone's tall figure through one of the doors. The once lovely black-and-white tile floor in the filthy hall was just barely better lit than the street outside. The elevator was out of order, so we walked up to the third floor. I couldn't stop thinking of how the residents of the building must feel to have those gangster guys standing on the front steps all through the neighborhood selling crack. At the same time, that was hip-hop. Crack, gangsters, and the Bronx. I was so close: no more than twenty blocks from 1520 Sedgwick Avenue, where DJ Kool Herc launched hip-hop culture with his legendary parties in the projects. Forty years later, hip-hop has become one of the most powerful driving forces of pop culture.

Akil cracked the door without removing the security chain.

"Come on in," he said, apologizing for his caution. "The other day, there was shooting at the neighbor's. I flipped out and had to go in there and tell him I got kids sleeping in here. Crazy fucking crackheads."

He invited us into the small home studio he had built in one of the smaller bedrooms. The walls were covered in graphite-colored foam, and on the desk was a beat-up white PC monitor and a small mixing board. A crooked stand stood in the center of the room, topped by a black microphone.

"So let me hear what you got," Akil challenged me.

"Huh?" I exclaimed. "I don't have any lyrics. I thought I'd get to hear some beats first and then I could go home and write."

"If you're a rapper, then rap," Akil responded, spinning his rickety chair toward the screen and moving the mouse to wake up the computer.

I struggled to hide my nerves. *I never should have smoked that spliff,* I thought. It only made my shyness worse. The dimly lit studio fell into total silence, aside from the clicking of Akil's mouse.

"Here's a beat for you," he said suddenly. "Now rap."

"Uhhh, I can't," I said lamely.

"If you can't rap whenever, wherever, you're not a rapper."

Tyrone broke in.

"He's from Sweden, Akil. He's an awesome rapper, I swear."

"If he's so awesome, then he'll prove it."

I froze. The last thing I wanted to do was disappoint anyone by rapping badly. But here it turned out that it would be worse not to rap at all. Although I made every effort in my attempt to rap, fear took over and I couldn't manage a single rhyme.

"Can't I take a beat home?" I begged. "I'll come back in a few days with some lyrics."

"You should be able to rap right now. But . . . OK."

For the whole subway ride home, shame pressed my shoulders into the gray plastic bench. The car was as empty as my heart. I had pretended to be something I wasn't.

For the first time since arriving in New York, I wanted to go back to Lund. That safe little city in the quiet little country I'd spent my entire upbringing referring to as Legoland.

As I finally got off the train at Times Square and walked over to Hell's Kitchen, where I shared a small apartment with three other Swedes, my thoughts were whirling madly in my mind: *I'm not a rapper at all. I should just head home to Lund and go to college like everyone else.*

One week later, I was once again breathing the stale air of Akil's home studio. I had my rhyme book in hand—a thick notebook covered in stickers, in which I'd written all the lyrics I'd produced in the past few months. I had written sixteen lines to the beat Akil had given me a few days prior. Akil gazed nonchalantly at me and pressed play on the computer.

Once my last line of rap had echoed over the drum rhythm played on Akil's halting PC, silence descended on the room.

"That's just not gonna do it," Akil said, scratching his chin. "Your flow. It's not good enough. This is New York, and if you're gonna stand out as a rapper, you really need a good flow."

Akil's judgment was crushing. It was the final nail in my rap coffin. With the wreckage of my boyhood dream and tears in my eyes, I got on the train home to Manhattan.

The so-called gold era of hip-hop was still underway during my six months in New York. Between 1990 and 1998, the most trendsetting hip-hop radio show was broadcast from the student radio station at Columbia University, on 89.9 FM. The program was led by the super-duo DJ Stretch Armstrong and his jocular sidekick Bobbito.

Each Friday, which also happened to be the only day I was allowed to wear jeans to the office, I was very tired. I never missed the show, and it was broadcast on Thursday between one and five a.m. This show was the first in the world to play new songs by all the most important rappers—Jay-Z, Biggie Smalls, Nas, Black Moon, Mobb Deep . . . Every week I sat next to the tape player, ready to record each new song. After a typical episode of Stretch and Bobbito, my mixtape contained several of hip-hop's most timeless creations.

When I returned to Sweden in the summer of 1995, my dream of becoming a rapper was dead. I had decided to start studying the history of economics at Lund University that fall.

It never happened. One sweaty July day, on the benches of the basketball court outside Vårfru School in Lund, I met a music producer from Copenhagen named Obi, whom I'd run into a few years earlier. He spurred me on, told me time after time that I was a good rapper, and tried to convince me to come to his studio just to try recording a song. I protested, but at last I agreed to come to Amager in Copenhagen and do a song. I wrote "Look Alive" in two hours—I'd never written a whole song so quickly. Obi was floored and said it was the best thing he'd ever recorded.

His compliments revived the hope that had died a few months earlier in a shabby studio in the Bronx.

I decided then and there to become a rapper. Again.

Fourteen years later, I got an email from one of my best friends, Claes, with the subject line: "Your song on Stretch and Bobbito." I opened the email and clicked on the link. On the raspy recording from the fall of 1995, you can hear the legendary hosts introducing a song by the group Timbuktu from Copenhagen: "Look Alive."

New York—the Mecca of hip-hop—had made me give up on my rap dreams but had also, without my knowledge, accepted me just a few months after pulverizing those dreams.

Eternally a visitor in my family's hometown, I trot around the wide boulevards full of a peculiar sensation. Harlem makes me feel just as white as a lecture hall at Lund University made me feel black. But it's there, in the space between—between races, between colors, between the narrative—that I have built myself a place to live. In the in-between-ness.

Perhaps it was the same for my grandfather Silas and great-grandmother BM. Far from the muddy misery of the cotton fields, they could at least walk around in their shiny shoes, furs, and wide-brimmed hats. Here in Harlem, they created their future. But maybe, once you've experienced true poverty, you can never quite escape it. Maybe Grandpa and Great-Grandma could no more shake off their origins than a cucumber can choose to stop being green. But they carried those origins with honor. There were many cautionary tales around them. Like my grandpa's older brother, Wade, who left the fields too, but instead of working hard for a better future wallowed in despair. He gambled, drank, and was a womanizer. And he died young, murdered in a dispute over a card game at the age of thirty-three. He was found dead one morning in a backyard in Harlem. Just another dead young black man. A "bad nigger."

In the latter part of the twentieth century, the word "bad" would be flipped around to mean the opposite in African American slang. To be "bad" meant daring to resist, daring to stand up.

"Not bad meaning bad, but bad meaning good," as RUN-DMC put it.

Wade's fate recurs in present-day América. In the past forty years, the prison population has increased by 500 percent, and today, in actual numbers, the country has the most imprisoned people in the world.

The United States has about 5 percent of the world's population but almost 25 percent of the world's prisoners. Resignation and nihilism are an epidemic among young black people. Life is lived and extinguished daily under the mark of violence and drugs, in the relentless pursuit of money and the battle to survive. Of the nearly 2.2 million prisoners in the US, almost 40 percent are black. Nowhere is structural racism more evident than in the US prison system. Black people are five times more likely to end up behind bars than white people are.

"Live with your head in the lion's mouth. I want you to overcome 'em with yeses, undermine 'em with grins, agree 'em to death and destruction, let 'em swoller you until they vomit you or bust wide open," Ralph Ellison writes in *Invisible Man*, describing his grandfather's last words to him. It was this sort of frozen virtue you could see both in Grandpa Silas and Great-Grandma BM as well as millions of black people all across the United States. It took a "mind your own business" attitude to survive in the early twentieth century. It was in many cases a feigned submissiveness that was as common as it was mocked in African American society.

To this day, the expression "house nigger" is one of the worst things an African American can be called. It was only the lightest or most obedient and cooperative slaves who were allowed to work inside the big house. They were considered, by the field slaves, to be collaborators. This internal cultural hierarchy, born among the plantation slaves, still permeates African American culture. Yet this mentality was and is a prevailing survival strategy for many African Americans.

Music and religion became places of refuge. I can hear it in Charley Patton's or Blind Lemon Jefferson's blues. The sorrows and joys of life need an escape valve. I hear it in Mahalia Jackson's and Sam Cooke's immortal songs, and it echoes in the poetry of Lauryn Hill and Chance the Rapper.

In 1964, Martin Luther King and Malcolm X had a hasty meeting after a press conference in Washington, DC. Afterward, King supposedly said that Malcolm was very eloquent but that their views differed on several points.

This was the only time they met face-to-face. But here, on the corner of Lenox Avenue and 125th Street in Harlem, in the absolute epicenter of African American culture, they will forever meet. In 1984, the east-west 125th Street, also known as the main drag of Harlem, was christened Martin Luther King Jr. Boulevard. Three years later, the north-south Lenox Avenue was given the official extra name of Malcolm X Boulevard.

In the time it takes for the light to turn green at that intersection, it strikes me: they did come together after all. Those two schools of revolution. Malcolm's "strike back with power" attitude and Martin's "love your enemies" strategy. Both giants were shot to death at the age of thirty-nine.

Had they been allowed to live longer, I'm convinced that their paths in the struggle would have run parallel in the end, instead of merely crossing briefly.

Harlem seethes with life. Teenagers playing basketball on the broadest sidewalks in New York, old men cackling in folding chairs in front of the tiny corner stores, artists spreading their collections of paintings on the ground. People caught up in loud phone calls, Jamaican dance hall music pouring from the speakers of passing cars. A frequent sight is the incredibly muscular guy who hangs from a street sign at 125th Street doing pull-ups. His entire workout routine happens out in the open. Kids jumping rope, teenagers going by in big groups, elegantly dressed elderly folks with carved wooden canes and gorgeous hats strolling by on the wide concrete sidewalks. Single moms with large flocks of children carrying huge bags of groceries, stiff-jointed retirees chatting loudly on the corners, vacant-eyed junkies staggering by. But there's nowhere near as many of those as there were in Dad's day, when the heroin epidemic had Harlem in a stranglehold.

Wherever I go in the United States, black folks talk about gentrification. How reinvestments in the slums force out the poor original occupants. "Urban renewal means Negro removal," as James Baldwin put it. It's happening in Harlem as well. The newly renovated brownstones are increasing in number, and the untouched, ramshackle buildings where the old Harlem folks live are becoming few and far between. Around here, Senegalese restaurants crowd in next to old barbershops; the Somali Swedish Mona's restaurant, Safari, rubs shoulders with H&M and other chains. Today you can even see something that was unthinkable when Dad and Mom were here: white middle-class families out for a walk with strollers and dogs, with no fear of the black folks.

One of the downsides of gentrification is that the black populace risks being pushed out by quickly rising rents.

"We must not lose Harlem, the symbolic capitol of black America," says Bayete Ross Smith, an artist and teacher I've just met at a concert at Red Rooster, a lively restaurant on Lenox Avenue. "We have poor people on welfare here, junkies and criminals living side by side with black workers and members of the middle class, and even the occasional white middle-class family who've moved into some of the flashy brownstones Harlem is famous for."

Every day, here in the neighborhood of Mount Morris, home to Red Rooster co-owner—and my friend—Marcus Samuelsson, I see a cross section of what Bayete is talking about. It truly is a diverse area. I wonder what BM, Madame, or Silas would have thought about the fact that so many white people now live in the traditionally homogenous Harlem.

Puerto Ricans and Dominicans have always lived in its eastern parts, and the whites kept far to the southwest, in the general area of

Columbia University. But for the past century, here in the heart of black Harlem—between Madison Avenue to the east and Morningside Park to the west—just about all the residents have been black.

During the Harlem Renaissance in the early twentieth century, the cultural landscape was dominated by ragtime, jazz, blues, poetry, and art. It was the first movement in American history to create an intellectual black high culture.

"This is the new Harlem Renaissance," an overexcited man screeches beside me in the bar where Bayete and I are chatting.

"That may well be true." Bayete nods at me. "Above all, you've got the rekindling jazz scene in Harlem. After several years of stagnation, where jazz was mostly played downtown, stages in Harlem like Shrine, Red Rooster, Smoke, Paris Blues, and Bill's Place are the destinations to hear rising stars. A majority of artists and documentary filmmakers of all skin colors choose to live and work in Harlem. Perhaps there's hope that the presence of white people in this particular part of the city doesn't have to mean the absence of black people."

During my walk home, I pass the outcropping of rocks that the early Dutch colonists called Slang Berg—Snake Hill—for the snakes that liked to curl up in the cracks between rocks. It was later called Mount Morris Park, but in 1973 it received its current name: Marcus Garvey Park. It's named for the Jamaican-born black nationalist and founder of the Universal Negro Improvement Association and African Communities League, the UNIA-ACL. Mr. Garvey's conviction that African Americans would do best to return to Africa rubbed off on my grandmother Madame.

His vision wasn't entirely successful. The few African Americans who heeded Garvey's and Madame's cry of "Back to Africa" had received permission to settle in Liberia. Soon after they arrived, they began to enslave the local population. The stolen people were forever changed, and there was no home to which they could return.

Black academic and activist W. E. B. Du Bois, who was one of Marcus Garvey's most vocal critics, maintained instead that the black population must be able to embrace its doubleness, to attain a new balance and find harmony in being both American and black.

> It is a peculiar sensation, this double consciousness, this sense of always looking at one's self through the eyes of others, of measuring one's soul by the tape of a world that looks on in amused contempt and pity. One ever feels his two-ness,—an American, a Negro; two souls, two thoughts, two unreconciled strivings; two warring ideals in one dark body, whose dogged strength alone keeps it from being torn asunder.

Garvey, for his part, called Du Bois a "white man's nigger." There were as many ideas to solve the problem of the black masses in America as there were skin tones of those who were counted among her citizens. From Du Bois's pale-yellowish-brown skin to Garvey's dark-chocolate-colored skin. Questions of cooperation and independence have frequently given rise to clashing schools of thought among African American intellectuals, as in the case of Martin Luther King and Malcolm X. The discussion continues even today—is it better to wait for the white establishment to give permission for black people to live with dignity, or to create those opportunities no matter what the powers that be allow?

I find the updated version of and role model for what a modern black person can be in people like Marcus Samuelsson. He was adopted from Ethiopia to Sweden and moved to the US at twenty-five. Today he serves Swedish gravlax on a bed of Ethiopian injera at his restaurant at 125th Street and Lenox Avenue. Swedes, Harlemers, tourists from all over the world, middle-class Americans, movie stars, rappers, ex-presidents, and Ethiopian immigrants find their way there and dine side by side every evening. Marcus is so used to surfing between his identities that it happens seamlessly. In most cases.

When President Obama invited Marcus to prepare a meal at the White House, Marcus asked, "Where the hell are all the black people?" All the paintings on the walls were of white people, and the only people in the room were white. When he went into the kitchen, he finally felt at home. Both white and black people were working there.

Du Bois's doubleness of the early twentieth century is Marcus's tripleness of the twenty-first.

"The Native American man, the Puerto Rican brown man, should stand united with the strong black man. We refuse to be held down in modern slavery."

It's the weekend, and the Black Israelites are out demonstrating. The man holding the megaphone is wearing a long black caftan, a black turban, and a hefty gold chain with a Star of David. His brothers in faith stand around his milk crate with their arms crossed. All wearing the same uniform.

I listen to the sermon as I wait for a green light at the corner of Malcolm and Martin. Across the street, the Nation of Islam is selling books and magazines. Two homegrown religious movements built on fragments of Islam, Judaism, and science fiction, on opposite sides of the street.

I keep walking down Malcolm's street. Harlem went from being dominated in the early 1900s by the white Jewish Lenox Avenue Gang, with infamous leaders like Gyp the Blood and Lefty Louis Rosenberg, to being colored in the seventies by the Black Liberation Army, whose systematic killings of the police soon got them stamped terrorists. And then came the street gang the Zulu Gestapo, whose outfits were inspired by Californian motorcycle gangs. Black bodies in leather vests and swastikas.

The streets of Harlem have always been full of pimps, dealers, and regular people. The legendary jazz club Minton's Playhouse still stands at the corner of 118th Street and Adam Clayton Powell Jr. Boulevard—where Dad wasn't allowed to play as a kid. It was too dangerous.

During the crack epidemic of the 1980s, this part of the city went completely downhill. Jazz vanished, as did the nice restaurants. Whole blocks were abandoned. Buildings stood empty and comparisons between Harlem and Beirut, in those days, were not so far-fetched. No one went to Harlem unless it was absolutely necessary. No one invested in the area. It was just poor. Like Allendale. Black and poor.

In 1973, my dad's film *For Personal Reasons* won an award at the Grenoble short-film festival in France. The movie is about a man who decides to murder a police officer out of sheer despair over the oppression he is forced to live with. As a twelve-year-old, I mostly thought it was cool that my dad had made a movie with shooting in it, and that Morgan Freeman's brother played the lead role. But twenty-eight years later, I wander through Dad's old neighborhood and realize how much Du Bois's double consciousness has marked black America.

How can you survive as a black person in the United States? How can you bear being constantly slapped in the face by the hand of society, being held in its stranglehold, without wanting to grab the first weapon you find and strike back full force?

Dad's paradoxical tug-of-war is between the fact that oppression drove him out of America and that, even so, he feels most alive right here on the cracked asphalt of Harlem.

I walk down to 110th Street. Maybe that impressive whitish-gray building on the corner of Lenox Avenue is the place where Mom and Dad first met. Despite my general lostness in Harlem, I still feel like my roots are sprinkled here and there in this beautiful part of the city. Dad has called almost every day while I've been here. He wonders if I've been to M&G Diner to have grits for breakfast, but he's dejected when I tell him that it closed. Have I run into his old friend Superfly? Are Saturday nights still crazy? I hear the longing in his voice and describe everything I see as vividly as I can. How the Lenox Lounge is abandoned, that there's a one-armed Jamaican beggar who sits on the median of Lenox Avenue every day, how stylish all the women are on Sunday afternoons. And I promise him we'll come here together soon. Maybe this is small comfort, but I think to myself that he's glad I'm here.

Dad never loved Sweden more than when he spent long periods in New York. As far back as I can remember, he has cycled back and forth between Lund and New York, with the ever-present dream of one day returning home. "Home" has always been spelled "U.S.A."

But despite their laments, Dad and his friends always found their way back to Lund. Anytime someone had just returned from a trip, they all showed up in Dad's kitchen to give an enthusiastic report about how wonderful it was to visit their homeland. They talked about the new music, the latest political happenings, what their families were up to, and how much better the food was there.

In 2012, I offer Dad a trip to the US. To his home.

One day we're drinking coffee at Red Rooster in Harlem and waiting for Marcus. He's always had a very special place in my dad's heart. Dad is incredibly proud of the enormous success Marcus has found in the US and Sweden. Nothing makes Dad happier than seeing black people excel.

On this particular sleepy afternoon in 2012, the usually bustling restaurant is half empty as it awaits the dinner rush. Marcus comes out of the kitchen with a big smile.

"Hey, guys! It's your last day in town, so I want to take you on a walk through Harlem."

"Do you have time, Marcus?" Dad asks.

"Yes, of course—let's go."

The September sun is warming the wide streets of Harlem, and Lenox Avenue is showing off its very best side. We walk a few blocks north as Dad shares his memories of the buildings and corners we pass. Marcus paints a vivid picture of everything going on here — new theaters, restaurants, and jazz clubs.

Suddenly, Dad whirls around.

"See that man?" he says, looking north along the wide sidewalk.

"Which one? There are people everywhere," I respond.

"The guy with the black hat."

"Sure, what about him?" I wonder.

"I think that's my friend Earl," Dad states with certainty.

"What? The one from the military? But, Dad, why would that be him?"

Dad's already moving faster than I've seen him go in a decade. When we finally catch up with the man in black clothes and that wide-brimmed hat, Dad is a little cautious.

"Excuse me, sir."

"Yeah?" the man in black says, turning around.

"I'm Madubuko."

"I'm Abdullah Bin Hassan Alhamdoulillah," the man says, his eyes narrowed and skeptical.

"It's me, Madubuko," Dad insists.

"S'il vous plaît," the man says, looking like he's gearing up for a fight.

"Earl," Dad exclaims joyfully. "It is you!"

The man's expression goes from puzzled to shocked until he finally erupts in a peal of laughter. They embrace warmly as Marcus and I, astounded, take out our smartphones and start snapping as many pictures as we can.

In each photo, Dad is sporting what has to be the biggest smile of the twenty-first century so far. After the long hug, the old friends Earl and Madubuko keep their hands on each other's shoulders, as if the moment might be lost as soon as one of them lets go.

They laugh loudly. "I just can't believe it! Alright, well ain't this something!" These two friends haven't seen each other in fifty years and have just happened to run into each other on a Monday afternoon on the northern tip of an oblong island where five million other people crowd the sidewalks and streets.

Earl's on an afternoon walk with his Jack Russell terrier Jane. He's wearing black gabardine trousers, a black shirt, a black vest, and a black Zorro hat with a silver band. He has a white carnation in his breast pocket.

"Shit, he's so stylish," Marcus whispers to me.

Earl notices that we're admiring his fashion.

"Always have a fresh white carnation at your collar, boys." He grins broadly and points to his chest. "Right, Buko?"

"That's right," Dad agrees. "Gotta look sharp!"

Earl's fingers are covered in silver rings, and I wonder—if this is what he looks like when he's walking his dog on a Monday, what does he look like on Saturday night when he's going to a party?

"Roberta's husband died," Earl tells Dad.

"Really," Dad replies.

"Yeah, he was into a lot of shit, though, you know."

"But Melvin's doing OK?" Dad asks.

"Yeah, man, that brother's around here somewhere. The old devil's still kickin'."

Once more, they're united in a long laugh.

"This is Earl, who I've told you so much about, Jason," Dad says, turning to me. "We were in the military together. Fort Benning, Georgia, 1958. You tell 'em, Earl."

"That's right," Earl responds. "It wasn't easy back then. Those Southern motherfuckers were no joke. I recall a sergeant we had. Remember, Buko, that cracker motherfucker?"

"Yeah, I remember."

"One time he said to me, 'Get in line, nigger.' You know, us northern black folks weren't about to let some white bastard talk to us like that, so I gave him a right jab, hit him in the cheek. But that fucker . . . He was huge. Didn't even blink. 'You're coming with me, Private Jones,' was all he said."

Earl is gesturing wildly and almost acts out the incident, making fists right there on the sun-drenched sidewalk as his dog Jane gives her master a pleading look.

"So I had to go before the sergeant, convinced he was gonna send me right to the stockade. Shit, I sure spent a lot of time in there."

Earl shakes his head and shoots Dad a meaningful look; my dad only smiles.

"But this time, I thought, I'd show him," Earl continues. "We walked down a long hallway, and suddenly I saw a bucket and a mop leaning against the wall. It only took a second. I grabbed the mop and swung around, aiming the handle at the huge sergeant's head. That's the last thing I remember."

Earl laughs heartily and wipes his forehead.

"My ass woke up on the bench in the stockade. That sergeant was no joke; he put my lights out in one second."

Dad chuckles knowingly.

As the old men chat, I think about the human need to experience life with others. The joy in Earl's and Dad's faces, because each can bear witness to the other's past.

"I remember your grandmother," Earl says, turning to me. "We called her A3. Her office was down there . . ."

He gestures toward the Empire State Building and Macy's and Wall Street, but also 116th Street, where Madame, aka A3 (for Adadie Afrikanwe Ajuluchuku), aka Lilian Davis—my grandmother with her many names—kept an office.

Dad and Earl continue to reminisce, exchanging gossip and updates. A lot has happened since 1963, or whenever they last saw each other.

"Do you have email?" Dad asks Earl.

"Well, I don't have a computer, but you can use one on the corner, in the shop the Indian owns."

Earl rolls his eyes.

"I swear, any bastard from any corner of the earth can come to Harlem, and in no time things are going better for them than they ever did for us niggers up here," Earl continues.

"Ain't that the truth," Dad interjects.

Their laughter echoes across the avenue until Earl excuses himself, saying he has to take the dog to the park, but he hopes we'll all meet again soon.

They hug one last time and go their separate ways.

"See, I told you guys it was Earl," Dad says triumphantly with a slow shake of his head.

He's found a person who, like a time capsule, can confirm that things really were as he recalls, back in the sixties when his youth played out on these hard-as-nails streets.

A group of boys on motorcycles swishes past on the street, one of the guys doing a wheelie, no fear for life or law.

"Yeah, niggers are still crazy up in Harlem," Dad says with a smile.

As I continue wandering up and down Dad's avenues on that warm October evening in 2015, an image of my great-grandmother BM pops up in my mind again.

Was that why she always kept a rabbit's foot in her handbag? Maybe Jesus wasn't enough of a savior. Superstition and the supernatural were always with her. A rabbit's foot for luck.

That's why Dad always has a horseshoe on the wall at home and one in the trunk of his car. Survival, for a poor black person in the United States, was such a long shot that magic became a deciding factor.

The left hind foot of a rabbit shot in a cemetery during a full moon has the strongest magical power.

Maybe I should get one too.

CHURCH SUNDAY

The door stands ajar. Although it's October, the sun is shining warmly, and the leaves along tree-lined Seventeenth Street are still as green as the awnings outside Gabriella's Restaurant in Birmingham, Alabama. An elderly man in a suit and a young woman in a white shirt and black pants stand and talk on the other side of the door. I stick my head in and ask if they're open for business.

"Of course, we are! Come on in!"

Along with my colleagues Lovisa Fhager-Havdelin and Camilla Nagler, I step into the restaurant. We work together at Teskedsorden, a Stockholm-based organization that works to counter prejudice, inequality, and racism. Thanks to either serendipity or fate, they are taking a trip to the American South, tracing the footsteps of the civil rights movement at the same time I'm in the US, and I eagerly welcome the opportunity to travel with them for a few days.

Just inside the door of the restaurant is a round table with a giant vase on it surrounded by plates of carrot cake and pecan pie wrapped tightly in plastic. Along the walls of the room, a soul food buffet is being served: deep-fried pork chops and chicken, macaroni and cheese, collard greens, beans, rice, sweet potatoes, creamed corn. Everything homemade.

It's noon on a Sunday. We've barely seated ourselves when the dining room is suddenly filled with people—old and young—mostly black but also a few white older ladies and gentlemen, all dressed in church-going finery. The men and the boys in suits and the women in colorful skirts with matching hats. Nothing in this establishment—neither the black-and-white photographs on the walls nor all these well-dressed people—would indicate that the year is 2015. It could just as well be 1963. But if it were, Lovisa, Camilla, and the white guests at the neighboring tables would be in one part of the restaurant, and I and the majority of the guests would either be in the back or we would simply have found another place to eat.

The menu would have been the same, though, and the radio playing jazz would have been on, and the streets would have been as deserted as they are today. Church Sunday is still sacred here in the heart of the South. Everything is closed, and just about everyone goes to church wearing their Sunday best.

Sunday, May 5, 1963, was the last day in the series of demonstrations by children against racism and segregation in these very neighborhoods in downtown Birmingham. The first day, hundreds of children were arrested. The prison cells were filled with children, from first graders to high school students. On the second day, the demonstrators—children—were bruised by water cannons and attacked by angry police dogs. But that didn't scare off the demonstrators, whose marches became known as the Children's Crusade.

Children continued to demonstrate the next day. On the fourth day, the march led to the prison where all the children who had been previously arrested were being held. Only then did the local politicians agree to sit down at the negotiating table, and a few days later, they reached an agreement stating that the city's public transportation would not be segregated by race, and that the imprisoned children would be released. The protesters, however, ended up expelled from school. The courage shown by Birmingham's children gave the civil rights move-ment national support and international attention.

Just as I helped myself to the last bite of deep-fried cutlet and gulped down the last drops of bottomless iced tea, one of the older white men bends down toward a black boy sitting in a high chair at what looks like the grandparents' table.

"You're a beautiful little boy, aren't you? Yes, you are. He's a pre-cious one."

He beams at an older black woman who was certainly in elementary school in 1963. "Oh, he sure is," she replies.

"Praise the Lord," replies the white gentleman, who likely also remembers the Children's Crusade demonstrations on the city streets.

Their short exchange strikes a chord in me. It's easier to dehuman-ize people if you never sit in the same room or take a meal under the same roof with them.

After the weakest cup of coffee I've ever consumed, we go back out into the sun. The streets are just as empty as before, and the traffic is so light, you can hear the birds singing. We cross Kelly Ingram Park, named after the first person in the US Navy to die in World War I. The park is now a museum under the open sky. The path through the small park is called the Freedom Walk, and everywhere there are statues and plaques that tell the story of the city's bloody struggle for the equal rights for its citizens.

On the other side of the park, a small group of well-dressed ladies stand in front of the long staircase up to the 16th Street Baptist Church and seem a little annoyed when I capture a series of pictures with my phone.

Just five months after the 1963 Children's Crusade in Birmingham, the usually quiet Sunday routine was broken by a powerful explosion. A six-feet-wide hole in the church's rear wall was torn open, several of the stained-glass windows were blown out, cars that were parked closest to the church were completely destroyed, and the windows in the buildings in the nearby neighborhood shook so violently that many were shattered. After the dust had settled, twenty injured people were found in and around the church. Survivors searched the church's basement, and there they found the burned, broken bodies of four young girls.

Before the sun went down, two more black children were murdered. Riots broke out. Birmingham burned. The Ku Klux Klan had carried out the bombing, part of their mission to spread death and terror among African Americans throughout the entire nation. The bomb attack on Sunday, September 15, 1963, is a permanent fixture in the people of Birmingham's consciousness and in the collective memory of the United States.

I find it hard to imagine the chaos of the bombing as I stand in front of the church, more than a half century later. Here and there, families stroll around the park. On a bench opposite me, three homeless people are involved in a lively discussion. Hardly any cars are visible on the streets, and the tranquility of the city gives me the peace and quiet I need to immerse myself in the stories behind the statues and plaques.

The next time we park our rental car, we're at Brown Chapel on Martin Luther King Street in Selma, the headquarters for what was called the Selma movement. The church, with its brown brick and white-painted windows and gables, looks like a gingerbread house. In front of the church, two large granite blocks have been erected. The names of those who died in Selma during the protests are carved into one.

On top of the slightly smaller of the two stones stands a large bronze bust of Martin Luther King Jr. A marble plaque bears the story of what the march from Selma to Montgomery came to mean for the civil rights voting movement in the South. Among other things, during the ten years following the march on Selma, the number of black elected politicians in the South rose from 72 to 2,586. Selma is in what has long been called the "Black Belt" of the US because of the overwhelming majority of black residents.

Today, it is a belt of unemployment, poverty, and hopelessness. Martin Luther King Street is bordered on both sides by two story apartment buildings. Unlike Birmingham, here you can't tell that it is a Sunday. Women sit on the curb talking, men sit silently along the house walls, children are running aimlessly around the brown-green planting strips between houses. Cars with huge chrome wheels drive around in caravans with blaring speakers sharing their hip-hop loudly for everyone to hear.

Brown Chapel is located in the heart of Selma's worst slum, a housing project named after African American inventor and scientist George Washington Carver. TripAdvisor issues warnings about the area. The locals have their eyes on us from the time we step out of the car and into the glowing sunshine. It doesn't feel as though we should stay here very long.

We move the car to the main street and take the symbolic walk over the Edmund Pettus Bridge. In 1965, the bridge was the scene of three significant demonstrations. The first march was brutally suppressed by the police before the protesters were able to cross the bridge, which forever gave the day the name "Bloody Sunday." Photographs of an unconscious Amelia Boynton Robinson, an activist and one of the leaders of the civil rights movement, were published worldwide.

Boynton Robinson was one of the initiators of the demonstration. She was 104 years old when she passed away in August 2015. During the last month of her life, she walked arm in arm with President Obama over the Edmund Pettus Bridge to mark the fiftieth anniversary of the bloody march.

The second demonstration in Selma also failed to make it across the bridge. But the third march, in which up to eight thousand people from all over the United States participated—white, black, indigenous, Latino, Catholic, Protestant, and Jewish—the protesters managed to cross the bridge. During the five days that followed, they continued to march over fifty miles to Montgomery. When the march finally reached Alabama's capital, it had swelled to twenty-five thousand participants. Martin Luther King stood on the stairs to the imposing white capitol building and spoke.

The sun burns our necks even during our short walk across the bridge. Edmund Pettus, whose name still adorns the bridge, was a senior officer in the Confederate Army and also bore the title of Grand Dragon of the Ku Klux Klan.

The woman who works in the souvenir shop next to the bridge shakes her head when discussing the questionable naming of the bridge, but she sees a point in not changing it.

"It is important to remember why we had to march over the bridge. All the structures and injustices that made thousands of people willing to risk their lives and their security still exist today. Let the bridge bear its racist name so we never forget."

Our day ends in a third city, Montgomery. We are at the top of Dexter Avenue at the stairs—right where Martin Luther King spoke fifty years ago. The street is completely empty—not a car or a soul in sight. The sun is setting, the light falls on the whitewashed walls of the Roman-inspired capitol building, and it shines against the dark-blue sky. This is the same building that became the presidential palace when the South seceded from the Union in 1860 and the American Civil War broke out. The so-called Southern White House is eerie in the twilight.

Martin Luther King's residence is just blocks away. Although closed up for many years, the house is now a museum. Along the wide avenue, there are plaques and signs that tell of the struggle that took place here half a century ago. Lovisa notes that all signs along the four-lane parade route have been set up in 2014 and 2015.

"Does it take that long to remember and acknowledge the story?" she says, amazed, and we walk on, each of us in our own thoughts.

Accepting the truth can take time for a person and even longer for a nation. In Sweden, for example, how many history textbooks talk about Sweden's passivity and silence during World War II? Is it possible to move forward if we don't acknowledge our roles in history, whatever they are?

The next morning, we wake up early for a side trip before our appointment with the Southern Poverty Law Center. As we drive along this highway, heading toward one of America's oldest and most renowned African American universities, Tuskegee University, it strikes me that I'm in a black Chevrolet with two white women.

How unthinkable this had been when Dad was young.

We stop at a gas station in Tuskegee. Lovisa jumps out of the car and points to a patchwork of worn gray asphalt behind the station.

"This is where Rosa Parks was born."

Standing on what, for most people, is just another piece of asphalt, but which is sacred land for us pilgrims, Dad's voice echoes in my mind: "Why do you want to go and track down old nigger's graves that have long since been paved over into parking lots?"

What Dad has wanted all along is for me to speak to living witnesses of contemporary black history. And so, when I returned from the States, he advised me to speak with Gloria Ray Karlmark, who was involved in one of the pivotal moments of the civil rights movement. In 1957, she was one of the nine black schoolchildren to integrate Central High School in Little Rock, Arkansas, under the protection of federal troops. The schoolchildren's fates became world news, and Gloria is enshrined in the annals of the black liberation struggle.

Stockholm's Royal Library café is full of students talking softly to each other, eating their lunches, or hunched over their keyboards. For a second, I am worried that the murmur of the room will drown out Gloria's quiet, calm voice so that I can't record the conversation properly. Without interrupting Gloria, I lean forward and move the phone closer to her.

It's a great moment for me. Gloria is a living example of what the civil rights movement cost in terms of human suffering and sacrifice. Being able to see and hear someone whose name and image are in the history books in person makes the story so real. History is alive. Gloria Ray has bright eyes and a round, friendly face, and she's wearing a white coat. Her hair is pulled into a knot and she keeps her coat on throughout our conversation. She begins speaking before I even have time to raise my coffee cup.

"My father was born in 1889 on a small farm in Arkansas. His dream was to educate himself. His father said that if my father could buy his way off the farm, he was allowed to go to school. So Dad worked his way through school to be able to fill the financial hole he created in the family home. He was finally accepted to Tuskegee and continued to work while he studied. He actually worked for Booker T. Washington himself, and he was also a laboratory assistant to George Washington Carver."

"Your dad worked for Booker T. Washington? That's incredible!" She nods.

"There were books everywhere in our home, but no trashy novels or romances. You see, my dad was an African Methodist and very strict. We couldn't even play music at home. Dad was very harsh. I remember that my older brother, Harvey Junior, came home with a rhythm and blues record, and when Dad discovered it, he took the disc and cracked it in two. 'That music is from New Orleans, and it is a city steeped in sin and depravity and symbolizes everything that keeps our people down.'

"There was a post in the garden, and my brother was often told to hold on to it while Dad beat him with his belt. The only time Dad struck me was when I got in the way of him hitting my brother. My brother refused to conform. He smoked, drank, played cards, slept around. He died of cancer at sixty."

Gloria stops for a moment and glances up at the ceiling.

"It was a constant struggle for survival. We always had to be mindful of the risks that came with the color of our skin. They lynched a man in front of our church one day, and my father said that this is what can happen to you if you strike back. Always turn the other cheek, or even better, turn your back and run in the opposite direction. We were taught to follow the rules and laws regardless of whether they were fair or not. White youths often teased us because they knew we did not dare to do anything back. To this day, I worry every time my children visit the United States. There, they're just black. The term 'common sense' is much more complex for a black person than a white person. We need to practice a higher level of awareness."

Gloria puts her elbows on the armrests before taking a sip of water. After a moment of silence, her gaze returns to me and she says: "It's just different there.

"When it was time for me to start high school in 1957, I wanted to go to Central High, because it was a white school, and, of course, the education was better than in black schools. On the first day of the autumn term, ten of us black students were escorted to Central High by a pastor and a woman named Daisy Bates of the NAACP. Before we had even reached the school, we were met by a large group of white men, women, and police officers.

"I remember it well, the morning when we opened the big gates to Central High School and went in as the first black students in a formerly all-white school," Gloria continues almost dreamily.

"After two hours, an anxious teacher came into our classroom and said that a mob had formed around the school. We were all terrified, hearing the chants from the mob surrounding the building. 'Race integration is Communism,' 'go home niggers,' 'no niggers in our schools.' They even hung black dolls from the big trees outside the school."

Gloria's eyes flash as if, six decades later, the pictures from that day were replaying inside her. She recounts how the roar of the mob grew louder. It wasn't until much later, after she and the other children had been safely escorted from the school, that the terror lessened in Gloria Ray's chest. One of her peers' parents was threatened with termination if his child didn't leave the school. That student didn't come back. Then there were nine black students left, and they came to be called the Little Rock Nine.

"The day after the angry mob forced us to flee from school, my dad sent a telegram to President Eisenhower, and that same evening, a soldier came knocking and delivered the president's answer: he promised to send soldiers from the 101st Airborne Division, the 'Screaming Eagles.' The day after that, we were picked up by a military convoy, and when we arrived at the school, the soldiers formed a corridor through the mob. The soldiers had bayonets on their rifles. I had never seen a bayonet before. Each of us then got a soldier as a personal escort who followed us throughout the school day, throughout the lessons and on the break periods. That's how it was for the entire year. The Screaming Eagles stayed until December and were then replaced by regular army troops."

Gloria tells me how, during that year, things were thrown at her in the corridor, and how she was called ugly names. Urine was poured in her locker so often that they couldn't get the smell out. One of the Little Rock Nine boys once had a brick thrown at his head and was knocked unconscious. The soldier escorts weren't allowed to enter the locker rooms, where the white boys could scare the shit out of the black students. The terror was constant.

"One day in the cafeteria, a white boy spit in my friend Minnie Jean's bowl of chili. It was the final straw for her. She threw the dish at the boy. She was suspended but still remained enrolled in the school. After a month, Minnie Jean came back, but she had apparently decided to resist her attackers. One day she called a student 'white trash.' Then she was expelled for good. Another of my friends got acid thrown in their face."

Gloria Ray learned not to meet anyone's gaze as she walked in the school hallways because it almost always led to verbal harassment. But one day, she met the eyes of a white girl named Becky. The smile Gloria Ray got from Becky was heartwarming. She was starving for warmth and kindness from the other students. The few white students who supported the black students also had to endure bullying and threats.

"I sent a note to Becky during the next class and asked if I could say hi to her next time. She wrote back and asked me not to because she didn't dare risk the safety or reputation of her family. I still have that note that Becky wrote. That short smile and the note meant a lot to me. They gave me a little hope and reminded me that there were actually decent white people. Something I had almost stopped believing."

Throughout her story, Gloria maintains a peaceful expression. I'm silently amazed that she can recount all these memories with such candid kindness and warmth, even when she remembers how some classmates put a nail on her chair in math class and how painful it was to sit on it. She didn't allow herself to react to the pain, intent on denying the racist students the satisfaction of seeing her suffer. Gloria and those of her friends who remained at the school learned not to cry and not to let their faces reflect either pain or grief.

Before the next school year, however, Governor Orval Faubus decided to close all the high schools throughout Little Rock. Better to have closed schools than to allow black students to be educated among whites. Gloria Ray and her seven remaining comrades were not allowed to continue on at Central High. In 1958, the governor ranked as one of America's ten most admired men in a Gallup poll.

Gloria and I have been sitting for almost two hours in the library's cafeteria, and it has become increasingly deserted around us. I begin to thank her for meeting with me, when she interrupts me and says, "One of the most uplifting events in my life was Obama's installation as president in Washington. All nine students from Little Rock were invited. My son came along. It was one of the proudest moments in America's history, especially for its black inhabitants. Huge crowds, cheering . . . the atmosphere was electric. That day, it felt like color didn't matter: we were just Americans. They say that the police did not arrest a single person in Washington that day."

"Did you think that Martin Luther King's dream was realized?" I wonder.

"In some ways, it was, that day. Finally proof that we can actually see past skin color. I am so happy to have experienced that moment, even if that was the only time." Gloria clasps hands over her stomach and straightens her back. She is proud and grateful for her life, after all she has gone through.

"I wish my parents had witnessed the day when a black man was elected president of the United States. Who during my dad's lifetime could even have believed it? The world has changed. People who look like you and my children are the future. You don't have blue eyes and blond hair—but you're Swedes."

FATHER'S DAY

A few weeks after I return from my trip to the South, I plan to travel from Stockholm to Skåne to visit Dad and celebrate Father's Day, which we celebrate in November in Sweden. You never know. He was so close to death in September. I don't want to realize a year from now that I should have taken the opportunity to celebrate one last Father's Day with Dad.

On November 9, my phone rings, waking me from my morning slumber in Södermalm. It's Dad's wife, Monique.

"Jason, hello?"

"Hi, Monique, how are you? I'll be there for Father's Day dinner tonight."

"Jason, your dad is very tired."

"What do you mean, very tired?" I quickly respond.

"He hasn't been able to walk since yesterday," Monique says softly.

"Monique, you have to call an ambulance right away. He was just seriously ill. Call an ambulance."

"OK, I'll ask your dad."

"No, don't ask him, just call the ambulance. Promise me."

"OK, Jason."

I hang up and call Anja right away to ask her to bike over to Dad and Monique's and make sure everything's OK.

"I'll head right over," my sister responds.

Twenty minutes later, I call Monique.

"Did you call an ambulance?"

"It's on its way."

Monique sounds lost, in shock. I call my sister again to get a clearer picture of what's going on in the apartment on Värnhemstorget in Malmö, even as I throw on my clothes and hurry to Arlanda Airport. Anja tells me that the ambulance arrived just as she got to Dad's apartment, and that they've taken him to the hospital.

Four hours later, I rush into the same emergency department I was standing in just six weeks ago. The same gray clouds outside the large windows, the same cold floor, the same collection of wrinkled, tired, aching souls fill the chairs and beds in the spacious waiting room.

I find Monique and Anja leaning over Dad, who's lying on a brown vinyl stretcher. We hug.

"How is he?" I ask.

"He's not feeling very well," Monique says, her eyes darting here and there.

She's in shock.

"Dad," I say, bending down close to his face.

He's the color of the Malmö clouds, and his eyes are half closed. His gaze is completely vacant.

"Dad, Dad," I repeat. "How are you?"

His eyes sweep slowly past my own and out the window.

"I'm here, Dad, I'm here," I say, trying to gesture at him to look at me.

He just keeps staring at nothing. His gaze reminds me of a deer that's just been run over. It belongs to a tormented creature that feels nothing but terror and confusion to the very end.

I turn to Anja and Monique.

"He's unresponsive. What happened?"

Monique tells me that he became very tired on Friday night, and by Saturday morning, he couldn't really use his legs and he started speaking strangely.

"Why did you wait so long to call the ambulance?" I demand, upset.

Monique just looks at me with sad eyes. I feel ashamed and give her a hug.

"It's going to be OK," I try, faking hope.

Suddenly, Dad says, "Toilet, I have to go."

"I'll take him," I say.

I press the call button, and a nurse comes to help. We lead Dad down the harshly lit corridor toward the bathroom.

"Should I come in with you?" asks the nurse.

"No, I can manage," I say.

Once we're in the bathroom, I try to talk to Dad and get him to sit down. But he doesn't hear me. He's delirious.

"I see there are white people in Harlem Hospital now," he says.

"I don't know, Dad," I say with a small laugh. "But I suppose so. Harlem isn't what it was. Lots of white people live uptown these days."

He thinks he's at the hospital in Harlem where he was born. I can't hold back the tears; they're running down my cheeks. I would rather Dad didn't see me cry, but he's so unaware of what's going on that he probably doesn't notice anyway. He's just sitting there on the toilet, twisting his head, his eyelids twitching. Suddenly Dad collapses.

"Sit up, Dad, you have to sit up."

He has to fight to keep his back straight, to sit up on the toilet.

"You just have to pee, right?"

He doesn't respond, just gazes down at the floor with his vacant eyes and falls forward. I realize now that he did more than pee. I was supposed to celebrate Father's Day with Dad, not have to watch him so helpless that he can't even go to the bathroom by himself. I press some folded toilet paper into his hand and guide it down and behind him. But his arms don't respond. He has no strength. I have to do it for him.

Throughout the years, whenever I'm being obnoxious, Dad always tells me, "Jason, I used to change your diapers, when you were too small and helpless to even know what you were doing. Don't ever forget that. Your mother and I were the ones who took care of you."

I also remember him telling me that he had to wipe his own dad's behind when he was sick with cancer and couldn't take care of his own needs.

"You'll have to do the same for me one day," he said.

At the time, I just shrugged off his words. My parents have always been constants in my mind. As long as I have existed, they have been there for me. I can always call them up and talk about ordinary things, ask for advice, or complain about my sorrows or failures. I am not prepared for the fact that, one day, they will no longer be there.

But now those thoughts and fears are crowding my brain. He is old and can't go to the toilet on his own. It's my turn to give back. With tears on my face, I clean Dad off and pull up his blue hospital pants. I call for a nurse to help us back to his room. When Dad is finally back on his stretcher, I leave the room to make a call.

"Hilmi, it's me, Jason."

My godfather, the South African surgeon, replies, "Hi, Jason, how are you?"

"Not good."

I feel the tears pressing into my eyes again.

"Dad is unresponsive, it's like his brain doesn't work. He can't even use the bathroom by himself."

"That doesn't sound good," Hilmi says.

"Could it be a stroke?" I wonder. "Is his brain bleeding?"

"Hmm . . ."

Hilmi thinks for a moment.

"It could be. But it could be something else too. Let's not jump to any conclusions before we know what's going on."

Several hours later, Monique and I are pacing back and forth as we await the results of Dad's x-ray. A nurse rolls his bed into the hallway and tells us that the doctor will come by soon to give us an update.

It's nearly midnight, and we've been at the hospital since early afternoon. Each minute we wait for information feels so long. I try to tell myself that Dad will get better. At the same time, the voice in my head says I must prepare for the worst, and an old email from Dad flickers through my mind. I received it on a Sunday evening in January of 2012.

> *Hi,*
>
> *I'm so glad we got to spend time together in Stockholm. I still have very special, warm memories of you and me in Stockholm. A lot of the time those memories come back to me when I'm in the city. But especially when it's dark, cold, and snowy. Here's the story:*
>
> *It was January 1977, and we were staying with the Browns in Rinkeby. It was so fun, all you kids playing together in the kitchen and the living room. You were just about to turn two, and I bought you a BRIO rocking horse. On the night before the eleventh, your birthday, I placed it beside your bed as you slept. When you woke up in the morning, you stood up, saw the horse, took the pacifier out of your mouth, and exclaimed, "A horse!"*
>
> *Then you hopped up onto it and started rocking. You didn't want to do anything but rock on it all day long. You were so happy, and I was too. That day, I realized what a joy it was to raise a child, and I've carried that feeling with me ever since. That moment, that day you sat on the horse, was the happiest moment of my life—honestly.*

Walking to Central Station with you today, on the way to my train, was yet another happy moment, and I hope you were happy too, even if the moment was short. We have to do it again someday: walk together, converse with joy, father and son. Thank you for being a wonderful son.

Love,

Dad

I cried when I read the letter, and I'm crying again now.

At last the doctor arrives. Our wait has been unbearable. She curtly informs us that Dad is bleeding between his brain and his skull and is going to be transported to the neurologist in Lund for emergency surgery. Then she turns on her heel and walks off. Monique and I don't have time to say a word. I call Hilmi again and tell him what's going on.

"At least it's relatively good news," he says.

"What? How can this be good?" I wonder.

"Well, your dad has what we call a subdural hematoma. The bleeding is outside the brain, but it's pressing against his skull and requires an operation so that his brain has room to function normally again. It's a routine surgery, Jason," Hilmi assures me.

Three operations, two weeks, and several bouts of fear and despair later, Dad is sitting in the TV room in the neurology wing of the hospital with no memory of what has happened in recent days. He tries to keep a firm grip on his fork to bring the large slice of cucumber to his lips. The procedure is painstaking.

My dad, so full of opinions and fighting spirit, has been reduced to a slow-motion version of himself. I reflect on how thin and wrinkled he has become. He seems to have aged at high speed. At last, he gets the cucumber to his mouth and watches me as he chews slowly. He makes a great effort and manages to say, "I'm old and I'm sick."

His face is slack. As if the many tiny muscles can handle neither a smile nor an expression of sadness. I see clear hints of his recent operations and hardships in that moment. I have grown used to his graying skin and the tubes sticking out of the back of his hand, wound in coarse white gauze. It's as if his flame is permanently turned down. It's gone from burning on five for several years to sputtering at a waning two.

I can't tear myself away from the devastating sorrow in his eyes. They seem so empty. Dad's eyes are more vacant than I've ever seen them, as if all his dreams have fled. Maybe what I see in him is regret; maybe he has realized that by now it's too late to repair everything that went wrong during the course of his life.

It's like he knows that death has its sights on him, is nipping at his heels, and that all he can do is accept this.

"You're not that old, Dad, and you will get better," I try to encourage him.

He can't manage to do anything but close his eyes.

WHITNEY
PLANTATION

One stuffy morning in March of 2016, Amelie and I step into a particularly dismal room with worn gray-blue walls and the sort of sluggish atmosphere you find in a workplace where nothing ever comes as a surprise. The gaze of the rail-thin woman with the furrowed brown face at the Avis counter is harsh, but it softens as she asks, "Will that be all, Miss Amelie?"

I can't hold back my laughter as we leave the office and wait for the terribly overweight rental-car guy to bring us our car.

"Hey, Miss Amelie," I say, imitating the rental-car lady's Southern dialect.

But I also know there's something about Amelie's eyes. Some sort of deeply attractive kindness that makes the world want to show her friendliness. Walking around a city with her gives you some insight into how immediate karma can be. I've seen the appreciation in the eyes of passersby, servers, retail workers, and now, even the counter staff at a dreary rental-car office.

According to the letters on its side, the silver Korean car we're assigned is called a Soul. And indeed, I have felt a lot of soul during this Easter weekend in New Orleans. The city has a soul as magnetic as Amelie. Her green eyes, her eyebrows like an eagle's wings, make me feel joy and hope; she moves with an ease that won't let me take my eyes off her.

My search for my roots led me to New York, and by some miracle, the vibrant megacity brought me the love of my life in the form of this Swedish woman, who had just moved to the city after two years spent working in China.

Although we hung around the nightclub until three this morning, waiting for the trans artist Big Freedia, one of New Orleans's most popular rappers, to take the stage, we got up early today to get out of the city and explore the Louisiana countryside.

The air is warm and humid, but not nearly as warm and humid as it will be in a month. The sky and our Soul seem to be in competition to see which can shimmer with the most silver. The thin layer of clouds is like a filter high above our heads, letting in a veiled light, which gives the bursting green swampland we're driving through a ghostly aura. It's far from Lund's low-hanging grayness, which weighs down the inhabitants like a thick woolen blanket for the better part of the year.

We pass a stretch of gigantic, rusty-red oil refineries, which protrude from the otherwise endless and impenetrable swamp like metal beasts.

"This looks just like in *True Detective*."

Our destination is Whitney Plantation, about an hour's journey from downtown New Orleans.

Ever since Simme and I walked across the fertile lawn at Erwinton Plantation in Allendale a few months earlier, *it* has been haunting me: the incomprehensible realization that slavery was real. Real people—my forefathers—were whipped, tortured, herded, and sold like livestock. I haven't been able to shake off the unpleasantness of feeling the bloody ground of a plantation beneath my feet. Nor of stepping through cotton fields that are flourishing like never before and seeing the enormous plantation homes of South Carolina still standing, freshly painted and renovated.

How can so little have changed? The laws . . . Sure, they were changed after the bloody, tireless struggle for justice during the civil rights movement. But there's still a world of difference between rich and destitute, between someone who can live a tolerable life and someone who is born into hopelessness, without a chance, without full rights.

The fields, the crops, the buildings . . . they're all still there. Unchanged.

Since that day, I have wanted to understand more.

How did my relatives survive? How did my grandfather's grandfather Jack Miller and his wife, Myla, live their lives?

I have eagerly devoured book after book about slavery. I've written and discussed, pondered and mused. It aches inside of me.

Then someone like Amelie shows up in my life, insisting that we visit a plantation she's read and heard about, no matter how tired and hungover we are. She knows that by understanding my roots, she'll have a clearer view of what's in my head.

Early this morning, she playfully smacks the sole of my foot. "Time to get up. This is important to me."

Funny how the universe works. My thirst for knowledge about how my grandmother and grandfather experienced the world led me to make my way to New York, and it's thanks to that I met Amelie. In loving her, I become closer to myself. It's as if chance knows better than my conscious brain what's good for me.

During our car ride, she calls out a reminder at regular intervals.

"Keep an eye out for alligators. If you see any, we have to stop and take a look."

"Will do," I reply from the passenger seat, my eyes still far too full of sleep.

The landscape is truly enigmatic in this part of the United States. Flat, endless stretches of forest grow right out of the water. Here, the sea owns the land. As we drive the seemingly infinite miles across the country's longest bridge, the Lake Pontchartrain Causeway, it's not hard to understand how Hurricane Katrina could make the water overflow and seize the land and forever change so many of the inhabitants' lives. Engineers in the state had long warned that the levees of Lake Pontchartrain needed to be fortified, but nothing was done here, in one of the most corrupt states in the nation. When Katrina swept in across the southern United States in 2005, it wreaked massive destruction upon New Orleans, among other places, and affected its poor population hardest of all.

My eyes begin to adjust to the bright sunlight. With each tree that flashes past the car windows, I feel even greater joy at being on the road with Amelie, on a road trip, our destination completely up to us.

After a long drive, we finally enter the small community of Vacherie, Louisiana, and I have a flashback to my arrival in Allendale a few months earlier. Poverty is visible everywhere. In the buildings, the shabby signs hanging over the gas station, the rectangular mobile homes, the rusty cars and tractors on the cracked concrete of the parking lots. Near one group of particularly tumbledown little houses, a man is half reclining on ramshackle steps. He seems to be passed-out drunk.

The black people who live here carry the inherited hopelessness I've read so much about in books and witnessed in Alabama and South Carolina. The unconscious man's slack body on the broken steps is in stark contrast to the leafy green vegetation around the buildings. It strikes me that the psychosocial consequences of poverty make the state of things look more like an illness than a socioeconomic condition.

Whitney Plantation is within a fifteen-minute drive of at least five other plantations. One of them is Evergreen Plantation, which you can see in Quentin Tarantino's spaghetti western *Django Unchained*, set in the South in the nineteenth century. It's in the scene where the main character arrives at the plantation dressed as an eighteenth-century dandy, in a cornflower-blue silk suit, and meets the slave owner Big Daddy, played by Don Johnson.

The country road we're driving down is edged by stately trees; their branches form a green ceiling over us, and Billie Holiday singing "Strange Fruit," that poetic, brutal song about lynchings, fills my head.

Beside Evergreen Plantation is Oak Alley Plantation, the largest, most impressive, and most-visited plantation in the area. The tour guides here walk around in antebellum clothing and, according to our guide at Whitney Plantation, never use the word "slave"—they're called "workers" instead. Tourists from near and far flock to the plantation every day to hear the guides' enthusiastic narrations about glorious life at one of America's most beautiful manors.

Oak Alley is not our destination, but we do park the car outside the tall metal fence to take a peek. An avenue of majestic, crooked oaks leads up to a large mansion supported by massive columns. It's like it was lifted straight out of the 1980s miniseries *North and South*, starring Patrick Swayze. It's the prototypical plantation house, and it looks exactly as it did when incomprehensibly brutal injustice was the custom here.

The only difference is that agriculture has been replaced by tourism and slavery by a low-wage workforce.

The Spanish moss still hangs from the giant oaks, but the descendants of slaves no longer have to worry about being dragged from their homes in the middle of the night, having a noose tossed over their heads, and being hoisted into the big trees to the cheers of white mobs.

In modern-day America, it seems the police handle this job instead. Until very recently, every fourth black person in Florida was denied the right to vote due to having spent time in prison. The fact that so many have been robbed of their civil rights and the opportunity for decent employment is evidence that many states in the US still have an oppressed lower class not unlike the one that existed during the time of slavery.

As I stand outside the gates and watch the white families in their sun hats pass through the showy entryway into the flowery garden at Oak Alley Plantation, I muse that the whitewashing of the bloody history of Louisiana and the USA is the greatest factor in why the inequalities are never evened out. The yoke of history can never be cast off if you don't first recognize that history for what it was.

For the tour guides to wear those wide period dresses that the slave owners' daughter and wives wore while the slaves were whipped behind the house is like going on a guided tour of Auschwitz led by someone in an SS uniform. I feel only anger, disgust, and hatred.

An admission ticket costs twenty-five dollars. More than any descendants of slaves in the area likely can afford or have interest in sparing, and this is to hear someone clad in the uniform of oppression talk about how wonderful it was to sit on the wide verandas and drink mint juleps in the shade while chatting about embroidery and village gossip. It's a slap in the face to those who died, bled, and toiled on these grounds, who brought in the money that allowed the house to be built and silk to be imported for the dresses. After the guided tours, the visitors are, in fact, offered mint juleps just to get a sense of what it was like to live there in the past.

Amelie and I hop in the car and drive the few miles down the road to Whitney. We're greeted by Cheryl, a short black woman with glasses, an alert gaze, curly hair, and crooked, chipped teeth. She speaks in a loud, clear voice and tells us that Whitney opened to the public the year before, and it's the only one in the country that exclusively tells the story of plantation life from the perspective of the slaves. Amelie almost chokes on her water, and asks, "Can you really be the only one in the country?"

"Yes, unfortunately, that's the case. At Oak Alley, you can hear all about how terrific life on a plantation was if you were white. But not what daily life was like for the slaves. But you can't go around thinking about it, because that'll just make you mad. The important thing is that y'all are here, and that here at Whitney, we tell history the way it actually was. The plantation was originally called Habitation Haydel, and it was founded by the German immigrant Ambroise Heidel in 1752. He bought the land and started planting indigo. Later on, his son switched the primary crop to sugarcane. Back then the production of sugarcane was labor intensive and took place under the most inhumane conditions. Basically, all of the West Indies were devoted to the cultivation of that granulated white gold, and all the work was performed by African slaves. The same was true in Louisiana."

Amelie and I, along with about a dozen other visitors, follow Cheryl out onto the plantation grounds. I have the same sensation as when Simme and I were at Erwinton. But my hatred and sorrow are deeper than what I felt then. Maybe because our sharp, well-informed guide leads us to a monument. It's half the size of a soccer field and made up of tall walls covered in large black stone tablets. On each tablet is the name of a slave, along with their occupation and where in Africa they came from. Lucien from Senegambia, Basse from the Congo, Maime from Senegambia, Alice from Senegambia . . .

From the start, Ambroise Heidel bought 101 slaves directly from Africa, primarily from what are now Senegal and The Gambia, but also from Angola, the Congo, Nigeria, and Ghana. He later bought another 250 slaves, also first-generation slaves from the coasts of Africa. The name of every single slave who lived at Whitney between 1752 and 1865, when slavery was abolished, is now carved in the shiny stone tablets we wander by in the humid air under the silvery Louisiana sky. Also, there are the names of the 2,200 slave children who died between 1823 and 1865—mostly of starvation, even though they were owned by one of the richest plantations in Louisiana.

Between the rows of names are also testimonies from the slaves who were forced to work here, who lived, suffered, and died here.

Another marster I had kept a hogshead to whup you on. Dis hogshead had two or three hoops 'round it. He buckled you face down on de hogshead and whupped you 'til you bled. Everybody always stripped you in dem days to whup you, 'cause dey didn't keer who seed you naked.

—*Leah Garrett*

Oh yes! They had straps and a whip and they'd better not catch you praying to God. When you prayed you had to hide in the woods.

—*Carlyle Stewart*

We wasn't 'lowed to go around and have pleasure as the folks does today. We had to have passes to go wherever we wanted. When we'd git out there wus a bunch of white men called the 'patty rollers.' They'd come in and see if all us had passes and if they found any who didn't have a pass he wus whipped; give fifty or more lashes—and they'd count them lashes. Ef they said a hundred you got a hundred.

—*Julia "Aunt Sally" Brown*

Our group moves among the stone tablets. Some have their hands to their mouths; others sigh audibly, but most just shake their heads during the quiet procession. Amelie reads testimony after testimony, her face full of sadness. I hold her hand, and at the end of the grove of stones, we embrace.

Cheryl gathers the group and leads us to the slave quarters, a group of gray-brown cabins slightly larger than sheds.

"This is where the slaves lived," she says. "When it became illegal to import slaves from Africa in 1807, the breeding of slaves began in earnest. Typically, the most fertile women were paired with the largest men in a cabin, and if the woman didn't become pregnant within a year, she was moved to be with a new man in a different cabin. The children who lived in the cabin weren't the biological offspring of either the men or the women who lived there. Children were always being sold. So people didn't live in family groups, although adults and children lived under the same roof."

I am startled. This means the splitting up of the African American family was done systematically from the start. The dysfunctional situation many children grow up in, in places like South Central in Los Angeles, or the Ninth Ward in New Orleans, with absent fathers and defeated mothers, might have been created or imparted back in the time of slavery.

It's like we're walking through a cemetery. I believe everyone in our group is affected by the pain and brutality that played out here. It's as if history has come to life. The horrified hush of our group is one I recall from my own past. In 1994, I visited the concentration camp Theresienstadt on a school trip. Although we were a goofy group of teenagers, the gravity of death was present in every step we took. That was the closest I'd ever come to being able to absorb how brutal human history is. Until now.

"Eighty percent of the slaves suffered from PTSD," our guide Cheryl continues loudly. "You can imagine how difficult it must have been for people with heavy psychological burdens to be friendly and empathetic toward each other. They could increase the odds of survival if they informed or worked against each other, so oftentimes there wasn't much solidarity among the slaves."

Amelie and I exchange somber looks. With every sentence Cheryl serves up to our group, the knot in my stomach twists more and more.

"A slave woman could not under any circumstances say no to a man. Rape was systematic and happened more or less every day. The rule was, if your mother was a slave, you were automatically a slave, no matter how light your skin was. A woman at Whitney by the name of Anna had fifteen children with fifteen different men. While Louisiana was under French rule, the slave laws followed Code Noir, which was a collection of laws instituted back in 1685 by the Sun King, Louis XIV. Among other things, it forbade the splitting up of slave families. The law provided slaves one day off a week and forbade torture or other cruel punishment. The slave owner was also required to educate his slaves in the Catholic faith. This completely changed when Louisiana was purchased by the United States in 1803. One difference was that the slaves were no longer allowed to become Christian. The slave owners believed that would lead to the slaves being humanized because they would be brothers in faith. Any sign of belief in God would bring strict punishment from the overseer."

Cheryl stops to let this information sink in.

"What's more, many methods of torture were systematized—such as hamstringing," Cheryl tells us. "They would sever tendons in the thighs of male slaves, and even cut off their ears. Another cruel punishment was buck breaking. A male slave would be bound over a barrel or a large stump, and other slaves would be forced to rape him."

Our group moves on across the grounds of Whitney Plantation. On this sunny, peaceful green paradise of an afternoon, it's hard to picture the terror, screams, and tears that must have been a daily routine here among the grand oaks and loaded pecan, citrus, and fig trees: essentially, black blood colored this ground on a daily basis. I close my eyes for a few seconds and imagine how the chirping of birds must have clashed with the whistle of the whip and the dull sound of flesh being torn from bone. How the odor of sweat and blood must have blended with the heavy aroma of orange blossoms and magnolia flowers. How the plantation owner's wife and daughters must have trained themselves to shut out the sounds of suffering around them. How they must have sat with their embroidery, chatting about weekend trips to New Orleans or gossiping about the neighbors, their voices growing louder and louder each time the whip cracked in the yard.

They're still turning that same deaf ear and blind eye at Oak Alley Plantation next door, I think. I can't believe they use the word "worker" instead of "slave" and serve cocktails instead of talking about what really happened on the plantation land two hundred years ago. How can people live with shutting out the truth generation after generation?

As the group walks up the white wooden steps to the plantation owner's house, I am surprised by how small and rustic it looks, until Cheryl, as if she's read my mind, rolls her eyes and says, "The family's house in New Orleans was much flashier than this one. This was mostly a workplace."

Each time Cheryl concludes a portion of the guided tour, she asks if anyone has any questions. No one says anything. I think we're all struck with the same feeling of incomprehension. How could this happen; how could it go on? How could this country be built in such a bloody manner?

My mind turns to the world map in my high school history book. Various arrows sprouted from the continent of Africa toward Europe and North and South America. On the arrows were the words "Gold," "Ivory," and "Slaves." Gold and ivory are still shipped wholesale and retail from the continent, and my old-world map sheds a macabre light on the constant stream of migrants risking their lives on crowded boats on the Mediterranean to reach Europe. If you were to update one of the arrows in my textbook, change "Slaves" to "People," the diagram would still be accurate today.

In school, I was frustrated that I never got to learn about Africa. The Eurocentric history I was educated in begins when the Europeans arrived in Africa but explains nothing about what life was like, about the societies, cultures, and traditions that flourished and developed before the colonizers landed. The same goes for the newspaper articles I read on a daily basis about the flow of refugees and migrants to Europe. Very little is said about these nameless people's origins and lives; instead, they're measured by the value or burden they will become to those of us in the rich part of the world.

On our trip back to New Orleans—the birthplace of jazz, the music created by slaves and their descendants, essentially the basis for all the popular music we know—I can hardly take in the suffering this powerful form of expression sprang from.

In the late nineteenth century, those black folks who didn't migrate north continued to live around the plantation. They still worked to sow and harvest the same crops as the slaves had, but instead they were day laborers. Like Don, my great-grandmother BM, grandfather Silas, and their families all were.

When black people could no longer be considered property with intrinsic value, the lynchings began. Terror as an everyday practice to keep the oppressed in check. Music was a vital escape both during slavery and in the years after its abolishment.

As our Soul flies across the damp Louisiana countryside, I think of how jazz, blues, rock, soul, funk, and hip-hop are an ode to humanity's unbreakable spirit. Soul was born out of tragedy, brutality, and terror. Sprung from the same soul that gave rise to the inherent cheerfulness and spark of life that George, Enid, Don, and so many more of Dad's friends allowed me to experience during my upbringing.

We accidentally take a wrong turn as we try to get back to the highway from the back roads we wound down to find Whitney Plantation and end up having to drive over an enormous bridge that crosses the Mississippi River.

"There it is, in all its majesty!" Amelie cries.

The river does look undeniably majestic. The same water that made it possible for the cotton, indigo, and sugarcane to reach Europe and the American East Coast. Its refined products that considerably improved citizens' lives, far from the sound of the whip and the slaves' screams.

I am just as far removed from the suffering that hides in the creation of my iPhone, my shirts, my plastic bowls from IKEA, the wine and espresso I drink, and the chocolate and bananas I eat. Is my ignorance and guilt as great, my blinders as thick, as those of people in the past? Did they even know what lay behind the dearly acquired bowl of sugar on their table or the cotton of their tablecloths? Are we as a species eternally condemned to be blind to the suffering of our fellow humans, or the inevitable cost of our comfort?

I feel a deep sense of relief when Amelie steers our Korean car into the picturesque neighborhood of Treme in central New Orleans. To interrupt the images of the brutality of slavery that have had a stranglehold on me, I ask her, "What should we eat today, Vietnamese, French, or Creole?"

THE DAY WILL
SURELY COME

"You can park here," Dad says, pointing at a spot ten yards ahead of the one I've just stopped the car in.

"But I just parked, and it can't be more than twenty-five yards to Don's place."

"I'm old, I can't walk that far," Dad says, upset.

"But you have to use your legs, or else you'll never regain your strength," I plead with a weak smile. "You really need to get a little exercise."

"Stop saying that all the time. I have no muscles."

"OK, you have no muscles."

"Stop being so cynical, Jason. You're never here, you don't see how sick I feel."

"You're not sick, Dad, you're healthy."

"You know nothing about how it feels to get old."

Dad shoots me a surly look. He starts to breathe faster; he narrows his eyes and refuses to make eye contact.

I drive the car into the spot he suggested, here on Dukatgatan in the residential neighborhood out past Rosengård. The hedges and trees along the street are showing their first buds; in three or four weeks, with any luck, we can expect the long-awaited Swedish spring to arrive. But for now, everything is cold, bare, and monochromatic. The milky-gray light and the colorless city don't put me in a very hopeful mood.

Dad's complaints make my heart ache. I just want to cry. Cry because he seems to have given up. Dad has put a tough autumn behind him, with an acute case of septicemia and three brain surgeries and almost three months in the hospital. His brain and body are still recovering.

I hop out of Mom's red car, which I've borrowed for the day, and walk around to open the passenger-side door.

Dad slowly looks up at me from the passenger seat.

"I bet you think I'm just lazy. You're always getting after me to use my muscles. But you don't know how it feels."

I don't say anything. I know it's not going to improve his mood if I keep picking on him. That only seems to have the opposite effect. I don't know if it's my own talent for self-pity I see in him that makes me feel this mixture of scorn and sadness, or if it's just my grief at watching Dad waste away before my eyes while nothing and no one, least of all he himself, can do anything to stop it.

"You're forty-one years old, Jason. I'm not about to fight with you. You don't know how to keep your mouth shut."

"Oh man." I sigh.

"Don't 'oh man' me. Why don't you just shut the fuck up!"

He has never spoken to me like this before, and it makes me sink even deeper into sadness. He's fighting for his life. He doesn't want to waste away either, but he seems incapable of doing anything about it. That comment does the trick. I zip my lips and avoid his gaze.

I can see Harlem through his eyes now. That hard look in his eyes, fostered in him by the streets of his childhood, is so familiar to me. It's a crucial part of the armor every resident of the ghetto must put on to keep from being destroyed by the ruthless streets. It's part of the gorilla suit you have to put on every morning before you go out, as Don talked about last time we visited him.

Dad has lived in Sweden for nearly fifty years, and there's not much ghetto left in this stooping, weak-legged man I'm helping out of the car, to the accompaniment of his sighs and grunts of pain. His once raven-black eyes have grown ice-blue with age. The melanin—the amino acid that gives color to skin, eyes, and hair, and whose natural quantity in a body determines whether that person should be considered black or white—is decreasing in Dad's body.

In two lifetimes, perhaps his great-grandchildren will be born with blue eyes and blinding-white skin. How will that drop of midnight, that melanin left in our line but watered down through the generations, reveal itself? It occurs to me that I might be the last in our family to care about my skin color, which spaces I'm welcome in, who might hate or try to degrade me based on the way I look. The last one to struggle with, experience, and be marked by what life as a nonwhite person is like.

"Look, there's Don," I say, pointing at the living room window of the small, sand-lime brick house on the outskirts of Malmö.

Don waves back at us.

"Express train approaching!" I shout to Don, whose face cracks into a wide smile.

Dad sighs at my sarcasm.

Coco, Don's energetic, shaggy mutt, runs out and barks sharply to greet us as soon as we've come through the gate and into the yard. To the right of the steps is a large lift that was installed several years ago. But Dad takes the steps, even though it takes him a few minutes to maneuver himself up and into Don's crowded front hall.

"Hey, Don," I shout in an attempt to be heard over the stereo, which is turned up to the max as always.

Bill Withers's unmistakably urgent voice thunders through the living room: "You want to take me to a doctor, to talk to me about my mind . . ."

"I'm playin' your theme song," Don calls cheerfully.

Dad's laugh erases the dark cloud of the grudge between father and son. A visit to an old friend is three times better for Dad's mood and spiritual condition than all the medicines and doctor's appointments in the world.

"Trouble in me is not related, to things I might say and do," Bill Withers continues as Don, Dad, and I embrace.

Instead of pizza, I've brought shawarma and rice for the men. As Dad and Don move in slow motion, sighing loudly as they settle into their chairs, I set out the white Styrofoam containers of food. The scent of grilled meat and garlic sauce rises to meet the sound of Bill Withers's voice. As Don sits down, he says, "OK, first things first, baby boy. Tell me about the diaspora. Tell me about the South and the people, are they still glued or are they doing alright?"

Don has always called me "baby boy." I've never doubted his love for me. Whatever Don says, positive or negative, it always sounds good. It's something about his raspy, animated, African American way of speaking. It's like you can hear that his voice contains a treasure trove of experience, even as it feels benevolent and attentive. The way he speaks makes you want to confide in him.

I explain that the situation for first-generation African immigrants in the US is better than that of the domestic black population. I spoke with people about Harlem's 116th Street, the area where Dad lived as a child and which is now called Little Senegal, and a lot of them say that group is doing very well in America. At least compared to the old Harlemers. The children of the Senegalese go to college. They have a future.

Don nods slowly, inserting little "uh-huhs," "alrights," and "yeah, yeahs" as I speak.

I haven't seen Don since the mid-March day last year when Dad drove me to the little gray house on the outskirts of Malmö in the hopes that Don would talk me out of going to South Carolina. Now Don wants a detailed report on the conditions in his former home state.

I tell him about how overwhelmed I felt when I saw a cotton field for the first time, on the fringes of Allendale, a few months ago. I tell him about my urge to stop the car and run out into the field to pick a few of the fluffy white tufts. How my fingers and back demanded an empirical experience of what my forefathers' main occupation felt like.

"Yeah, yeah, you had to get the feel of it, huh," Don says with a mysterious smile.

As if I had gotten to peer through the keyhole into the crazy state he was born in eighty-three years ago.

"He didn't feel how it was to pick a whole bale of that stuff, though," Dad throws in.

Don wonders if anyone has explained to me how to pick cotton.

"Nah, I just assumed it was in my genes," I say, because I know that sort of comment is guaranteed to unleash peals of laughter from the two old black men.

"You gotta use your fingers and get way into the pod to manage to get that whole thing out clean," Don responds once the laughter has subsided. "You don't want to get any of the shell, you see, you just want that cotton."

"Seems like you've got skills in the cotton area," I reply, teasing Don a little.

The happy face Don's been sporting since we arrived transforms in a flash to one of utter seriousness. He rests his fork on the edge of the small white Styrofoam box and turns his eyes on me as he speaks in short, scornful sentences.

"Man, I grew up in those fields. From the time I was five years old, I picked cotton."

"What? You worked in those cotton fields?"

"Oh yes, baby boy . . . At six o'clock every damn morning, my grandmother and I walked to the fields. I would swing a burlap sack over my shoulder, and then it was time to start picking."

Even as Don's gaze is on me, it's as if he can see images of the dewy mornings when he walked barefoot into those fields, a little boy with a sack almost as big as he was. I've known Don as long as I can remember, but I never knew anything about his childhood. I've never understood the legacy of slavery, or the symbolic or real-world meaning of the cotton field, for someone like Don. Until now. Maybe that's what these old men wanted to spare me last year when they tried to convince me not to visit the South.

Now that I've seen the fields, the plantations, and the hopelessness of the ghost towns, all I can do is shake my head. A great sorrow awakens inside me when I realize that the old man sitting before me with his looming posture and otherwise so lively laugh had to experience this even at the age of five.

"After a long day, you take your sack of cotton to the gin, and they weigh it and then decide how much they pay you for it. We were sharecroppers, man."

Don shakes his head. He describes what befell the black population of the South after slavery was abolished. For those who didn't move north to work in factories, there was no other option. You kept doing what you had done as a slave. Picking cotton, chopping sugarcane, harvesting rice, picking indigo . . . instead of being a slave, you were a day laborer. Instead of the overseer's whip for incentive, you had the burden of needing to earn enough money to pay rent to the plantation owner for your little shack and to put food on the table.

Don squeezes his eyes closed and pokes his fork at the plate of shawarma, which he hasn't yet touched.

"We didn't get much for the cotton we picked. The white man took most of our earnings, and we were left with hardly anything. It was slavery man, plain and simple. Slavery."

Don stops, just as Dad so often does when his gaze turns inward, looking back through his life.

"You see, the same whites who owned the cotton fields also owned the only store in the area. That's where we bought sugar, coffee, flour, lard, tobacco, and other necessities. We didn't have no money, of course, so we bought on credit, and then we were forced to go back into the fields to earn some and pay back for what we owed the store . . . The whole system was rigged. Arranged to keep us blacks in our place. At the bottom."

As Don goes on, full of sadness, I look at Dad, whose eyes are also fixed on an imaginary horizon.

"We never had a chance, man, never. Not to this day. We were pickers, man. My grandmother, my aunts, my uncles . . . We only earned a little over fifty dollars in a whole year. That's how it was, in the forties."

Dad whistles, shakes his head, and looks at me.

"You see, Jason, fifty fucking dollars . . . If that ain't slavery, I don't know what is."

I break the silence that follows by describing the hopelessness that shocked me so deeply as Simme, Alluette, and I explored Allendale. We found ourselves in the midst of what Eddie Glaude calls an "opportunity desert" in his book *Democracy in Black*. These are places where hope, a future, opportunity, and chance have long since fled, leaving behind nothing but poor black people moving back and forth between the ruins of houses, streets, and hope.

Now Don, like Dad, slowly but resolutely begins to shovel forkful after forkful of shawarma, rice, and salad out of the white boxes on the rickety little coffee table before them. My testimony about the dismal reality for poor people in the South doesn't surprise them. They shake their heads and exclaim between bites.

"Boy, I'm tellin' you."

"Yeah, ain't nothing new about that."

"The Man got it all figured out."

"You didn't have to go all the way there to tell me that."

Resignation has been so deeply rooted in them since childhood that any information about the United States is reflexively put through a filter of cynicism and observed with the most critical eyes. At the same time, the avenues of nostalgia are always open, and Don and Dad often interrupt their lamentations to recall memories in dreamy voices: a song, a smell, a taste, a street, or a movie from their distant homeland. These pauses of loving retrospection are always followed by a brief moment of silence, only to be interrupted by political comments.

"Man, look, Hillary Clinton got all the money behind her. But look at what the young people want. They see clearly now, social democracy is what is needed to lift the country up. Maaan, nobody wants that stank ol' woman in office, she and her old man done fucked the country up enough already. She should just lay up and enjoy her pension and let somebody else fix America."

Don and Dad look at me to make sure I'm listening. Don goes on.

"That's why I like Trump. You know America is done, finished. The place has been so fucked up for so long. Somebody has got to pull the worms outta the can. And that's what Trump, for all his foolishness, is doing. We all know he's a loudmouth buffoon, but at least he's saying what so many white people in that country have been thinking all along. He's bringin' all of it out of the closet. Finally."

Dad is silent as Don lays out his analysis. In my eyes, their view from this quiet residential neighborhood in Malmö to the United States is limited, and I'm dumbfounded by their interpretation of the situation in the country. I've been witnessing these conversations for as long as I can remember. As a kid, I always took their dogma as truth; in my twenties, I didn't bother to sit with them; in my thirties, I responded to their declarations with wild protest. Now I find myself just being quiet and listening. Don preaches on.

"You see, now you have white people suffering. In a way that they haven't experienced before. That's why so many of them are committing suicide. They're being evicted, they're on food stamps, their cars are being repossessed. So, you see, now they're almost in the same boat as me."

Don is aglow as he describes the collapse of the American white middle class as the main reason someone like Trump can come as far as he has in a presidential election.

Dad tells us that Uncle Obi is volunteering for the Trump campaign and recently held his first pro-Trump speech at a rally in Baltimore. This information makes me feel a little ill. How can the world be so messed up that someone as far down the ladder of society as my uncle is completely convinced that he has to back the most toxic and ignorant presidential candidate in modern history just to bring about some sort of change? It's so cynical that all I can do is shake my head. What can I say to these men?

Don smiles rather secretively and shifts his line of thought.

"Black people have been suffering since we got to America, so we're used to it. We learned to survive through the most obscene hardships one can imagine. But the white man isn't prepared for that. He ain't ready, and he don't know what the fuck to do now that reality is biting him in the ass."

The thick, grave atmosphere lightens when Dad fires off a burst of laughter that ropes Don in as well. A good laugh seems to be the only medicine for tragedy. I find myself feeling less certain about my instinctive objections to their cynical attitude about Donald Trump. They're right, of course. But it's too fucking much to sit there praising a racist ass like Trump. I can't join in, no way. But I keep my protests to myself.

"I'll tell you who else I like," Don says in a challenging tone. "Putin."

"What?" I respond. "He's a fucking Fascist."

"Shiiit," says Don. "Who isn't? What do you think Trump and the rest of them are? They're all tumors sprouting from the same goddamn sickness. But Putin challenges the system, and the Western world has no idea how to deal with that Russian. They never have. Putin's playing chess. He makes his moves, moving his pieces into Crimea, then Syria. What the fuck is the US supposed to play for a countermove now? Man, if it hadn't been for the Russians, the whole of fucking Europe would belong to the Nazis now. And what did they get from the West? Not a damn thing. They were frozen out and opposed because they were Communists. Man, listen . . ."

Don stretches in his seat and extends an index finger.

"Anyone who challenges the West, I'm for. The oppression they've subjected the nonwhite world to for so long, it has to fucking stop. Whatever the cost. Just look at ISIS. They've really given the Western world something to sink their teeth into. The US and Europe have no fucking clue how to take that bull by the horns. The world has changed. There's so much more fear now, everywhere. The white man still wants to present himself as innocent. As if nothing is his fault."

Don bats his hand as if he's trying to shoo away an annoying fly.

"Ah, I love Trump," Don repeats with that mysterious expression. "Clinton is a joke. Trump is shouting out loud what all those other fuckers have always whispered."

As Don and Dad exchange high fives, I realize there's nothing I can say to make them or Uncle Obi change their minds. Their cynicism has become pathological. In their case, maybe it's just easier to hope as much of the white world burns up as possible, the world that has oppressed them, their families, their forefathers.

Recently, when I was having coffee with the African American activist Casey Gerald in Brooklyn, he said, "Where I grew up, we learned that hope was dangerous. It was irrational to have hope. It was absurd to dream."

Don, Dad, and Casey are all born of a reality I will never completely be able to understand, no matter how many journeys I make. The great difference between them and me is that I grew up believing that I have certain rights that no one can take away from me, while they grew up with the certainty that society would never lift a finger to help them—in fact, society would destroy them for the tiniest misstep.

But in the untidy house under the Skåne clouds, the atmosphere remains cheerful despite the topic of conversation.

"Dick Gregory said it best," Don continues. "The white man lives in the penthouse, which is why more white people commit suicide than blacks do. You know, if you already live in the basement, there's nowhere to jump from."

Don's laugh sounds like someone keeping time by shaking a jar of pebbles. The rhythmic clatter starts out loud, only to quickly subside, and the conversation resumes. Dad interjects, "Dick Gregory was important to us. But another favorite was Muhammad Ali. In 1960, right after he got back from the Olympics in Rome, he went to a restaurant that had previously refused to serve him because of the color of his skin. He just walked right in and slammed his gold medal on the counter, to which the waitress said, 'We still don't serve niggers.' 'That's OK, I don't eat them,' Muhammad Ali countered quick as lightning."

"Man, he really was the greatest," Don interjects, turning to me again. "Now you're just back from the US, Jason. You've seen it. The racist American system isn't just something you've read about in books and newspapers anymore."

Don's and Dad's attempts to warn me off gaining these eyewitness experiences in the South have completely vanished. Now, instead, they give me proud looks and encouraging words. Maybe they're impressed with my determination, or maybe they find some comfort in the fact that I now understand a little more about their backgrounds and the conditions they grew up in.

"Know what we did when we were kids?" Don asks. "On Saturday nights, when the theater had performances downtown, we went there and stood on the steps and took off our caps. The white men on their way in would rub our heads, and if we were lucky, we'd get five or ten cents for our trouble."

"What do you mean? They rubbed your heads?"

"Yep," Don says, aiming a sly look at me. "Like we were Aladdin's lamp."

Dad's whole body is shaking with laughter.

"It was good luck to rub a black boy's head. Understand what we mean now? That whole country is fucked up. Always has been. I've been through so much racism in my life, you have no idea . . ."

"That can still happen today, in Sweden," I respond. "It's happened to lots of people I know. White people want to feel their African hair."

Don bows his head and mumbles something as if to demonstrate what used to happen on those theater steps seventy years ago.

"Have you been to Cuba?"

"Yes, twice."

"Alright, alright." Don nods approvingly.

"Obama was just there," I add.

"Man, I'm not talkin' about your hero, I'm talkin' about my hero. You, Jason. Have you been there?"

"Yes, I have, Don."

"Great, great, isn't the music incredible?" Don says.

"Yeah, it was something else. The closest I've come to the feeling of Havana is New Orleans. But in Havana, you don't have to see Confederate flags flying."

"Sure you do," Don responds. "Lemme tell you, when I went around selling at squares and markets in this country, I always brought some Confederate flags with me. They sold like hotcakes. Confused, ignorant boys would come up to me and ask, 'How much is that flag?' 'One hundred eighty-nine kronor,' I always said. 'All the flags are eighty-nine kronor, except the Confederate flag.' 'Why's it so expensive?' they wondered. 'Because being racist comes at a cost,' I said. 'If you want to hang up that rag, you'll have to pay for the privilege.'"

Dad cracks up and I can't help but join him after Don's lecture.

"Was that your racist tax, Don?" I ask.

"Exactly." He chuckles. "Same as with a Nazi flag. Of course, you can buy it, but it's not cheap."

Don straightens his back and suddenly changes tack.

"Jason, you're number one. You've come so far in this country, much farther than I believed any of us ever could. You have no idea how proud I am."

Don's quiet, serious voice tells me he truly means it. I'm just so not used to receiving this kind of recognition from the older generation.

"When I see you on TV or read about your progress in the paper . . . Man, it makes me feel so damn good. I swear to God. It makes me happy. You give us hope, Jason."

Don's eyes tear up. As usual, I find it very difficult to accept compliments, and I don't know what to say. I smile nervously and squirm in the creaky chair and try my best to accept this unexpected, sincere praise from one of the people I've looked up to most of all in my life.

"Fuck Marco Polo, I choose you." Don laughs. "Your travels, your words, your songs. They lift me up. One day you're in the Congo, you're in Ethiopia the next, and the day after that you're in Alabama. Goddamn, boy. None of us here has ever before done what you do."

The older men slowly rise from their chairs, and their walkers roll through the mishmash of books, records, and papers to stop in Don's little front hall.

Don's sentimentality surprises me. The man I've known almost all my life, and who, like Muhammad Ali, always has a witty response at the ready, who always takes an ironic approach to the injustices of the world and so often responds to hardships with a laugh. Don, whom I've always admired for his coolness, charm, and intelligence, really sees me now. As an adult. I suppose I've been wishing that Dad would see me the same way. I'm so unprepared for his sentimental comments that I have to squeeze my eyes closed to keep the tears from coming. Here in Don's hall. In front of Dad.

When I meet Don's moist eyes, I think about how every human, from the time they're born until the time they die, is a universe of memories, dreams, plans, sorrows, desires, and convictions. In listening to Dad's and Don's testimonies and stories, I am given the opportunity to remember what I never had to suffer through. I am grateful, so fervently grateful, that my gathering tears retreat, and instead I find I want to break out in the hugest smile I can.

"May the spirits always be with you, Jason," Don says. "As long as they're by your side, I know I will be there too, even when our old bodies are rotting in the cold fucking dirt of this place. That knowledge is enough for me."

Before Dad and I leave, I take out my phone and play "The Day Will Surely Come" by the 1930s gospel group the Swan Silvertones. Don sets the brake on his walker and sits on the rail between the grips, taking off his cap with the Ethiopian Lion of Judah coat of arms and resting his hand on the crown of his head. The same head that was offered up, seventy years ago, to white men in the hopes of earning a few cents. He closes his eyes and shakes his head in time with the beat, and once again, I witness the healing power of music. Singing might be the most formidable armor available to black people the world over, to survive in a system that has forever been rigged against us, a system full of death traps.

But Don and Dad survived. They broke out of their respective opportunity deserts and did something no one else around them dared to do. They left the ghetto for a place where they believed they could live rather than just survive. They are success stories, just as my grandfather is. The very fact that they're still alive is a statistical deviation. And with their brains and their honor basically intact.

As the Silvertones' tenor starts in on the second verse, tears run down Don's furrowed cheeks. I know him and he knows me. It's like I'm coming home.

"I know the day will surely come, the day will surely come," these long-since-dead voices rasp from my iPhone speakers, and the comfort the voices provide is still as potent as it was nearly a century ago, just after grandfather had left Allendale, when this song was recorded.

PICKING THE PIN

Malmö's early summer has made the sun-drenched living room almost unbearably warm, and my forehead and palms are damp. After almost a year of nagging and reminders, Dad has finally agreed to sit down with me and read through all the letters that have been hidden away in the red faux-leather suitcase.

And he's letting Simme film us. Now that I'm holding the thick white stationery, dated September 8, 1973, and I see the well-formulated but caustic sentences my grandmother tapped out on her typewriter, I understand why Dad has been putting off digging through these letters and hearing the voices from his past.

> *My Dear Madubuko,*
> *You and Elaine have chosen a lifestyle from which retreat is difficult, if not impossible. No world will open its heart for either of you. Neither the black world nor the white world will allow you in . . .*

Dad is sitting motionless in his favorite black easy chair. He's wearing a pea-green short-sleeved shirt and has drawn the belt tight through his blue jeans; his suspenders are just as tight. In the past few months, his weight has plummeted because of his illness, and even though all his pants are too big, they just have to stay put.

For the moment, his blue gaze is vacant and he's staring straight ahead, past me even as I'm sitting directly across from him. His face is pinched, and all the tiny, copper-colored wrinkles hint at the deep pain inside. It's as if he's looking into his own heart.

He breaks the uncomfortable silence with a heavy sigh.

"I should have burned that letter too," he says at last. "All of her letters were cruel."

Dad's eyes focus on me again.

"Your grandmother never understood what I wanted from my life. Even though she sacrificed so much to fulfill her own dreams, she could never understand why I chose the life I did."

He closes his eyes, an expression of exhaustion on his face, but he looks up again after a few seconds.

"I remember one letter where she claimed I had only moved to Europe to 'swim in a sea of white women,' and her recommendation was for me to act as 'Negro' as I possibly could. She wrote that I should drink, fight, and play cards as often as I could, that I should act as ignorant and stupid as I possibly could. I burned that letter as soon as I finished reading it. For her, it was the ultimate insult to be called or act like a 'Negro.' She often called your grandfather that. For her, a Negro was someone who lived up to all the stereotypes of what a black man was: irresponsible, addicted, abusive, criminal, and ignorant."

I'm so eager to read more of my grandmother's letters, but it's impossible to shut Dad's newly opened floodgates.

"When I came to Sweden, I saw that some black people really did act that way. Like Earl the Pearl, an African American who came to Malmö in the sixties and became a pimp. Prostitution was out in the open in Malmö back then. In American ghettos, the pimp has often been seen as some sort of folk hero, a master of his own fortune, no matter the cost. The ultimate revenge for some black men was to prostitute white women. As if to say to the white man, 'You don't want to give me my rights, you don't want to give me a job, you don't want to treat me like a human. Fine, then I'll take your woman, your mother, your daughter, and make her my slave. The way you forced me to be your slave.'"

When Dad pauses for breath, I hold up the letter. I want to keep reading. Dad is used to my impatience and raises a finger so I'll allow him to continue his train of thought.

"But like with all pimps, everyone who lives by the law of the street, Earl had a tragic fate. He tried to leave the criminal life behind, and he opened a reptile store in Växjö and was in a relationship with a woman. In the end, he couldn't shake his bad habits and went to prison for abusing her. As far as I know, he was deported from Sweden. He's probably sitting on some corner in one of the ghettos of America, talking shit with the old men in the neighborhood, or else he's buried in some unmarked grave. Earl acted like a 'Negro.'"

Yet another piece of the puzzle slides into place in my mind. Because I recognize the worldview that Dad ascribes to my grandmother. For as long as I can remember, Dad has used the same word for certain black people in Lund and Malmö, people he doesn't think behave with dignity. Even though he's always held his head high and never bowed down to the white man, Dad's story about his parents shows me how ingrained these high standards are in him.

Like original sin. With a black body comes great responsibility. You learn to smile wider, be friendlier and more responsible, work harder, and choose your words with much greater care. As if having black skin is a punishment. You are forced to carry the knowledge inside you that your worth and everything you've fought for can be taken away from you at any moment with a single word.

Nigger.

My eyes light upon the woven African fabric in blue, red, and yellow that's draped over the leather sofa to Dad's right. He raises one hand to get my attention.

"She was a good writer, your grandmother, but she seldom had anything kind to say. I can't remember a single time that my siblings or

I called her 'Mom' in her presence. Or a single time that she said she loved me."

Dad leans back and gazes at the ceiling. I seldom hear him criticize his mother. Although, over the years, it has emerged more and more what an unusually bad parent she was.

If it had been up to him, Dad probably would have preferred to leave the red suitcase hidden among layers of boxes, bags, and dust in the attic. At the same time, there was something that prompted him to save the letters. Could it be that these folded, wrinkled, yellowed documents are the only concrete evidence Dad has that his parents took the time to talk to him? Maybe he never felt as much love from them as when they went to the trouble of sitting down, composing a letter, and making their way down to the post office on Lenox Avenue in Harlem to send it to Sweden.

The contents of the three big, thick envelopes in the suitcase are all Dad has left of his parents—this is his bridge to the life he once lived in the United States. It wasn't as if opportunities grew on trees for a poor boy from Harlem who wanted to get a university education. In Lund, he could study for free, in English. *But was it really free?* I wonder as I sit in Dad's sunny living room with all these dusty letters full of words from a time gone by, full of voices long since silenced.

I observe Dad, who's still sitting motionless in the leather easy chair, staring at the Persian rug under our feet. I take a deep breath and continue reading the letter from my grandmother out loud.

The two of you ought to broaden your horizons by adopting an orphaned child from Vietnam. This would internationalize your lives and bring you some dignity, which would inspire respect. The adoption would be guaranteed to change you, and also many aspects of your stubborn relationship, for the better. Furthermore it's very IN right now to adopt a Vietnamese child . . . you could

easily adopt three or four children of different ethnicities
and have your very own little United Nations household.

"What kind of mother writes so sarcastically to her own child?" I ask, turning to Simme.

Simme moves the camera lens closer to Dad's face as I read him the letter.

"Wow, Buko, your mom was a hard woman," Simme says, peering out from behind the camera. "How did you respond to a letter like that?"

"I didn't. I was furious every time I got a letter from her and realized how cruel she was. Every time. That's why I burned so many of her letters. She was a woman with very strong convictions. But she wasn't a good mother. No way . . ."

My grandmother had a round face, a big mouth, and silvery hair, and she spoke in a loud voice. One of her hands was under my chin while the fingers of the other combed through my hair. She wasn't addressing me; these were just joyful cries to the world at large.

"Oh, what soft hair! What a beautiful boy!"

She had a black fur coat and dark clothing. After the protracted and numerous pinches of my cheeks and comments about my hair, we walked with Dad to an Indian restaurant at Fourteenth Street and First Avenue.

The year was 1980, and this is my only memory of my grandmother Madame, born Lilian Davis around 1920.

"Why does your mom have silver hair?" I asked Dad as we stood on the sidewalk outside the restaurant after we'd parted ways with my grandma.

"It's a wig," he replied.

How weird for that old lady to have a wig on, I thought.

When she had a stroke and unexpectedly passed away in 1982, I asked Dad why she had died. He said she'd died from eating too much Kentucky Fried Chicken. I didn't understand how anyone could die from eating chicken. My grandfather's death—from a brain tumor, also in 1982—was expected, but my grandmother's came as a shock to the family, and it took years for Dad to recover after losing both his parents so suddenly.

I never got to know these people. But the stories about them remain. Such as how my grandmother once shipped a Cadillac from New York to Conakry, Guinea, when she worked for the US embassy. According to Dad, it's possible that it's still in use somewhere in West Africa—in that part of the world, there is such need that the most unlikely and inventive repairs are made to keep cars functioning.

My grandmother's framed Bachelor of Arts diploma still hangs in a place of honor in my father's office. Every time I ask him about the diploma, he beams with pride as he rises from his favorite chair and takes it off the wall. Not many African American women received degrees from Columbia University in 1959.

After being influenced by Marcus Garvey's apostle Carlos Cooks, who carried on the message that African Americans ought to be repatriated to Africa, she changed her name to Adadie Afrikanwe Ajuluchuku. Gone was the slave name Lilian Davis.

Dad recalls how Carlos Cooks used to bring a small stepladder to the corner of 125th Street and Lenox Avenue, from which he would preach his message of strengthening the African American identity.

Afrikanwe was still a poor woman from Harlem. She worked as a substitute teacher and started an apartment-rental agency to finance her studies. On weekends, like so many in the black ghettos, where swing—born out of Southern misery, carved from the same tree as jazz—had started a revolution, she went out dancing. She'd met Grandpa at a dance at the Savoy Ballroom on 140th Street and Lenox Avenue. He was thirteen years older. Grandpa loved jazz, while my grandmother preferred classical music.

Grandpa was a steady man who kept his eyes on the sidewalk and thought you should be thankful for what you had, and she was a whirlwind striving for something greater, her eyes on the horizon. They say Grandpa could move on the dance floor. Maybe it was his Lindy Hop skills, his charm and style, that spoke to my grandmother—or maybe he was just a good, safe man.

They married and had one baby, and soon another. Dad was born Warren, and my aunt Chinyelu was born Brenda. Afrikanwe was only twenty when Dad was born. At twenty-three, she left my grandfather. He didn't understand her talk of getting an education, learning French, or moving back to their mother continent of Africa. While Grandpa put lye in his hair to straighten it, Grandma had stopped processing her hair with chemicals. She was proud of her African curls. She despised servility. Driven by whispers and cries from the streets about rights and struggles, she wanted more. She refused to join the ranks of the quiet black masses of the inner city.

She was unusual for her time, my grandmother.

In 1951, Madame/Lilian/Afrikanwe showed up outside Dad's school. She ordered him to get in her car. Grandpa had just given Dad a bicycle, and his first thought was that he couldn't leave it.

"But, Mom, if I come with you, someone will take my bike."

"Forget the bike, boy," she said. "There are other bikes. Now get in the car."

Dad hesitated. But at last, he leaned his bike against a tree and hopped into Grandma's car.

Once my grandmother had gathered her four children and brought them to an apartment in West Harlem, she sent them—without a word to my grandfather—across the Atlantic to West Africa. To Nigeria.

Grandpa was furious when he learned from my great-grandmother that his children had been sent away. He couldn't find out where they were. He tracked down my grandmother time and again, begging and pleading with her to bring the children back. Once, they fought so loudly on the street in Harlem that two police officers appeared, and Grandma told them Grandpa was threatening her. The police carted Grandpa away with a strict warning to let the woman be, or else they would throw him in the clink. It was pointless for a black man to argue with the police in 1951—no matter how innocent he was. It didn't much matter what the law said—whatever the police said was law. So, in the end, Grandpa gave up the hunt for his children.

Once Grandma was divorced from Grandpa, she remarried and had two children with the Pan-Africanist Balfour Linton, who died just a few years later. After that, Grandma remarried again, this time to the Nigerian journalist Melie Chukelu Kafundu Ajuluchuku, who was studying in New York.

In 1996, Dad published a book he had written about his early childhood and his years in Nigeria, *Not Even in Your Dreams*. No publisher in the United States wanted to publish it. Eventually, a small, obscure publisher in England printed it, but Dad had to take care of distribution and sales himself.

In the book, there is a photograph of Afrikanwe and Mr. Ajuluchuku taken in 1951. They're not smiling, but their arms are linked and they're wearing identical black coats; he has a suit and tie, and she's got high heels on. It was to him she sent her four children after exchanging their slave names for African ones. Dad went from Warren to Madubuko, my aunt Brenda became Chinyelu, my uncle was given the name Obedike, and my other aunt became Nana. For Afrikanwe, the dream of Africa was real. The world was much larger than Harlem.

As Grandma said in her own defense when her mother asked why she wanted to send her children away: "I can't live with my children growing up here in America and becoming ignorant Negroes. Should they walk around with straightened hair, drinking and gambling away their money like the rest of the inhabitants of the ghetto? Warren will be stabbed on the street before he turns sixteen, and surely Brenda will become a mother by the time she's fifteen. They must be rescued from Harlem. Let the rest of these semiliterate wretches kill each other on these streets. My children are getting out of here as soon as possible."

To Dad, she said, "I want you to grow up proud. Proud of your African heritage."

When Dad wondered what their African heritage was, she said, "Your origin is the life our people lived before the white man tore us away from the soil of Africa and shipped us across the Atlantic in chains. Your heritage is the history of the African people, and who we were when we built the empire. We are a proud people with a proud history and strong cultures. It is our duty to learn who we are so we will know where to go in life. The segregated United States is no place for my children. So you will grow up in Africa instead."

Dad wondered if he could bring the electric train he'd received from his father for Christmas the year before, and he asked what would happen to his nice bike. Grandma gave evasive answers. He never saw that bike again, and it would be many years before he saw the train.

Dad also wanted to know how often his father would visit. Grandma firmly replied that Grandpa had no idea how dire the situation was, when it came to equality between the races in the US. If it were up to Grandpa, Dad and his siblings would have spent their whole lives in the ghetto.

"Your father is so ignorant, Madubuko," my grandmother said time after time.

But my grandfather was of the opinion that he had already managed to get out of the ghetto. For him, Allendale was the place where black people would never attain freedom and make their dreams come true. He had reached great success—he had come to Harlem and gotten a job that paid him every week. No one else in his family could boast the same thing. He had succeeded. So why shouldn't his children grow up in Harlem?

For my grandmother, Harlem was just a place to corral poor, black bodies so they could live on charity in the white city. She often said that black people in the US would never attain equality with their white fellow citizens. Dad, who was only ten years old at the time, asked if all white people were evil.

"They might not all be evil, but black people would do best to keep to their own kind," she responded. "Whites and blacks can't live side by side and be equally free."

Grandma simply couldn't live with the knowledge that in so many parts of the country black people still couldn't vote, eat in the same restaurants as whites, sit in the same bus seats, or use the same drinking fountains. The ones black people were allowed to drink from in Grandpa's home state of South Carolina were still labeled "Colored Water."

Her conviction was so strong that she did the most unmaternal thing a mother can do—separate from her children. She remained in Harlem to save up for a university education.

Dad writes in his book that, before they parted ways, Grandma told him, "You'll thank me for this. You don't realize it now, but one day you'll understand, Madubuko. I'm sacrificing my love for you so that you can get away from these streets and from certain death."

I doubt Dad recalls exactly what his mother said to him, and something inside me says that the woman who wrote the cruel letter we just read probably wasn't as pedagogical as Dad describes her in his book. Time softens sharp edges. Even a bad parent can inspire fond memories once enough years have passed. Dad probably wants to remember the ideological magnitude of her decision to send her children to Nigeria, not the harrowing emotions in his chest that resulted from being forced to spend six years in a strange country with people they didn't know and who didn't love them.

Nana, Obedike, Chinyelu, and Madubuko's mother's choice changed their lives forever. When Nana died in the summer of 2016, she had spent her whole life in Nigeria. She didn't return to the United States until just before her death. By the time her cancer was discovered, it was too advanced, but Nana decided to go to the US in the hope of finding better care.

Nana grew up without parents and, in the end, without her siblings. The bitterness of being abandoned in Nigeria never left her. She didn't want to have anything to do with her siblings, whom she presumably felt had abandoned her too. She only had sporadic contact with Dad, Uncle Obi, and Aunt Chinyelu. She married a Nigerian politician and had four sons, all of whom moved to the US.

The four siblings' relationships have been complicated and full of conflict.

Their new stepfather, MCK Ajuluchuku, was from the Igbo tribe of southern Nigeria. He was an activist and journalist who fought for the liberation of his people and was an active participant in what many years later resulted in the Biafran War. He already had two wives, and they were the ones tasked with making Nigerians of the four children his American wife sent to Africa. First and foremost, the siblings were to be disciplined. At that time in Nigeria, children were essentially property; they had no rights, and they were absolutely forbidden from making their voices heard.

They almost never heard from their mother, and their father had no idea where his children were, so the group of siblings was completely at the mercy of their new reality.

In Nigeria, food was first served to wife number one and her family, and on down the ranks thereafter, in descending age order. So Dad and his siblings always received food after everyone else, and Obedike, the youngest, always filled his plate last of all. Hence the golden rule in my father's house: the youngest gets their food first. They get first choice when it comes to cuts of chicken or lamb.

Dad recalls how one of his stepmothers, Victoria, furiously explained the rules of their new home to the confused siblings from Harlem: "If you think you can come here and decide how you want things to be, you are mistaken. This is Africa, not your America, where children talk back to adults, and worse. Here, children do as they're told without asking questions. Your mother wrote to me that you're to be raised up as Africans, and that we are to do our best to get rid of your American habits. So now you know. As long as you're living here, you have no right to anything. Is that understood?"

It must have been the hardest for Nana and Obedike. For one example, it's tradition in Nigeria for meals to be eaten with your hands. Your right hand, to be precise. You only use your left hand when you go to the toilet. Four-year-old Nana was left-handed, and she was beaten by Victoria each time she touched her food with her left hand. Sometimes Nana was locked up in a closet instead of being allowed to eat dinner. Soon Nana was almost as good at using her right hand as her left.

As the older brother, Dad became his siblings' protector and often tried to strike back and shield them when they were punished. Which meant that he was beaten fairly often as well, but by his stepfather rather than his stepmother. Usually with a rod or a belt, and the number of blows varied depending on his degree of disobedience. Sometimes Victoria rubbed salt or chilies into the wounds left by the lashes.

"It was no joke in Nigeria," I recall Dad telling me. "They took absolutely no shit from us kids. Especially not from the American children of a third wife who wasn't even there. I think our stepmothers were jealous and angry that our stepfather had so many wives, and they took it out on us. 'Go to the woods and fetch a good stick,' Victoria would say. It couldn't be too thick or too thin. It had to be flexible, like a riding crop. If you brought home a bad stick, you got extra lashes. So we were complicit in our own punishment. Worst of all was watching my siblings being whipped. But how do you protect children from their guardian? There was nothing I could do to make our stepmothers treat us more kindly. All I could do was get in between and mouth off enough to be the one who received punishment instead of Obi, Nana, or Chinyelu."

Another creative method of punishment during Dad's time in Nigeria was called "picking the pin." You had to stand in the center of a room on one leg, then lean over and keep your balance with only one finger on the floor. If you fell, you were whipped.

The siblings learned to speak both Igbo and Yoruba fluently. Their American accents quickly transformed into the British English they were taught in school. Slowly but surely, Dad and his siblings became more Nigerian. In a picture at the very back of Dad's book, all of them are lined up in a yard. Nothing about the black-and-white photograph, where Dad is wearing a long, embroidered caftan, with his hair combed into a part, would suggest that they are a group of siblings from Harlem.

When Dad talks about his time in Nigeria, he seldom mentions the painful memories. Instead, he goes on and on about how good the Nigerian food was. *Fufu, egusi*, stockfish, okra, all the exotic tastes their new country had to offer. Food Dad still loves. He also frequently talks about how he learned to be proud of being black. There weren't alcoholics and junkies on every corner as there were in Harlem. In Nigeria, people walked around with ironed shirts and straight backs.

After six years, Dad managed to send a message to Grandpa in New York by way of a contact at the American embassy in Lagos. Grandpa had basically given up on trying to persuade Grandma to bring the children home. Instead, he had remarried and had two new children.

When Grandpa finally got the message from the American State Department that his missing children had been found in Nigeria, he polished his shoes until they were shiny, put on his nicest tie and a freshly pressed jacket, and headed for Midtown Manhattan. A government official in a dark suit received him in a small office high up in a skyscraper.

"Mr. Robinson, I have a letter to you from your son," the official said, handing Grandpa an envelope.

Dear Dad,
I hope you remember me. I'm your son Junior and I'm
writing to you from Africa. Brenda and I were sent here
by Mom. She didn't come with us and we've been here
alone for several years. Please help us come home to you,
Dad. Please help us.
    Love,
    Junior

I can only imagine how Grandpa's heart must have ached when he read his only son's words. What did he feel? Did he think he'd been a bad father since he hadn't managed to protect his children from such a fate? How did those guilty feelings affect him?

In *Not Even in Your Dreams*, Dad describes how his stepfather called him into his office one day and said, "I've received a letter from the American Department of State. They claim I'm holding you here against your will and apparently someone also wrote to them that the children are being beaten. Do you know who could have written to them?"

"It was me," Dad replied firmly.

"Right, that's what I expected," his stepfather said, resigned. "But let me show you what you'll be going home to."

His stepfather held out an English-language newspaper with an article about the nine black schoolchildren in Little Rock, Arkansas, who needed a military escort in order to attend an all-white school.

"Is this the country you so badly want to return to?" he asked, pointing indignantly at a picture of the black children surrounded by screaming white people.

"This is America. This is your country. With the color of your skin, you will never be treated as anything but an animal there, and now you'll have to go back."

Then he threw the paper on the desk and shouted at Dad to get out of his sight.

For six months, my grandfather attended various meetings with the State Department. He even wrote a letter to the mayor of New York, asking him for help to bring his children home. After all these years, he wasn't sure he would ever see his son or daughter again.

In 1957, Madubuko and Chinyelu finally returned to New York. They were met at the airport by Grandpa and several relatives. The newspapers were there, taking pictures of the reunion, and later on, the siblings were even photographed with the mayor. The relatives cried and applauded and hugged the children, all at once.

When I read Dad's story of his time in Nigeria and recall all the stories I've heard throughout the years, I realize what a turbulent relationship he had with his parents.

Only now do I understand why Dad is always so particular about the family sticking together, why all those dinners around the table are important. Why he makes sure that the younger members of the family are allowed to have a voice and always lets the youngest be the first to help themselves to the food.

The fact that I've been blind to this for so long makes my conscience sting the same way it has so many times before when I've felt like I've treated Dad unfairly.

A few weeks before Christmas, he told me for the first time about his reunion with Grandpa.

"The scene at the airport was extremely emotional, Jason. Chinyelu and I cried, and your grandfather cried. That might have been the only time I ever saw him cry. Or . . . maybe he wasn't exactly crying, but his eyes were definitely wet when he hugged us that first time after six years of involuntary separation. I also remember the feeling of sleeping in a real bed again. I was so grateful to be back in the United States, with my family. Back to the place, the streets and culture, where I belonged. But it was also difficult to connect with my old friends again. So many years had passed. Their experiences and development were dramatically different from the life I had been living. We saw the world and our skin color through different eyes. Nigeria forever changed me. For better and for worse. I gained some sort of insight into another way to carry the blackness of my skin during those years. It was a secret the black citizens of the US hadn't yet discovered."

But his reunion with my grandmother was not as joyful. Dad walked into her office on 116th Street in Harlem and asked why she had sent them to Nigeria.

"I know you think I don't care about all of you, but I do," Grandma replied in a quiet voice. "I care about all my children. I thought it was best for you to grow up in Nigeria."

"I want you to make sure that Nana and Obedike are brought home as soon as possible. They're beaten every day in Nigeria; they have to come home now."

She quickly changed the subject and asked Dad what he wanted to do now that he had returned to the United States.

Dad said, "I want to go to college. I want to get an education. I want to go to Yale and study law."

Grandma leaned back in her office chair and burst into scornful laughter.

"You'll see that there's no room for a black man with such big dreams in this country. This isn't Africa, this is the United States. Your father is a poor server. He can't pay for school or send you to any college. Get a job. Forget Yale."

Grandma's words brought tears to Dad's eyes. How could his mother, who had managed to make her own dreams of getting a university education come true, be so discouraging? Especially after everything she'd subjected her children to in Nigeria?

A few months later, Grandma ordered my then seventeen-year-old father to come down to Times Square with her. They were going to a recruitment office for the United States Armed Forces, housed in a small, boxy kiosk that's still standing at the southern edge of the square. Grandma brought dad into the little glass kiosk and enlisted him in the military. Suddenly, he owed the state at least four years of service.

Once again, she abandoned Dad. She did the same to Uncle Obi, who was sent to the Vietnam War shortly after he returned to the United States many years later.

Around that time, when the 1950s had so recently given way to a new decade, Grandma was hit hard by the zeitgeist, and her Pan-Africanist convictions grew even stronger. Kwame Nkrumah had just become the first democratically elected president of Ghana, Patrice Lumumba had become the first free prime minister of the Congo, and Julius Nyerere had become the leader of the free Tanzania. The whole continent was bubbling with revolution and a belief in the future. Africa was on its way to breaking free of the yoke of colonialism. At least, that's what people thought.

In the United States, the civil rights movement had gained speed, and the Montgomery bus boycott had brought Martin Luther King Jr. to the forefront as one of the strongest leaders of the movement. It was a time of black awakening in both the US and Africa.

For Afrikanwe, the dream of an Africa free of white control was greater than the dream of black equality in slave-state America. In her eyes, the latter was an impossibility. Black people could only be free in Africa. So, in 1960, she moved to Conakry, where she worked as a secretary to the first president of Guinea, Sékou Touré. She also conducted English-language broadcasts on Radio Conakry.

I imagine that Grandma was living her dream. At last she could live in a society that was led by black people, where her black skin didn't make her a second-class citizen. For such a political woman, the spirit of the times must have been electric.

Everyone in Conakry called her Madame—that's where she got her nickname.

BM thought her daughter's Pan-Africanism was nothing but baloney. As long as you were literate and had a job, you had made great strides compared to previous generations.

"What you mean, back to Africa?" she said, according to Dad. "We in Harlem. Why you wanna go to Africa? Black people in America ain't got no business goin' to Africa. All you gotta do in life is stay black and die."

In a brief interlude on the 1972 record *Ghettos of the Mind*, Bama the Village Poet expresses exactly this internalized oppression of the inhabitants of the ghetto. Maybe the ghetto lives in the hearts and souls of its residents. It becomes more than just a physical location made of asphalt, brick, and concrete. It becomes a mentality, a culture that keeps people in place, their heads bowed, with an invisible hand. In the end, resignation and oppression become part of their DNA. In the end, people submit to the situation. Just as the slaves on the plantation did.

Convinced as Grandma was that black people could live free, proud lives in dignity, she wanted more from life. She practiced what Bama wrote about: "The Right to be Wrong."

It's nearly dinnertime in Dad's apartment on the fifth floor on Värnhemstorget in Malmö. The sun has set behind the grand trees of Rörsjö Park, its expanses on view outside the living room window, and it's finally starting to cool down. My back aches from sitting on the green stool and plowing through all these old written words for hours at a time.

But I keep reading the letter from Grandma. Dad is still in his chair, quiet, his hands folded across his belly. He tilts his head forward, his eyes half closed.

You have better luck than your father, who turns to whiskey to drown his sorrows over being a miscegenist, a habit for which his liver will undeniably pay the price. Take my words for what they're worth. The sum of them all is meant as advice to you, to hold tight to your marriage, if possible. Or to use once you've found a new, better wife. It's time for you to realize that you no longer belong in the black world, unless you become a negro pastor. A tax-exempt chicken-eater . . .

As always,
Madame

I drop the letter on the floor. Floored by the words. By my grandmother's cruel voice. How could she say those things to her son? After she'd sent him to Nigeria for six years and forced both him and his brother into the military, she wrote hateful letters to say that his choice of my white mother as his partner made him a traitor to her and his race.

I want to say something to Dad, but I can't find the words. I don't know how to offer him any comfort. At last, I lean forward and say, "Dad, I know it must have been hard for you, all these years in Sweden. How could you live with the pain of leaving your city, your parents, your siblings and friends behind? And you had to deal with the torture of having one parent laying guilt on you because you're not at home, while the other guilted you for not being black enough."

Dad smiles and nods in agreement.

"Jason, thanks for seeing that. Honestly, thank you."

He turns to Simme.

"Simon, are you filming this?"

"Of course, Buko, this camera doesn't miss a thing," Simme is quick to respond.

Dad's expression grows thoughtful. Just as I'm wondering what's going on in his head, he turns to Simme, looks straight at the camera, and says, "It's not every day my son actually understands the sacrifices I've made so we could live the lives we have in this country."

As we read through the letters, he looked as if he had just been punched in the gut, but now he seems to come to life. He tries to straighten his back, clasps his hands over his stomach, and turns to me.

"All the things you take for granted—free health care, education, the fact that you can walk down the street without someone trying to rob you, that you've shaken hands with the prime minister and the king . . . None of this would have been possible if you'd grown up in Harlem. You might not have lived to see forty-one. Or maybe you would have ended up in a prison cell like so many other black men your age. I rescued you and me from a certain fate, Jason. Just as your mom rescued me from Harlem. When Madame sent me and my siblings to Nigeria, our eyes were opened. It made me realize that the world was bigger than Harlem, bigger even than New York. There was a place where black people were proud and held their heads high. Nigeria showed me what black people can be. Even though the land was colonized by the British for many years, people held on to their culture and their unshakable pride. If it hadn't been for my time in Nigeria, and the fact that I got to see things my friends in Harlem couldn't even dream of, I wouldn't have been able to lift my eyes to the horizon. My experiences prompted me to seek out something better, and in the end, that brought me to this small, cold country. You got to grow up free. That's thanks to your grandma and your mother."

Following Dad's long speech, we go back to plucking letter after letter from the thick envelopes.

"Don't you want to read some letters about my academic career in this country?" Dad asks, waving an envelope.

"Dad, I'm most interested in the family letters. The personal and emotional stuff."

Dad rolls his eyes and shakes his head.

"What are you going to write in your book? That we were all slaves who picked cotton, or what? That we were a gang of poor wretches who didn't know any better? Write about our dignity and our struggle instead. Write about the positive aspects. Our achievements. Our merits. This whole house is full of diplomas that demonstrate my merits. Why aren't you interested in that?"

I make an effort not to contradict him. Even though I've been trying to explain why I want to read the letters for almost a year, Dad doesn't understand. Or perhaps he doesn't want to understand that I want to hear about the dreams, mistakes, and hopes, about my family's struggle to survive.

"Dad, this handwritten letter must be from Grandma too," I say, holding up a sheet of paper that's quite a bit smaller than the others.

I hand it to him.

"You want me to read it right now?" Dad asks, looking resigned, letting the hand holding the letter fall to his lap.

"Yes, I really do."

He slowly brings the letter closer to his face. I reach for a pair of reading glasses on the bookcase beside us and pass them to dad, who looks at me curiously.

"So you truly want me to read this?" he says, reluctantly putting on the glasses.

"Yes, Dad."

"You're right. The letter is from your grandmother."

> *Dear Elaine,*
> *How are you? BM and I are well, thank god. I'm assuming you and your husband are also in good health . . .*

"Dad," I interrupt. "Are you the one she's referring to as 'your husband'?"

"Yes, I'm telling you, she was a tough fucking woman," Dad says with an audible sigh.

He hands me the letter, and I keep reading.

> *You must not be fooled by your husband's smoke-screens about writing a dissertation or his dreams of becoming a documentary filmmaker. You can also let him know that he forgot to congratulate his father on his birthday . . .*

Dad snorts and leans back in the chair. His eyes are blank. He looks exhausted. It seems he has no words left; he just shakes his head in silence. The reading glasses have slipped all the way down to the tip of his nose. On the coffee table to his right is the plate with the remains of the chicken Simme brought for him, now reduced to a pile of tiny bones. I stand up and draw the thick white curtains aside to let in what's left of the daylight.

Never before have I looked at Dad with such compassion. The guilt over those he left behind remained with him, a lingering burden, and letter after letter hit him where it hurt most.

Simme tries to offer some comfort: "Maybe she was just jealous of you, Buko. I mean, you were free . . . you did manage to get an education, after all, and get out of Harlem. She stayed up there for the rest of her life, and all she could do was write nasty letters to you."

"Yes, maybe you have a point, Simon," Dad responds, slightly heartened by the thought. "I never understood that woman. But you need to know this."

He shakes one finger.

"I never cared what she thought. Never," he repeats loudly. "I knew what I wanted. I knew what was good for me."

Dad sinks back in the chair again after this last exertion. The wrinkles that form a valley on either side of his nose, and down over his cheeks, like parentheses around his mouth, deepen again, and his exhaustion takes over his face.

"She wrote letters to me frequently, and each one contained some sort of cruelty. Then I don't know what happened, because in 1979, her tone changed and she became much more affectionate."

The volume of Dad's voice decreases with every sentence; he almost whispers the last words.

Books and photographs crowd the large bookcase that covers the entire southern wall of the spacious living room. Pictures of family members and holidays. Books about the struggle for black liberation, about the law and anti-racism, stand in rows. On one shelf, exactly at my eye level as I sit on the green wooden stool across from Dad, is a Lionel steam locomotive and three cars, on their original rails. It's the same train set Dad got for Christmas in 1950, the one he wasn't allowed to bring to Nigeria. Dad has tucked a cotton ball into the smokestack of the black locomotive, to be the smoke.

"Now I've reached the point where I'm starting to feel a little depressed," Dad says after a while, his voice sluggish. "All I want to do now is cry, go get in bed and rest. Fuck . . ."

He takes off his glasses and rubs his eyes and looks down at the floor.

"I'm sorry, Dad," I say with an edge of guilt in my voice. "I know how hard this is for you."

"You have no idea, Jason. One thing's for sure. I'm going to burn these letters."

Dad sinks even further into himself, his head drooping until his chin almost touches his green shirt, and whispers, "I'm going to burn every last one."

A GOOD JOB

I'm sitting in a hotel room in Umeå. The sun is high in the Västerbotten sky, and I don't think there will be many minutes of darkness on this June night. The sound of the BBC news streams from the flat-screen TV in the recently renovated hotel room. All I'm wearing is underwear, and the brown pleather of the easy chair feels cool and damp against my back. Although the internet is slow, I'm trying to download a hefty file from Simme. It's the footage of the other day in Dad's living room.

I can't escape the sting of my guilty conscience from forcing Dad to go through all the letters. I've never seen him so worn out before, so broken down, so small. What if he hasn't been able to sleep? What if he's plagued with guilt and regret?

Ever since we dug that red suitcase out of Dad's dusty storage room last year, I've been pressuring him to let me read more. But I should have suspected what awaited us after Enid read that letter from Grandpa on that August evening last year. Should I have prepared Dad somehow? How could I have? Should I not have invited Simme to film us? It's too late to do anything about it now, but I have to make sure to call Dad to see if he's feeling OK.

Grandma's letters were crueler than I ever could have imagined, yet they're not surprising. After all, I'd heard the stories about Madame. But there was something about all those letters from Grandpa that struck a note of deep sorrow within me. Especially the letter dated December 2, 1974, where Grandpa wrote:

Dear son and daughter,
How are you? How is the little baby? I pray to God you
are all well. I'm doing very poorly. Christmas is coming
soon, and I don't want to celebrate yet another Christmas
without you. I'm so terribly alone. Bring the baby and
come home. Please, come home.

Grandpa is talking about me. I'm the baby. Although I wasn't born until several weeks after Grandpa penned those pleading words in black ink, in his looping handwriting on the thin Air Mail paper.

I picture him sitting alone in his favorite red easy chair with its plastic cover. On the shelf beside him is a small gray radio, and the commentators are calling the Yankees game. The wood-paneled TV is playing the Red Sox game. Despite the loud voices, he can't hear anything.

Something heavy expands in Grandpa's chest. Maybe he's recalling the feeling of those difficult years when his son was missing. Abducted by his mother and sent to Africa. Maybe that's why Grandpa can't bear to be away from his son even now. Even though he knows Dad is off chasing his dreams.

Why does he chase such crazy notions? Can't he just live here in Harlem? Like I do? Just look at how well he's done for himself. He still doesn't have much money, but he's sober, at least; he has his own apartment and pension.

He thinks back to when he was a child and young man in Harlem, living far from his own family, and that brings him to write letter after letter to my dad, begging his son to come home. Home to Harlem, home to him. What my grandfather doesn't realize, in all his loneliness, is that his letters and pleas cause guilt. Grandpa is feeding and fattening a guilt in Dad's chest that will never subside.

Grandpa never knew his own father. None of his children remember Grandpa ever mentioning his father, and despite my many questions to all my relatives, I've never learned his name. Maybe Grandpa's fatherlessness is what made him always want his children near.

It sits deep within Dad, this guilt and sorrow over abandoning his father, my grandfather.

I realize that this scenario is only repeating itself. All the times Dad has called and texted me, wondering when I'll return home to him. All the times he's said he misses me and wants me to come home and be beside him. What Dad is doing is sowing the same guilt in my chest as his own dad planted in him. It's sprouting inside me as well.

I can't live with the idea that I will bear that guilt, that chafing conscience, for the rest of my life. The chain of guilt and dysfunction that has run through our family for generations and centuries must be broken.

I don't want to pass this on to my future children. I must find a way to transform the guilt I carry in my chest into sympathy and empathy.

All my life, I've contradicted Dad, argued with him and landed in conflict with him, every time I feel like he's treating me unfairly. After every fight, I feel worthless and mean. Until today, I've thought I must defend myself against Dad's guilt-trips to keep myself from becoming like him. But now I realize that empathy might be the key that unlocks the chain of guilt once and for all.

I think back to something Dad told me the day before yesterday. "The incredible thing about your grandpa," Dad said, "was that when I did come home to him, he wouldn't turn off the radio or the TV. He always wanted baseball on. So he sat there in his chair, absorbed in the commentary. It was like, in the end, baseball was more important than I was. But at the same time, I know he just wanted me there in the room. To keep him company. He just wanted to know that if he looked away from the TV, I would be sitting there. His son."

Dad's words make me think of all the times I've come to his house to find the TV showing the news, or a documentary, as he just sits there in his chair, his eyes glued to the screen, while I sit silently on the couch next to him. Now and then, he looks at me, smiles in satisfaction, and keeps watching the TV. Yep, his son is only a glance away.

From the hotel room in Umeå, I can see Grandpa more clearly than ever before. I see him waking up in his little two-room, four-hundred-square-foot apartment in Harlem. How it takes effort to get up off his sagging mattress and stretch his old, aching back. Morning is the time of day when Grandpa feels old and worn out. All those years of serving plates and bending his back for the guests have settled in his muscles and bones. He walks over to the wardrobe and takes out a dark suit. The whole room smells like the mothballs he sticks in the pockets of his jackets to keep the fabric from being eaten up by pests. He puts on a white shirt and a tie, then heads down to Lenox Avenue for the short walk to the subway. Sometimes he says hello to the old men sitting outside the corner store. They chat about the weather and yesterday's baseball scores, and then he walks down the stairs to the crowded subway platform to wait for his train.

He's stylish in his suit and hat, with his cane. At work, he puts on an apron and carries plate after plate to the hungry guests. At night, when his shift is over, he shrugs back into his jacket and takes the long train ride back home to Harlem. Now, as he strolls home along Lenox, the street is full of action. He goes to the West Indian barber and takes a load off on the worn leather sofa. On the coffee table in front of him are the day's papers. He opens a copy of the *New York Post* and reads about events in the world and the city. He chats a little with the barber about what's been going on in the neighborhood that day. On his way home, he zigzags between the junkies hanging out on the wide sidewalk. He's watched as more and more zoned-out drug addicts arrive in the neighborhood. But he doesn't bother them unless they bother him. If any of them get in his way, they'll get a taste of the cane. What they don't know is that the brass shell at the tip can be removed to reveal a spike, so the cane can be used as a weapon if needed. Everyone in the neighborhood knows that Grandpa is tough.

He slowly walks up the stairs, unlocks the door, and steps into his apartment, where he takes out a plate and eats a dinner made up of leftovers—what the guests of the restaurant didn't finish. Maybe, today, he has a piece of sirloin and a few cold potatoes. Baseball commentary streams from the radio. He spends an hour sitting in his favorite chair, and this is the time of day he feels most alone. That's when he rises from the chair, walks to the bureau, and takes out a piece of stationery and a blue-ink pen to write a letter to his son. All Grandpa can think about is his loneliness and how much he wishes his son would come home and help fix the hot plate that's been broken for six months and tell him all about what happened at work.

Grandma's letters were probably easier for Dad to dismiss and burn, as callous as they were. But Grandpa's words are so imploring. In letter after letter, he begs his son and daughter-in-law to come home to him.

How did Dad live with all these letters landing in his mailbox day after day? How did he explain to Grandpa that he couldn't return? How did he explain to him that his dreams were bigger than Harlem, greater than simply earning money and putting food on the table?

In Grandpa's world, there was no such thing as an existential crisis. Anxiety and depression were something for the more privileged classes. He was a breadwinner. He served food to restaurant tables and, in so doing, put food on the home table as well. He was proud of his job as a waiter. "Get yourself a good job," he often advised his son. By that he meant be a janitor, doorman, waiter, or taxi driver. "A good job." An honorable job.

Grandpa never retired; he worked until the cancer took over and finally kept him from performing his duties. He died at the age of seventy-five.

Grandpa carried the Robinson name to his grave. He lived at the same time as Langston Hughes, Ralph Bunche, and Paul Robeson. The Harlem Renaissance was going on around the corner; Jelly Roll Morton, Fats Waller, and Duke Ellington were playing their way into the collective history of the world. Culture, music especially, was the valve for everyone in Harlem, no matter their perspective, conviction, or starting point. Music was something to gather around. Jazz, soul, funk, blues.

But Grandpa didn't write, didn't sing, never chanted.

He just worked.

SOLOMON'S SONG

I'm wearing a pair of blue pants I found in a small secondhand store on Avenue B and E Eleventh Street in the East Village. The clerk said they were from the forties. Grandpa's sand-colored trench coat is on a hanger, reflecting the pale light of this Stockholm afternoon.

It's all I have of him. I seldom wear it, but I often take the coat out to look at it and wonder what Grandpa looked like in it, where he bought it, and what the city sounded like in the days when he wore it. It's an artifact. It's a portal to all the history that happened before I was born or old enough to be an active participant.

I'm also wearing a tie I really like. It came in the mail yesterday. I found it online and bought it from a small shop in Los Angeles that sells authentic 1930s ties. I imagine Grandpa had a similar tie when he was my age. It's short and wide. As ties were back then.

Grandpa Silas told my dad that a person should always have a dollar in his pocket. With a dollar in your pocket, you still had a chance. Hope, made of green paper.

I seldom carry cash in Stockholm. But I always keep a dollar in my wallet. My lucky dollar.

I put on a record. Duke Ellington's "In a Sentimental Mood." The pants, the tie, the jazz . . . I'm thinking about Grandpa. Otherwise, I probably would have put on Kendrick Lamar. The agitator, provocateur, thinker. The kind of person Grandpa never pinned his hopes on.

I'm a rapper. I travel around and perform for people and sing songs I've written. Not entirely unlike Duke Ellington. Hip-hop would have been as impossible without jazz as my existence would have been without Grandpa. "It don't mean a thing if it ain't got that swing." Grandpa lived for jazz. What would Grandpa have thought to hear me call rapping an honorable job?

The last time I saw my grandpa was in 1981. I was just shy of six years old. It was Father's Day, and Dad and I visited him at home in Harlem. Dad had gone all out and brought fresh lobster from the South Street Seaport. I didn't even dare to look at those red shellfish; their claws scared me.

I recall standing barefoot on Grandpa's plastic-covered sofa and dancing around. Dad came into the room with a lobster claw in his hand, pretending to chase me. I was terrified and began to cry.

"Aren't you too old to cry over a lobster claw?" Grandpa sighed from the easy chair he was rooted to.

I have a photograph from that day. I'm sitting on Grandpa's lap, my fingers resting on his large hand. The blinds are closed. Grandpa is wearing a brilliant-white shirt with a pen in the breast pocket, and he has his silver nylon stocking on his head. It looks like I've just told him something, and he is looking at me with encouragement. Now, when I hold this photograph in my hand, I feel a burning inside. A wish awakens—I wish we'd had more time together. That I could have more of my grandfather than just a coat and a faded photograph.

Grandpa always wore that nylon stocking indoors to protect his relaxed hair. He continued to wear it out of habit even after the chemicals had made every last strand fall out.

There's a picture from 1998, when I released my first album, with the R&B group Excel. On my head, I have a nylon stocking. Not to protect my hair. I just thought it was a cool look. After all, I have my mom's straight hair. A white person's hair. Not teeny-tiny tight curls like

Grandpa and Dad and everyone else on that side of the family. "Tight-ass nigger naps," as one of my aunts calls it.

Only when I was fourteen and began to embrace my blackness did I wish I had the same kinky hair as Grandpa, Dad, and my aunt and cousins. What Grandpa needed caustic chemicals to attain, I had from birth, but instead I wanted what he was trying to scorch away. What Dad traveled to Sweden for—the opportunity to get an education—I had from birth. But I wanted to go back to Harlem. I traveled there every night with the music and my pen and paper.

The other day, Dad told me that, in Grandpa's day, black people didn't like being called "black." It was considered derogatory. Back then, they wanted to be "Negroes." If you wanted to be really rude to a black person when Grandpa was young, you called them "BAJB": "Black African jungle bunny."

If I have kids, they'll probably be the color of the sand on Lomma Beach. What would Grandpa advise me to tell these children? How should I convey the experience of being black, brown, less white to them?

Dad has always told me I must never forget that the world will judge me based on the color of my skin. My constant counterargument was that Dad's worldview is too black and white, but I have been reminded that I'm not white more times than I can ever forget.

It's deeply ingrained in my behavior to always scan each new room I step into. Will my color or my name work against me when I walk into the bank or a gas station, with the police or my neighbors, at a job interview, at the bar? My internal system of checks borders on paranoia, and sometimes, an almost self-fulfilling sense of inferiority. It can also make me stuck-up, arrogant, and self-pitying to a destructive degree.

Skin color is more than just a broad palette of pigmentation. It's much more than the melanin that gives my skin its reddish-brown color.

I look like I do because of the way my great-grandmother's Cherokee blood mixed with my paternal grandfather's yellow-brown skin, my paternal grandmother's deep-chocolate color, my maternal grandmother's milk-white German heritage, and my maternal grandfather's Slovak origins. The part of me that's descended from African slaves, and which makes my skin anything but white and my hair not totally straight, is what cries out the loudest. It's those drops of midnight that make all the difference. It's what strangers' eyes notice first, what may prompt them to form preconceived notions about who I am and what I'm like. Indeed, many of my most painful childhood memories are related to not being accepted for who I am.

Blackness has been both a burden and a gift. The majority of people on this planet are not white. But many people still observe, analyze, and explain the world and themselves through the lens of whiteness. Myself included, for so long. My blackness was hard to love. I spent a lot of time being ashamed of it.

That shame, or the memory of it, is still crystal clear within me. It's like a thistle in my chest that sometimes pokes me and stings for a while, but for the most part, it rests there, safely surrounded by flesh.

My blackness is like water that has been filtered through generations of bodies and now rests in my hands, my belly, my forehead, my ass. It's always with me, and one fine day, I will send it onward to yet another generation, which in turn will be able to influence what it means to live a life bearing these drops of midnight. Grandpa bore his skin as best he could, and Grandma was driven by her blackness to make decisions that conflicted with her motherhood. I don't know how to explain what my skin color feels like; it's omnipotent. Beautiful. It encompasses everything.

The color of my skin has caused me to question my entire existence at times. My experiences of racism have sometimes made me hateful, have been transformed into self-contempt. But my impulse reaction to being called slurs has always been anger. Anger and tears.

For most of my life, I have proclaimed myself half American, half Swedish, half white, half black. But now I choose to say I'm both white and black, both Swedish and American. German, French, Slovak, African, Cherokee. All these identities belong to me. I've gone from being half to double, and in that seemingly tiny semantic shift lies one of my greatest strides of identity. Doubleness is infinitely better than halfness.

Perhaps my children will go through life unconcerned about skin color, ethnicity, and belonging. Maybe the world will become better than it has been, able to see them in a loving light no matter their shade. On the other hand, maybe they'll be the first of my grandfather's bloodline to be almost white, and thus be spared the effects of racism, so difficult to eradicate. But that thought is too sad for me to bear. That I should have to wipe out the melanin in their genes to spare future generations the complex, brutal obstacle course of racism.

I look again at the photo of Grandpa where he sits so deeply sunk in his threadbare easy chair with a stoic expression and a nylon on his bald head. Maybe he, too, pondered who he was on his long Sunday walks along the broad avenues of Harlem, beyond the dutiful waiter who always had shiny shoes. I wonder what Grandpa would have said about my search for my roots. Who are my people? Where is my home? Probably:

"Son, don't think about that nonsense. Get yourself a good job, put food on the table, and look sharp."

I double-knot the short, wide green-and-white tie around my neck, put on the worn coat and my freshly polished brown leather shoes, and go out.

EPILOGUE

Standing in the hallway of my apartment in Södermalm today, the evidence of the passing of time is clear. I navigate among the little rubber fish, plastic stars, wooden building blocks, regurgitated bits of bread, and old tangled headphones that trace the route taken by my daughter, Maxime, before she was put in the stroller and rolled out into the April sun. Amelie is waiting outside with her, and I have just run up to find Maxime's ever-elusive yet essential accessory, her pacifier. It is 2019, and she is turning one in three weeks. Maxime, Amelie, and I have just returned from a long stay in Los Angeles. Sweden, Stockholm, this apartment all feel both foreign and familiar. Like we're visiting a past life. A museum of who we were, back then. My jar of cotton from the Allendale fields is still standing in its place on a dusty corner of my desk. Silas's trench coat is still hanging in the closet. But Maxime's presence is everywhere, and it is what gives me the feeling of growth, of progress. With her comes a new way of measuring time: in diaper changes, feedings, new teeth, acquired skills, the longer barrages of proto-words that she often starts her day with.

Maxime is the second generation of Madame and Silas's lineage to be born in Sweden. The African part of her heritage is only visible in the latte-colored skin right under her fingernails and the slight wavy curls on the back of her neck. It occurs to me that she will probably be able to pass. But cultural advancement will be measured by whether she ever feels she needs to or wants to.

I feel a new bond has formed between Dad, Mom, and myself, and I have found myself thanking them. I realize, now, the amounts of love, care, patience, and hope that go into bringing up a child.

And I must say, Uncle Obi was right: becoming a grandparent truly has breathed new life into my dad. He'll be turning seventy-nine in a few months. His health is better than it was, but he's still frail. I don't disagree with him as vigorously as I once did. I understand better now.

I've realized recently that my feelings of otherness and homelessness are stronger in Sweden than in the United States. All I can think of now is when and how Amelie, Maxime, and I can move back across the Atlantic. Every inch of me is longing to reverse the migration of my parents.

When I enter a room in Sweden, my reflexes are trained to gauge the effect, the consequences, of my presence. When I'm in the US—in New York or Los Angeles—those reflexes relax. Yes, the brutal structures of racism and oppression and the culturally ingrained segregationist attitudes are much more visceral in the States, and the scars run deeper. But still, I'm rarely the only person of color in the room. Blackness is not alien to Americans in the same way it is to Swedes.

I've just ended a long hiatus from writing songs and performing. In a few weeks, rehearsals for a pan-Scandinavian tour commence, and I look forward to them with renewed energy because now Maxime will be with me, and there is so much I want to show her.

Under a pile of magazines she must have yanked from the living room, I find her green pacifier with its leather string that attaches to her jacket. I put it in my pocket and go out.

ACKNOWLEDGMENTS

This book wouldn't have been possible without all of your help. You have my undying gratitude.

Mustafa, this project would never have happened if you hadn't encouraged and urged me to write. Since then you have been the shepherd, Virgil, Yoda, and Moses all in one. You led this fumbling novice author through the wilderness and all the way to the finish line.

Amelie, for your unfailing support and unflagging pep, for offering me sanctuary on Park Avenue, where I found the peace and the time to find and get all of these words out of my head, and for giving my heart a home. The air, always!

Madubuko, for all the years of wisdom and inspiration, and for patiently, if sometimes reluctantly, answering all my questions and telling me about our history.

Elaine, for always being in my corner no matter how hard the wind was blowing. Your energy and joie de vivre have always been the wind in my sails.

Simon, if you hadn't come to New York with me on that September day, none of this would have come to be—not the book, nor love, nor my new life.

Björn and Lili, for always being the ones to back me up, fix things, and guide my ship in the right direction.

Marcus, you are inspiration in human form.

Alluette, without your guiding hand, I wouldn't have found my way back to my village of origin.

Don, for all the wisdom, support, and encouragement. The day will surely come.

Monique, for your support always.

Anja, for your way of seeing people, and you've had my back since day one.

Uncle Obi and the whole Linton family, for your love and encouragement.

Auntie Juanetta, Jimmy, Tony, and Michael, thank you for your hospitality and love.

Gloria Ray, for so generously sharing your story with me.

Elizabeth DeNoma, thank you for believing in this book and helping me to realize its publication in English.

Judith Bloch, thank you for taking the painstaking time to weigh, sift, and distill all these words and helping me tell my story.

Marcus Hoffman, thank you for shepherding this book to a new home in the United States.

All my love to all of you!

Jason Diakité
New York, April 2019